The Social Construction of Free Trade

The Social Construction
of Free Trade

THE EUROPEAN UNION,
NAFTA, AND MERCOSUR

Francesco Duina

PRINCETON UNIVERSITY PRESS

PRINCETON AND OXFORD

Library of Congress Cataloging-in-Publication Data

Duina, Francesco G., 1969–
    The social construction of free trade : the European Union, NAFTA,
and MERCOSUR / Francesco Duina.
        p. cm.
    Includes bibliographical references and index.
    ISBN-13: 978-0-691-12353-0
    ISBN-10: 0-691-12353-5 (cloth : alk. paper)
    1. Free trade.   2. Free trade—Social aspects.   3. Regionalism.
4. Trade blocs.   5. European Union.   6. Canada. Treaties, etc. 1992
Oct. 7.   7. MERCOSUR (Organization)   I. Title.
    HF1713.D85 2006
    382'.71—dc22

                                                              2005043243

British Library Cataloging-in-Publication Data is available

This book has been composed in Sabon
Printed on acid-free paper. ∞
pup.princeton.edu

Printed in the United States of America
1 3 5 7 9 10 8 6 4 2
10 9 8 7 6 5 4 3 2 1

To Angela

———————————

CONTENTS

LIST OF FIGURES AND TABLES

FIGURES

TABLES

A NOTE ON TRANSLATIONS

THROUGHOUT THE BOOK, the names of government departments, lobbying groups, associations, trade unions, and other entities appear in their original language. Most are mentioned once, or more than once but in the same few pages. For those, I provide English translations directly in the text on their first appearance. A few names appear repeatedly throughout the book. I translate those names below. Only figures 5.1 and 5.2 contain some terms for which I offer no translation, since these are for ministerial units of secondary importance to the discussion at hand.

- AK-Samvirke (Denmark): *National Association of Unemployment Funds*
- Asociacíon Latinoamericana de Libre Comercíó (Latin America): *Latin American Free Trade Association*
- Centro Feminista de Estudos e Assessoria (Brazil): *Feminist Center for Research and Assistance*
- Comisión Sociolaboral del Mercosur (Mercosur): *Social and Labor Commission of Mercosur*
- Consejo del Mercado Común (Mercosur): *Common Market Council*
- Conselho Nacional dos Direitos da Mulher (Brazil): *National Council for Women's Rights*
- Coordinadora de Centrales Sindicales del Cono Sur (Mercosur): *Association of National Trade Unions for the Southern Cone*
- Declaración Sociolaboral del Mercosur (Mercosur): *Social and Labor Declaration of Mercosur*
- Grupo Mercado Común (Mercosur): *Common Market Group*
- Instituto Nacional de la Familia y de la Mujer (Uruguay): *National Institute for the Family and Women*
- Ministerio de Economía y Producción (Argentina): *Ministry of the Economy and Production*
- Ministerio de Educación y Cultura (Uruguay): *Ministry of Education and Culture*
- Ministerio de Trabajo, Empleo y Seguridad Social (Argentina): *Ministry of Work, Employment and Social Security*
- Ministerio de Trabajo y Seguridad Social (Uruguay): *Ministry of Work and Social Security*
- Mujer a Mujer (Mexico): *Woman to Woman*
- Red Mexicana Ante el Libre Comercio (Mexico): *Mexican Network Against Free Trade*
- Secretaría del Mercosur (Mercosur): *Mercosur Secretariat*

ACKNOWLEDGMENTS

ONE PERSON ALONE cannot hope to understand the current and past legal, political, and social landscapes of dozens of countries in three continents. When three regional trade agreements are added into the equation, the task becomes daunting. When writing this book, I thus sought help from a number of people and organizations.

Special thanks go to the many government and regional trade officials from Europe, South America, and North America who kindly met, spoke by telephone, or corresponded via electronic mail with me during 2002, 2003, and 2004. I was especially lucky to interview several government and Mercosur officials in Argentina and Uruguay during a trip to the region in July and August of 2003. Our conversations covered a range of topics: women's rights, the dairy industry, labor issues, the nature of Mercosur law, and much more. In Argentina, I benefited in particular from extended conversations with Ruben Cortina and Gerardo Corres (Ministerio de Trabajo, Empleo y Seguridad Social), and Maximilano Moreno and María Juana Rivera (Ministerio de Economía y Producción). In Uruguay, I had enlightening conversations with Daniel Muracciole and Ana María Santestevan (Ministerio de Trabajo y Seguridad Social), and Beatriz Etchechury Mazza (Ministerio de Educación y Cultura). My meeting with Manuel Olarreaga (Secretaría del Mercosur) was also very helpful in shedding light on the nature of Mercosur law. Special thanks go to Maricela Viera in Uruguay (Ministerio de Trabajo y Seguridad Social) for her patience with me: throughout 2002, 2003, and 2004 she provided me with insights, documentation, and key contacts.

I traveled to Brussels in early 2004 to meet with representatives of European-level women's groups and of the dairy sector. Cécile Greboval (of the European Women's Lobby) was most welcoming and informative. Henriette Christensen (Secretary General of the European Council of Young Farmers), Mauro Poinelli (of Coldiretti, a major Italian agricultural lobbying group), and Pierluigi Londero (of the European Commission) were especially gracious. On that same trip, I visited Copenhagen to investigate how the Danish state has managed to provide migrant workers from other EU member states with unemployment benefits. There, too, I found exceptionally kind and knowledgeable people. I must thank Professor Ove Pedersen of the Copenhagen Business School for helping me obtain appointments with senior administrators there, as well as for his valuable comments on the project. Special thanks also go to Ingmar Jørgensen of AK-Samvirke and Jørgen Kappel, Head of Division at Arbejdsdirektoratet (National Directorate of Labor), for meeting with me. In the case of NAFTA, I must thank two lawyers—who wished to remain anonymous—from the Office of the United States Trade Representative and the United States Department of Commerce for sharing with me valuable insights about the nature of NAFTA law.

Representatives from dairy companies in Europe, South America, and North America shared up-to-date and reliable information with me on the location and activities of production facilities of their organizations, either through electronic correspondence or telephone conversations. I ultimately interacted with representatives from over twenty-five companies—both private and public. In the case of NAFTA, I also benefited from a conversation with David Phillips of *Dairy Foods Magazine* regarding the industry landscape in North America and the impact of NAFTA law on companies.

On the academic side, a number of insightful and generous readers offered invaluable advice on all aspects of the manuscript. As is always the case in these endeavors, they receive credit for the positive qualities of this book while I am of course responsible for its shortcomings. I would like to thank John K. Glenn, a sociologist and the Director of Foreign Policy at the German Marshall Fund, for many useful conversations and for reading multiple drafts of chapters. Once again, he proved to be a great intellectual partner. Professor John L. Campbell from Dartmouth College read all chapters of this book with his usual rigor and provided me with many detailed comments. I will remember fondly our conversations in Copenhagen, Denmark, and elsewhere. Professor John A. Hall of McGill University offered both much encouragement and sophisticated criticisms of early and later drafts of the book: as in the past, he has been an amazing inspiration. The comments and academic work on NAFTA and EU law of Professor Patrick Glenn of McGill University influenced much of chapter 3. Professor Paulette Kurzer of the University of Arizona wisely urged me to think about the wide array of factors that drive regional market building. The work and comments of Professors Robin Stryker of the University of Minnesota, Vivien Schmidt of Boston University, and Michael Oliver of Bates College shaped this book in many ways.

On the editorial front, I am most thankful to Tim Sullivan at Princeton University Press for his interest in the project, insights, and guidance. My good friend Patrick Lohier, a professional editor and writer, volunteered to read parts of the manuscript and improve my writing. It was a remarkable gesture of friendship. My research assistant, Craig Saddlemire—an undergraduate at Bates College—read through several drafts of the manuscript and offered many useful comments. He was also instrumental in conducting primary searches, reviewing the literature, and searching for contacts. Jason Buxbaum, Mashfiq Haque, Jamal Smith, and Erin Russ—

also undergraduates at Bates College—helped me with the coding of hundreds of laws. Lorelei Purrington, Area Coordinator for Sociology at Bates, gave me extraordinary administrative help with the preparation of the manuscript.

Various versions of the chapters and book were presented at professional conferences throughout the years. I am thankful in particular for comments I received during 2002 from audience and panel participants at meetings of the American Sociological Association, the Society for the Advancement of Socio-Economics, and the International Conference of Europeanists organized by the Council for European Studies at Columbia University. I discussed some of the evidence found in chapters 3 and 4 in the journals *Economy and Society* (Duina 2004) and *European Law Journal* (Duina and Breznau 2002).

The research trips and other expenses I incurred while writing this book could not have been possible without the financial support of Bates College. I benefited from two Faculty Development funds. My colleagues in the Sociology Department were amazingly supportive of my ideas and endeavors. My thanks, therefore, to Professors Emily Kane, Sawyer Sylvester, and Heidi Chirayath.

Throughout, my dear wife Angela supported me with patience and much wisdom. This project, and indeed much of my academic career, would not have been the same without her. It is to her that I dedicate this book.

ABBREVIATIONS

ACSSMW	Administrative Commission on Social Security for Migrant Workers
AFTA	ASEAN Free Trade Area
ANCE	Asociación de Normalización y Certificación del Sector Eléctrico
AOC	Apellation d'Origine Controllée
ASEAN	Association of Southeast Asian Nations
BPWE	Business and Professional Women—Europe
CAP	Common Agricultural Policy
CER	Closer Economic Relations Trade Agreement
CET	Common External Tariff
CUSFTA	Canada–United States Free Trade Agreement
EC	European Community
EDGE	Coalition for Women's Economic Development and Global Equality
EEC	European Economic Community
EIWH	European Institute of Women's Health
EU	European Union
EWL	European Women's Lobby
EWLA	European Women Lawyers Association
FEFAF	European Federation of Women Working in the Home
FMM	Foro de Mujeres del Mercosur
GATT	General Agreement on Tariffs and Trade
IMF	International Monetary Fund
LTC	Ley de Contrato de Trabajo
MM	Mujer a Mujer
NAAEC	North American Agreement on Environmental Cooperation
NAALC	North American Agreement on Labor Cooperation
NAC	National Action Committee on the Status of Women
NAFTA	North American Free Trade Agreement
NAO	National Administrative Office
REM	Reunión Especializada de la Mujer
RMALC	Red Mexicana Ante el Libre Comercio
RTA	regional trade agreement
SADC	Southern African Development Community
TEC	Treaty of the European Community
TEEC	Treaty of the European Economic Community
TEU	Treaty of the European Union
WTO	World Trade Organization

PART I

Introduction and Theoretical Framework

Chapter 1

VISIONS OF FREE TRADE

THE CLOSING OF THE twentieth century and the opening of the twenty-first witnessed an unprecedented proliferation of regional trade agreements (RTAs). As Europe pushed for the completion of its regional market, a stunning number of countries in North America, South America, Africa, and Asia rushed to form regional markets of their own. Between 1990 and 1994, officials from the World Trade Organization (WTO) were notified of thirty-three new RTAs, more than doubling the total to sixty-eight (Frankel 1997: 4; International Monetary Fund 1994). Then, between 1995 and 2001, another one hundred RTAs formed. A patchwork now covered much of the world. As one observer wrote, RTAs had become "almost a craze in the sedate world of economics, springing up here, there and everywhere" (Urata 2002: 21).

Numerous academics, journalists, and other observers commented on this trend. Most assumed that the majority of RTAs could be understood as expressions of a single phenomenon: a widespread embrace of the principle of free trade. Largely uninterested in comparative questions, they then proceeded to investigate three pressing issues: the causes of this collective turn to free trade, the future of the global economic system, and the local consequences of RTAs for the environment, workers, and other matters. Few wondered whether the presumed similarity of RTAs was, in fact, accurate. *The Social Construction of Free Trade* challenges this undifferentiated view of RTAs and, in so doing, offers one of the first systematic comparative analyses of regional market building across the world.

The starting premise of the book is that the pursuit of free trade in any given region is a *social* endeavor. Much like national market building, it occurs in the midst of rich institutional and political contexts. Market officials take action, but powerful constraints limit their choices. Traditions, structures, values, and norms along with the preferences of powerful actors define the range of what is possible. Societal players, in turn, respond to a broader marketplace by expanding their reach across national borders. Yet which players do so and what, exactly, they engage in depend on the specific opportunities presented to them and the position of those players in their respective environments prior to integration. We thus observe continuity between the shape of RTAs and preexisting local realities. We also observe the *uniqueness* of any given RTA: each is the result of a widespread desire for regional free trade pursued in very particular local conditions. RTAs are remarkably different creations. This book explores and accounts for their distinctiveness.

The evidence presented in the next chapters has direct implications for three topics of much current debate: globalization, the nature of markets, and the spread of neoliberalism. First, contrary to the fashionable claims of globalization theorists, the local still matters. Enduring differences across geographies still shape social life. Second, despite the belief that most economists hold about the spontaneous rise and functioning of markets, we see that social actors make markets in specific contexts. Third, the spread of neoliberalism at the end of the twentieth century was not, as most observers have assumed, a homogenous affair across the globe. As is true for many other economic doctrines, neoliberalism offered a general blueprint for economic activity but no instructions for its practical deployment in real life. To be sure, some of these observations are not novel. Until now, however, they have been articulated with evidence from nation states rather than regions of states. The focus on RTAs brings new evidence to bear on these issues.

The specific focus of the book is on two major areas of difference among RTAs. The *first* difference concerns the legal systems crafted in pursuit of free trade. In any market, sustainable buying and selling requires that participants share some basic understandings of the world. On the one hand, they must subscribe to similar views of what is being exchanged and of other items and entities associated with that exchange. Unmet expectations engender disappointment and the dissolution of relationships. Thus, for instance, consumers, importers, and producers in a given market must share similar views about what yogurt, beer, and credit cards are without need for recurring explicit discussion. Patients and doctors must similarly agree on the basic elements of a routine physical examination. And clients at a real estate law firm generally assume that their attorneys know the difference between commercial and residential buildings. On the other hand, participants must also subscribe to certain ideas about what is desirable in the world. Life in the marketplace is complex and unpredictable. When engaging in buying and selling, participants must feel confident that business will be reasonably safe, orderly, and fair. Thus, in any given market there must exist numerous notions that guide everyone's behavior. There must be broad agreement, for instance, over whether purchased goods can be returned, food labels should list all ingredients, or racial discrimination in hiring is acceptable.

Regional market building poses special challenges. Historically, most markets have formed slowly over time in tandem with gradual adjustments in the worldviews of market participants. By contrast, the building of regional markets is a deliberate process where barriers to exchange are quickly removed and peoples from diverse backgrounds are expected to interact with each other. The process therefore poses the challenge of standardization: definitions and normative viewpoints about the world must be brought into alignment. This is a major task, since it requires fundamental changes in subtle and sometimes implicit notions about the world.

RTA officials have responded differently to this challenge. In some areas, they have aggressively sought to standardize the world; in others, they have adopted a more laissez-faire approach. The primary tool for standardization at the regional level has been law. This means that in some RTAs officials have erected complex legal architectures rich with standardizing notions about the world. In other RTAs, by contrast, we observe minimalist legal architectures. The latter are often matched by a tendency to encourage participants to trade first or simply rely on standards set by other international organizations (especially for technical matters) and, if problems arise, to turn to reactive conflict-resolution mechanisms.

RTAs differ not only in the complexity of their legal architectures but also in the very targets and content of their laws. They differ in what they standardize, even though similar products are being traded across countries. Thus, for example, in one RTA apples may be subject to standardization (for instance, laws may define varieties of apples) while in a second RTA computer monitors are subject to standardization (for instance, the chemical properties of liquid crystal display screens are specified), even though in both RTAs apples and monitors are bought and sold across national boundaries. There also exist differences in the very content of standardizing law when, in fact, similar subject matters are targeted. The laws of two RTAs, for instance, may define and regulate child labor, medical conditions, and the use of food additives quite differently.

The *second* claim concerns the responses of societal organizations to regional integration. Different interest groups, businesses, and state units develop regional structures and programs in different RTAs. In one RTA, for example, we may observe the rise of environmental groups with transnational membership bases and objectives. In the same RTA, we may also observe that computer manufacturers have expanded their production infrastructures across national borders, while state labor departments participate in new regional-level coordinating bodies and have developed specialized domestic units to deal with the movement of medical professionals. In another RTA, we observe different dynamics. There, we may note the rise of regional associations of wildlife hunters, the expansion of furniture manufacturers, and the internationalization of transportation departments.

In some cases, analogous organizations develop regional structures and programs across different RTAs. But those cases still see important differences across those organizations in terms of specific structures and programs. If, for instance, farmers emerge at the regional level in two RTAs, their members' profiles and their objectives are likely to vary. Similarly, if textile companies expand internationally in two given RTAs, what exactly they produce will differ.

What helps *explain* these differences in law and organizational developments? *The Social Construction of Free Trade* proposes a political-institutional explanation: with regard to both law and organizations, a combination of institutional factors (above all, legal traditions) and political factors (above all, the preferences of powerful actors in society) is at work. This combination in most cases ensures that RTAs offer much continuity with existing conditions on the grounds in the member states and that RTAs acquire their distinctive character.

Specifically, in the case of interventionism versus minimalism in regional law, the presence of civil- versus common-law traditions in the member states of each RTA is of great importance. Civil law represents an attempt to codify the world a priori so as to facilitate social life. Common law is a reactive, case-by-case, and thus gradual approach to regulation. The former is more idealistic and rigid, the latter more pragmatic and flexible. RTA officials instinctively veer towards interventionism when they operate in spaces where member states share traditions of civil law: it is the logical solution to the cacophony of national laws. Officials are naturally inclined towards a minimalist approach when they operate within common-law traditions. There will be times, of course, when not all the member states of a given RTA share a similar legalistic approach. In those cases, officials opt for a regional legal system that matches those that are most prevalent in the member states. The choices of market officials receive the crucial support of key powerful actors (leading economic groups, civil society associations, politicians, and so on) that have flourished in those dominant regulatory environments.

As to the targets and content of regional law, we consider again existing legal principles in the given subject area and the preferences of powerful societal players. When crafting regional laws, officials turn to the predominant domestic approaches in the member states: they regulate mostly that which is regulated at the national level and they articulate principles that more or less replicate, at the regional level, shared national principles. Here too, of course, officials can at times craft regional laws that depart from existing principles in one or a few of the member states. Such departures, however, do not deprive regional law of its roots in the legal principles that are shared by most, if not all, of the member states. Pressuring market officials to follow national legal approaches are powerful actors. With a vested interest in translating at the regional level those legal environments in which they have grown, these actors have a great stake in RTA officials' developing specific types of laws that will solidify their position in society. In many cases, their influence ultimately determines, within the boundaries of the permissible, the final character of any given regional law.

Organizational changes in RTAs also reflect existing institutional and political contexts. Those organizations that develop regional capacities have typically operated in domestic legal environments that have prepared them for expansion. Seldom do weak domestic organizations respond to integration by asserting themselves at the regional level. At the same time, the very presence of regional law (itself an institution) in certain areas of social life has an impact on organizations: regional law creates incentives for organizations that have the necessary resources to become transnational. This happens differently for different types of organizations. The presence of regional law on certain topics encourages certain interest groups to develop regional capacity to lobby and guide the direction of such law. The standardization of certain products and processes encourages certain firms to expand their programs and structures at a regional level. Regional law, in turn, poses for state administrative units problems of oversight, implementation, and reporting that are more readily addressed by developing regional capacity. Thus, in a given RTA, we are likely to see the parallel evolution of law and societal organizations in certain spheres of social life. As regional law takes shape and offers the underpinnings for an economically integrated area, organizations adapt by expanding their operations in tandem with such law.

The evidence for these claims concerns three RTAs in Europe and the Americas: the European Union (EU), Mercosur, and NAFTA, the three most important and, occasional crises notwithstanding, best functioning RTAs in existence. We shall examine NAFTA's minimalism and the interventionism of officials in the EU and Mercosur. We shall also see how EU, Mercosur, and NAFTA officials have differed in what they target for standardization and in the content of their standardizing definitions. For that, we will turn to three subject areas within the realm of economics: the rights of women in the workplace, dairy products, and labor rights. Only EU officials have generated rich notions on working women. Only Mercosur officials, by contrast, have standardized the world of dairy products. In all three RTAs, officials have generated important notions surrounding labor rights, yet their definitions and visions vary significantly.

We will then consider the evolution of three types of organizations in the same three areas of economic life. Here, too, the three RTAs exhibit remarkable differences. We will learn about the development of regional-level women's groups in the EU, but not in Mercosur or NAFTA. In Mercosur alone we will observe dairy companies rushing to expand their operations across borders. In all three RTAs we will note that national administrations have developed units and processes with regional capacity in the area of labor rights but, crucially, that those units and processes are particular to each RTA.

The argument and evidence presented in this book directly challenge the recent writing of a number of academics, journalists, politicians, business leaders, and other observers of globalization. The most aggressive theses were put forth in the late 1980s and early 1990s, following the collapse of Communism as a viable option for organizing human societies (Zakaria 2000). There is now an extensive and sophisticated literature on the topic. Edited volumes offer interesting overviews of its breadth and variety (Lechner and Boli 2000; O'Meara et al. 2000; Berger and Huntington 2002). We shall not review that literature here,[1] but only refer to some of its most important claims, all of which point to a decreasing relevance of the local as a place of difference. Three strands are especially important.

Some proponents of globalization suggest that the world is becoming an increasingly homogenous place. They describe the impending arrival of single models for political, cultural, economic, legal, and other types of systems (Fukuyama 1992). Central to their view is the end of variety. In the political realm, for instance, they note that democracy is becoming the only acceptable form of governance for any community (Diamond 2000). Dictatorships, empires, and other models possess little or no legitimacy: the world community and its spokesmen, such as the United Nations, ostracize them. Without either recognition or access to external resources, nondemocratic communities are unlikely to survive for long. Similarly, the only sustainable form of economic life is some type of market capitalism. Socialism, various forms of protectionist systems, and other approaches to economic life are unrealistic and untenable. The collapse of the Soviet Union was but one indication of this. China and India are now moving towards market capitalism gradually, with impressive results for both. Countries in Eastern and Central Europe, such as Estonia and Poland, offer similar examples (Arrighi 2000; Burtless et al. 2000).

A second set of globalization theorists point to increased international cooperation. As human communities in various geographical locations adopt similar systems—political, cultural, and other—they also enter into very close relationships on the world stage, creating transnational or supranational structures to solidify their relationships. Thus, democratic countries participate in international democratic institutions and sponsor nongovernmental organizations to help formerly communist or socialist countries transition towards democracy (Mendelson and Glenn 2002).

---

[1] For excellent reviews, see Guillén (2001) and Steger (2003).

Capitalist countries in turn create international capitalist institutions, such as transnational corporations, and organizations like the IMF or the World Bank (Korzeniewicz 2000). And those concerned with the degradation of the environment and various forms of injustices worldwide join organizations with global agendas and solutions (World Commission on Environment and Development 2000; Amnesty International 2000). To these commentators, we are witnessing the rise of a global village where the boundaries of the traditional nation state are being eroded in favor of a global, cosmopolitan system.

A third group of proponents acknowledges that the world remains full of variation and idiosyncrasies. They also note—in an argument that applies most directly to culture—an unprecedented level of access to that which is different. For example, culinary traditions remain strong, yet foods of diverse origins are available everywhere. In Europe one can eat Cantonese, while in Moscow one can eat Brazilian (Warde 2000). The same applies to music and other forms of art. Again, national traditions remain strong and some even become revitalized, even if they are inevitably influenced by others. What is different is the availability of different artistic traditions (in recordings, live performances, exhibitions, via the Internet, and so on) throughout the world. What applies to culture applies to other spheres as well. As information travels effortlessly across the globe, politicians and economic actors can gain exposure to alternative systems, approaches, and ideas. No nation state can be separate from the world as might have been the case as recently as a few decades ago. Until the mid-1950s, for instance, the Kingdom of Nepal was virtually isolated from the rest of the world. Today, the Nepalese people are well aware of events and systems outside of their small country.

This book challenges these visions of a global world, and especially those related to homogeneity and global cooperation. With regard to homogeneity, it offers evidence that RTAs represent difference—in their architecture and in the societal changes that they engender. These are meaningful differences: they affect whole populations and a variety of businesses, associations, and state structures. They are also rooted in institutional, political, and, therefore, ultimately also in historical and cultural contexts: hence, they are enduring differences. We do not live in a world of converging societies, but in a world where the local—in its multiple dimensions—still matters. As to global cooperation, the book suggests that RTAs represent either an admission that efforts to forge a global economic system have so far failed or a recognition that societies are not ready to fuse themselves into a single economic system. Either way, RTAs represent smaller arenas for economic cooperation, suggesting, even if indirectly, that the vision of global institutions may either be untenable or still only be achieved quite far into the future.

This book naturally aligns itself with the critics of the globalization thesis. But while many of these works have sought to "rescue" the "national" from the "global,"[2] only some have pointed to the importance of the "regional." This book contributes to this smaller but also growing body of research. It is worth recalling here some of the most important examples. One is a famous piece by Ohmae (1993) describing the rise of heavily interdependent regional economic systems, comprising portions of nation states. It was paralleled by several works arguing that most trade across nations happens in very circumscribed areas, such as that encompassing Japan, Europe, and North America, or the whole of Southeast Asia (Hirst 2000). Others focused more on culture and politics. Huntington's (1997) famous book describing a world divided along the lines of major civilizations—such as the Western, Eastern Orthodox, Latin American, Islamic, and Japanese—is a good example. The next chapters offer evidence of an intriguing combination of regions with unique legal and organizational characteristics.

This book directly speaks to a second important topic: the nature of markets. For almost two decades now, economic sociologists have challenged in strong terms the neoclassical economic assumption that markets emerge naturally out of the human desire to trade: that markets "are spontaneously generated by the exchange activity of buyers and sellers" (Abolafia 1996: 9). A number of supporting structures and factors must instead be in place before exchanges can take place. In important works, Abolafia (1996), Fligstein (2001), Campbell and Lindberg (1990), and others have examined what, exactly, those supporting structures might be. Abolafia speaks of "rules, roles, and relationships" (1996: 9). Fligstein speaks of "social structures, social relations, and institutions" (2001: 4). Others speak of shared understanding about the commodities and actors involved in the exchange (Spillman 1999; Zelizer 1992).

Clearly, this book contributes directly to the idea that markets require much support to emerge and function. The book is above all an exploration of how RTA officials have worked to build spaces where regional markets can flourish. Yet, this project departs from the existing literature in important ways. Its comparative-regional focus is unique: there exist a few comparative works on market building at the national level, but there are no works on market building across multiple regions. We note in fact

---

[2] There are by now many interesting examples. In a representative work, for instance, J. Glenn (2001) showed that the embrace of democracy at the end of Communism across the world ushered a new wave of superficially similar, but in fact quite different, democratic regimes in Eastern and Central Europe. In a second example, Hall wrote that the post–Cold War period continues to be the period of the nation state: "the powers of the nation-state have varied, but this very variation has allowed them to survive" (2003: 2). See also Campbell (2004), Hall (2000), Paul, Ikenberry, and Hall (2003), Solinger et al. (1999), and Weiss (2003).

only some works on single RTAs—typically the EU (Fligstein and McNichol 1998). A comparative-regional analysis, then, is needed: Do regional markets require supporting structures? What are these structures, how do they come about, and are they identical across markets? What can account for variation across markets? What are the implications of such variation? If the study of national market building, in all of its variety, has proved rewarding, the study of RTAs is likely to yield a whole array of new and exciting insights.

In addition, we should note that RTAs represent a very particular genre of market building. Most existing analyses consider markets that have developed slowly over time, with the direct and indirect participation of numerous players only on occasion conscious that they are working towards the establishment of a particular market. In these accounts, markets emerge from the confluence of several events and trends. One recalls, for instance, Zelizer's (1992) account of the emergence of the life insurance industry in the United States. The process unfolded over several decades as the economic situation of working parents, culture, religion, and family structures underwent complex—and often unrelated—changes. By contrast, RTAs represent deliberate, explicit attempts to create regional markets in very short periods of time. This amounts to a very different kind of market creation: intentional, faster, programmatic. Our attention in this book is thus much less on proving that markets require supporting structures and far more on examining and comparing the choices that certain individuals and groups of individuals have made, in different places, to construct their respective markets.

The book addresses a third important debate: how a particular economic ideology—in this case neoliberalism in the 1980s and 1990s—has led to remarkably different outcomes in different places. The literature is not only about outcomes, but also concerns the very processes and mediating mechanisms by which ideas are put into practice: the translation of abstract concepts into real-life policies. The argument is quite straightforward. Scholars recognize that the 1980s and 1990s saw a widespread rejection of Keynesian principles of economic management that put a premium on state intervention. Policymakers everywhere turned to the free market as the potential solution to economic stagnation and declining standards of living. The move required restructuring existing state and social structures and instituting mechanisms that would reduce interference with economic life. Initiatives included the deregulation of domestic industries, bureaucratic downsizing, the privatization of state enterprises, the reduction of subsidies, and welfare reforms. Yet, the same scholars argue that the pursuit of broadly similar economic principles led to different outcomes thanks to the very unique processes and mediating mechanisms through which they were pursued. Neoliberalism did not lead to convergence across countries, as some observers thought it might (Boltho 1996).

In the case of outcomes, these scholars write that leaders engaged in neoliberal reforms proved selective in their choice of what principles and goals they would pursue. The specific framing and articulation of policies varied. Similar policies had disparate and sometimes unpredictable impacts in different countries (Campbell and Pedersen 2001a; Fourcade-Gourinchas and Babb 2002; Guillén 2001; Hall and Soskice 2001a; Schmidt 2002). As Campbell and Pedersen note:

> Despite increased capital mobility and the potential for capital disinvestment, insofar as labor market institutions are concerned substantial variation remains among the OECD countries in terms of the degree to which they approximate the neoliberal model and, in fact, some clearly do not. . . . [There is no] race to lower corporate tax rates . . . nor [is there] a convergence in government subsidies to business. . . . [T]his is not to say that convergence is an illusion. . . . [There] is evidence for convergence, but with an engaging twist (2001b: 271).

Fourcade-Gourinchas and Babb offer a second illustrative example in their analysis of "the neoliberal transitions" of Chile, Mexico, Britain, and France (2002: 536). "We argue," they write, "that important *differences* remain in the way each of these nations came to liberalize its economy" (536).

The processes and mediating mechanisms responsible for such variation include institutions, culture, politics, and other variables. "In institutionalist terms," argue Fourcade-Gourinchas and Babb, "the emergence and path of the neoliberal regimes was socially constructed through the mediation of national institutions and culture" (2002: 536). Campbell and Pedersen, in turn, observe that "a variety of historically given factors—many of them institutional, such as formal political institutions and discourse institutions—subsequently limited the range of solutions that were either politically available or discursively imaginable to policy makers" (2001b: 257).

This book confirms the insights of these works on how broadly similar principles of free trade (which are elements of a neoliberal philosophy) found unique expression in different places, as processes and mediating mechanisms translated abstract principles into reality. The evidence presented in the next chapters suggests that indeed a gap exists between abstract ideas, where indeed we find similarities, and their real-life pursuit and manifestations, where differences abound. In line with existing works on neoliberalism, the book also emphasizes the role of institutional and political factors in bridging that gap.

Yet *The Social Construction of Free Trade* also departs in important ways from these works on neoliberalism. Most of the existing research concerns the national as a source of difference: variation occurs across nation states and, therefore, nation states continue to be distinctive economic and policy entities. The unit of analysis in this book is, by contrast, the region. The book thus investigates the spread of neoliberalism on new empirical grounds. If convincing, moreover, the next chapters also point to some dilution of national distinctiveness. Countries all over the world have accepted the objectives of regional integration. They have lost some of their legislative autonomy while a number of their organizations have acquired a strongly transnational character. The conclusion is that the nation state matters less, then, as a place of difference and has instead become a piece of a larger construct.[3]

Before turning to the theory and analysis in the next chapters, we should review the turn to regional integration, the most important RTAs in existence, and the place of RTAs in the history of trade. This chapter ends with an overview of the rest of the book.

THE TURN TO FREE TRADE: BASIC CONCEPTS AND MAJOR EXAMPLES

RTAs constitute efforts to establish single economic spaces across a select number of member states. RTAs are thus neither national nor global: they are regional. This section offers a brief overview of RTAs at the end of the twentieth century: their basic characteristics and the most important examples, including the three case studies of this book—the EU, Mercosur, and NAFTA.

There are four basic elements to any modern market: goods, services, capital, and labor. We may think of goods as physical entities, such as apples, rubber, processed food, computer monitors, and cellular telephones, but also intangible items, such as a software program or a song. Services generally entail some sort of activity performed by somebody for the benefit of a second party. Examples include haircuts, taxi rides, brain surgery, and legal representation. Capital involves sums of money directed towards some form of investment, such as those in stocks, real estate, or private companies. Labor refers to workers of all types and in all industries and sectors.

RTAs aim at the creation of regional markets: spaces where some or all goods, services, capital, and labor can circulate freely across a given number of member states. This, by definition, requires the removal of barriers to the circulation of those entities. What are those barriers to trade? There

---

[3] Though we must acknowledge that the regional contains many elements of the national, as argued earlier in this chapter and throughout this book.

exist two types: tariff and nontariff barriers. Tariff barriers are taxes imposed on whatever is being exchanged as a result of its crossing the boundaries of member states. Imposed typically to protect domestic economic actors from foreign competition, they are to be removed gradually over time across sectors of the economy. Reduction follows different schedules and progressions depending on the industry in question. Industries deemed to be particularly incapable of withstanding a sudden exposure to foreign competition (because of unusually high cost structures, for instance) are generally protected longer from liberalization. Tariff barriers also include taxes imposed on trade between any given member state and a country outside of the RTA. When different, those taxes can cause disruptions to competition and ultimately trade within a given RTA.[4]

Nontariff barriers are far more varied and difficult to categorize than tariff barriers. The most obvious include quotas, subsidies, fiscal incentives, and other forms of support used by national governments to help certain industries or players. Quotas limit the quantities of a particular product that are allowed to enter into a country from the outside. They amount to a direct form of intervention on trade that clearly interferes with the natural demand for a product. Subsidies are a bit subtler: a government offers makers of certain products financial support, often on a volume basis. The result is tantamount to lowering production costs: thus, less efficient domestic producers (i.e., producers with higher cost structures) can afford to set their prices lower than foreign competitors, as if they enjoyed lower costs. The outcome is a distortion of trade in favor of domestic producers. Fiscal incentives involve any type of tax break awarded to producers, either during production or after. The effect is similar to a direct subsidy: producers can afford to price their products lower than they otherwise could.

There are then more subtle nontariff barriers—of central importance to this book—all of which ultimately concern fundamental viewpoints

---

[4] Consider, for instance, two countries from the same RTA in Africa imposing different taxes on Chinese steel. Different taxes will translate into differences in the price of steel and, therefore, in costs for those companies in those member states that utilize such steel. If those companies produce an identical product, under normal economic conditions they will be pricing that product differently: the company paying more for steel will charge the higher price. The resulting disparity in price will serve as a barrier to free trade between those two nations. Customers in the two countries, presumably interested in lower prices, will buy only from one company. The other company will have no opportunity to sell its products. When prices are instead leveled, consumers will presumably be indifferent to which product they will turn to, and trade between the two nations will boom. The solution to differential tax structures with third party trade is the elimination of those differences, something that is typically done with the imposition of a common external tariff. There are other advantages to the elimination of those differences, such as increased bargaining power vis-à-vis third countries (Wise 1994: 83).

that people and societies hold about the world. These include regulatory regimes in a variety of realms, such as the environment, consumer health, labor rights, safety, and others. When different from country to country, these regulatory regimes have adverse consequences on trade. They give rise to cost differentials among producers. Consider, for instance, a steel manufacturer in one country who, unlike its neighbor in the bordering country, does not need to comply with tight sulfur emissions into the air or with high minimum wages. Differences in regulatory regimes also generate hygienic or quality problems, product incompatibility issues, and so on. Nontariff barriers can also be "softer" than law: they may entail differences in inarticulate expectations that market participants hold about the world. Consider, for instance, the expectations that people from different countries can have about all aspects of a visit to a grocery store, the characteristics of wheat beer, or the equipment available at a ski resort. If not aligned, these expectations can harm market building.

Economists have devised a basic categorization scheme for RTAs largely based on what elements of the economy are affected by the integration process, and much less so on the choice of RTA officials over what tariff and nontariff barriers ought to be eliminated. This is probably due to the fact that the texts of most RTAs often very explicitly identify what elements of an economy they wish to liberalize and provide only general guidance for what types of barriers should be removed. It is in fact quite clear that all RTAs concern most, if not all, goods. The majority concern some capital and services. Only a few address labor.[5] These differences drive the current categorization of RTAs.

The least ambitious are "sectoral cooperation agreements." These are typically agreements concerned with goods in particular sectors of the economy, such as grain, coal, or fish. What are misleadingly called "free trade agreements" generally target most or all goods but only at times services and capital. Labor is typically excluded. "Customs unions" are typically free trade agreements with the addition of a common external tariff (CET) to undo tariff differentials between member states and third parties outside of an RTA.[6] One of the most comprehensive attempts to create a genuine free trade area are common markets. They are like custom unions but apply to the entire economy: goods, services, capital, and

---

[5] The predilection for goods is a reflection at once of the importance of goods for any given market (especially the less advanced ones) but also of the relative ease with which goods may be targeted. Perhaps more importantly, it is a reflection of the fact that goods are the most likely to be traded across borders with high frequency even before any agreement to craft regional markets is reached. Producers of goods have also traditionally pressured political leaders most forcefully to pursue regional markets.

[6] See note 4 for an overview of the purpose of a CET.

labor. This typology differs slightly across sources and scholars, and there exist additional combinations not mentioned here.[7]

We can consider the most important RTAs currently in existence in the context of this categorization. Table 1.1 identifies five key RTAs. It draws from their original texts but also takes into account later revisions and expansions.[8] The most advanced of all RTAs is certainly the EU: a full-blown common market.[9] Six countries signed the original Treaty of the European Economic Community (TEEC) in Rome in 1957: West Germany, France, Italy, Belgium, Luxembourg, and the Netherlands. Article 1 of the treaty stated the objective of creating a common market: an area where the trade of goods, services, capital, and labor occurs free from tariff as well as nontariff barriers (Articles 3 and 23 of TEEC). As a common market, the European Economic Community (EEC) would have a CET regime separating the member states from the rest of the international economy (Article 23 of TEEC). Of course, the members subscribed to the goal of generating wealth in a balanced, harmonious fashion. Major social disruptions, increases in poverty, and environmental degradation must be avoided. Progress must be balanced and gradual (Article 2 of TEEC).

A series of enlargements increased the number of EEC members. In 1973, Denmark, Great Britain, and Ireland joined. Greece would do the same in 1981, and Spain and Portugal in 1986. Austria, Finland, and Sweden, until then members of the European Free Trade Area, would become members in 1995.[10] In May 2004, ten additional countries from mostly Central and Eastern Europe joined the common market: Cyprus, the Czech Republic, Estonia, Hungary, Latvia, Lithuania, Malta, Poland, Slovakia, and Slovenia.[11]

---

[7] There exist, for instance, economic unions: arrangements with all the characteristics of a common market plus the "complete harmonization of government spending and procurement as well as the co-ordination of the operations of central banks" (Yeung, Perdikis, and Kerr 1999: 19). See Frankel (1997: 12–17), Gibb (1994: 24), and Yeung, Perdikis, and Kerr (1999: 18–19) for examples of RTA typologies.

[8] Note that table 1.1 does not include the Asia Pacific Economic Cooperation. Formed in 1989, the organization is not an RTA proper: it relies on voluntary actions by the member states, rather than on formal agreements, to liberalize trade. See Urata (2002: 23) and Mattli (1999: 9).

[9] As the reader will see shortly, the term EU officially refers to much more than the European common market. In this book, the term EU is used to refer to the common market. In certain passages, the term is obviously used to refer to the entire European project.

[10] The European Free Trade Area was formed in 1960 and later joined by a number of countries unwilling to join the EU's common market but still interested in free trade for goods and some coordination for agriculture. Great Britain and Denmark had been members until their move into the EU. The current members are Iceland, Liechtenstein, Norway, and Switzerland.

[11] In this latest enlargement, most of the older member states have opted to close bor-

Importantly, the EEC was itself only one of three treaties signed by the six member states and, later, by the new members. In 1952, those countries agreed to form the European Coal and Steel Community. This was in effect a treaty to establish a common market for coal and steel and, for that purpose, a supranational policy-coordinating body (the High Authority). The ultimate primary purpose of the European Coal and Steel Community was, however, geopolitical: to ensure international supervision of Germany's coal and steel industries (both central to war making) as well as to make German industries dependent on those of its neighbors (thus making military conflict much less appealing to Germany). In 1957, the same six countries also signed a treaty in Rome establishing the European Atomic Energy Community. In 1968, the three communities—the European Coal and Steel Community, the European Atomic Energy Community, and the EEC—were then collectively organized under one governing system called the European Community (EC).

By 1968, tariffs imposed on internal trade were eliminated and a CET erected. The EEC required the elimination of nontariff barriers. Yet, progress on that front stalled for many decades, much to the frustration of leading business corporations (Mattli 1999: 77–80). In 1986, a comprehensive plan—the Single European Act—was devised to remove all nontariff barriers to the movement of goods, services, capital, and labor. By 1993, the member states had a more or less functioning common market.

The year 1993 brought in a number of important changes to the overall structure and objectives of the EC, though these changes did not affect the common market project directly. At Maastricht, the member states agreed to change the name of the EC to the European Union. The title change was meant to symbolize closer economic and political union among the member states and the related approval of new arenas of cooperation: monetary unification,[12] a Common Foreign and Security Policy, and Justice and Home Affairs. The resulting Treaty of the European Union (TEU) of 1993 thus had three "pillars": the EEC (now confusingly called the European Community and whose founding treaty, the TEEC, is now known as the Treaty of the European Community [TEC]), the

---

ders to migrant laborers from the new member states for some years, at least in key sectors of the economy.

[12] A voluntary European Monetary System had been established in 1979 to coordinate and stabilize exchange rates. In 1993, most of the member states (Great Britain and Denmark being the exception) agreed to the creation of a European Central Bank and the eventual introduction of a single currency: the euro. The euro circulates today in twelve of the twenty-five member states (Great Britain, Denmark, Sweden, and the newest member states being the exceptions).

TABLE 1.1
Overview of Regional Trade Agreements

	Members (2004)	Elements of the Economy	Progress to Date	Key Additional Dimensions
EU (1957) *Common Market*	Austria, Belgium, Cyprus, the Czech Republic, Denmark, Estonia, Finland, France, Germany, Great Britain, Greece, Hungary, Ireland, Italy, Latvia, Lithuania, Luxembourg, Malta, the Netherlands, Poland, Portugal, Slovakia, Slovenia, Spain, Sweden	Goods, services, capital, and labor	Mostly complete, especially with goods	Monetary union; foreign policy; internal security cooperation
Mercosur (1991) *Common Market*	Argentina, Brazil, Paraguay, Uraguay Associate Members: Bolivia and Chile	Goods, services, capital, and labor Important exceptions in goods include the automotive and sugar sectors	Significant, especially with goods; common external tariff planned for 2006	
NAFTA (1993) & Side Agreements on Labor & the	Canada, Mexico, United States	All goods, selected services, all capital, no labor	Significant, especially with goods	

Environment *Free Trade Area*				
AFTA (1992) & Associated Services and Investments Agreements *Free Trade Area*	Brunei, Burma, Cambodia, Indonesia, Laos, Malaysia, Myanmar, the Philippines, Singapore, Thailand, Vietnam	All goods, services, and most capital Important exceptions in goods include unprocessed agricultural products and slow progress with rice and sugar; in investments, portfolio investments are exempted	Fair in goods for tariffs though poor for nontariff barriers; poor in services and capital	In the context of ASEAN, agreements on security, crime, preventive diplomacy, transportation, and other areas
SADC Protocol on Trade (1999) *Free Trade Area*	Angola, Botswana, the Democratic Republic of Congo, Lesotho, Malawi, Mauritius, Mozambique, Namibia, Seychelles, South Africa, Swaziland, Tanzania, Zambia, Zimbabwe	Goods and services	Progress on liberalization of goods; difficulties with services and with ratification of protocol by all member states	Various agreements on political cooperation, energy, crime, natural resources, and other areas

Common Foreign and Security Policy, and Justice and Home Affairs.[13] Additional, and less important, treaties followed Maastricht.[14] At the time of writing, a Constitutional Treaty that unifies and revises in a single document all the key texts of the EU has failed ratification in France and the Netherlands, and is thus highly unlikely to come into being in its current form.

A good measure of economic integration success is the increase of one member state's exports to the other member states as a percentage of that country's total exports since joining the bloc. Cameron (1998) has analyzed EU figures for 1958–95. With the exception of Ireland and Greece, member states show an average increase of 25 percentage points from the time of entry to 1995. These and other measures clearly depict a highly integrated economic area.

Mercosur represents a second rather impressive effort at forming a common market. Mercosur brings together Argentina, Brazil, Paraguay, and Uruguay as full members and Bolivia and Chile as associate members. It is the third largest trading bloc in the world (after NAFTA and the EU), and the second largest common market (after the EU). The Treaty of Asuncion of 1991 set out the bloc's objectives, while the Protocol of Ouro Preto of 1995 set out its institutional structure. Mercosur, like the EU, aims at the establishment of an area where goods, services, capital, and labor can circulate free from tariff and nontariff barriers. It also aims at the establishment of a CET (Article 1 of the Treaty of Asuncion). As with the EU, the founding documents emphasize that economic integration and growth are not to be obtained at the expense of major environmental degradation or social disruptions (Preamble to the Treaty of Asuncion). The original and very ambitious objective was to establish a common market by 1995. The Protocol of Ouro Preto set out a clear tariff reduction schedule and identified the automotive and sugar sectors as temporarily exempt from liberalization. It also identified a CET for nine thousand product categories (the CET ranged from 0 to 20%, with an average of 14%), though each government was allowed to exempt three hundred products temporarily (until 2001 for most goods).

The linear and automatic tariff reduction for intra-area trade of goods occurred more or less according to schedule. By 1995, approximately 95% of all internal trade was free from tariffs (Carranza 2003: 69). The erection of a CET regime in 1995 was imperfect and riddled with excep-

---

[13] The European Coal and Steel Community expired in July 2002 and the European Atomic Energy Community is still part of the TEU but in effect irrelevant and on its way to being expired.

[14] The Treaty of Amsterdam of 1999 and the Treaty of Nice of 2000 concern above all the structural adjustments that the EU had to undertake to accommodate the ten new member states joining in May 2004 and those joining later.

tions, so much so that leaders agreed to aim for 2006 as a target date for full deployment. The liberalization of services, capital, and labor also remains a challenge. Nonetheless, if we again use—as a measure of integration success—the increase of one member state's exports to the other member states as a percentage of that country's total exports since joining the bloc, we find that the average figure for Mercosur member states for the period 1991–2000 is impressive: 33 percentage points.[15] In absolute numbers, intra-area trade increased from US$4 billion in 1990 to US$20 billion in 1997 (Carranza 2003: 69). Intra-area trade accounted for 20% of all trade in 1999, up from 11% in 1990 (Mecham 2003: 378), and remained close to that figure even in the crisis years of 2001 and 2002.

Various political and economic shocks, such as Brazil's currency devaluation in 1999 and Argentina's economic crisis of late 2001 and 2002, have so far challenged but also strengthened Mercosur (Carranza 2003). The election of Luiz Inácio "Lula" da Silva as President of Brazil in 2002 and of Néstor Kirchner as President of Argentina in 2003 brought new energy and optimism to the area (Southern Cone Report 2003). Both men have openly committed their administrations to working towards the realization of Mercosur's objectives and even towards the formation of a broader South American trading bloc by linking Mercosur with the Andean Community.[16] Efforts on the latter front received a boost in September 2003 after the collapse of WTO negotiations in Cancun, Mexico (Forero 2003; Gazeta Mercantil 2003).

Progress in Mercosur is especially noteworthy when the failures of previous integration efforts in the region are taken into consideration. In the words of a prominent scholar of the region, these brought decades of "failures, disappointments and formalism" in South America (Castañeda 1994: 313). Signed with the Treaty of Montevideo of 1960, for instance, the Asociación Latinoamericano de Libre Comercio brought together the current Mercosur member states plus Chile and Peru. In 1961 the membership expanded with the joining of Ecuador and Colombia and, in 1967, with the arrival of Venezuela and Bolivia. The treaty called for the elimination of tariffs and other restrictions on most trade within a twelve-year time period and ultimately the formation of a common market. In fact, the member states failed to take concrete steps at tariff removal and the portion of international trade from the member states that was intraregional trade remained steady at 10% (Gwynne 1994: 193; Mattli 1999: 141–42).[17] The association was eventually reconstituted in 1980

[15] Estimates calculated from data available in International Monetary Fund (1995, 2000, 2002).

[16] The Andean Community includes Bolivia, Colombia, Ecuador, Peru, and Venezuela.

[17] Latin America witnessed a number of integration projects in the 1960s. The Mercado Común Centroamericano (Central American Common Market) was also born in 1960 with

under the name Asociación Latinoamericana de Integración Económica (Latin America Integration Association) with the much more modest function of fostering economic cooperation through bilateral agreements among its member states.

If the EU and Mercosur represent the two most impressive common markets in existence, NAFTA is undoubtedly the most impressive free trade area in place. Put into effect on January 1, 1994, NAFTA constitutes the largest marketplace in the world.[18] Built on the foundations of the Canada–United States Free Trade Agreement (CUSFTA) of 1988, it comprises Canada, Mexico, and the United States. Its paramount objectives, laid out in Article 102 of the NAFTA text, are the elimination of all tariffs and of a combination of nontariff barriers to the trade of goods by 2003, though sensitive sectors were given until 2008 (Annex 302.2). NAFTA also aims at the liberalization of capital movement (Chapter 11) and selected services (Article 102, Chapter 12).[19] Unlike the EU or Mercosur, NAFTA has no provisions for the liberalization of labor or the erection of a CET. Two corollary agreements on labor and the environment— the North American Agreement on Labor Cooperation (NAALC) and the North American Agreement on Environmental Cooperation (NAAEC)— specify additional trade and policy measures.

Progress in NAFTA has been rapid (Abbott 2000: 543–46). By January 1, 2003, following scheduled tariff reductions, almost all trade in the NAFTA region began to flow tariff-free. If again we consider increases in a member state's exports to the other member states as a percentage of that country's total exports since joining the bloc as a sign of closer integration, NAFTA may be said to have been a moderate success. The average increase is 2.5 percentage points for the period 1994–2001. Interestingly, while Canada and the United States have experienced increases (7 and 4 percentage points respectively), Mexico has not (around −3.5 percentage points).[20] In any event, Canada and Mexico are now the United States' number-one and number-two trading partners.

Though certainly less successful in practice, Asia and Africa have their

---

Costa Rica, El Salvador, Guatemala, Honduras, and Nicaragua as members. A CET was in place by the year 1966. All but 8% of trade was made free from tariff barriers in little time. Then, in 1970, Honduras withdrew from the common market and shortly thereafter went to war with El Salvador. Soon afterwards, the project collapsed (Mattli 1999: 145). The Andean Pact of 1969 then brought together five countries from the stagnant Asociación Latinoamericana de Libre Comerció: Chile, Bolivia, Peru, Ecuador, and Colombia. The pace of integration in this case was considerably slower than for the common market (Gwynne 1994: 193).

[18] NAFTA member states had a combined GDP in 2003 of US$11 trillion. The GDPs of the EU and Mercosur in 2003 were, respectively, US$8 trillion and US$700 million.

[19] Article 1201 exempts financial services and air transport.

[20] Estimates calculated from data available in International Monetary Fund (1995, 2000, 2002).

own assortments of free trade areas. Born in 1992 with the Framework Agreement on Enhancing ASEAN Economic Cooperation, the ASEAN Free Trade Area (AFTA) was intended as a free trade area for all goods with the exception of unprocessed agricultural products. AFTA at first included Brunei, Indonesia, Malaysia, the Philippines, Singapore, and Thailand. It later welcomed Vietnam in 1995; Burma, Laos, and Myanmar in 1997; and Cambodia in 1999. The mechanisms for tariff reduction were set in the 1992 Agreement on the Common Effective Preferential Tariff. The agreement envisioned a reduction of tariff barriers to 5% or less by 2008 as well as the elimination of all nontariff barriers. The member states then committed in 1995 to reducing barriers to trade in services (ASEAN Framework Agreement on Services) and, in 1998, to the liberalization of investments (with some exceptions, including portfolio investments) by the year 2010, though later that became 2008 (Framework Agreement on the ASEAN Investment Area).

Progress in tariff reduction for goods has been less than impressive, but nonetheless real. Tariffs on intraregional trade of goods fell, for instance, from 12.7% in 1993 to 6.4% in 1997 (Stubbs 2000). Impressively, trade among the member states doubled over the period 1992–2002 (Economist 2002a). Nonetheless, the deadline for full implementation was moved several times, until in 2003 it was set for 2010 for the original six members and 2015 for the remaining members. Countries also stubbornly refused to lower tariffs in major sectors: Malaysia on imported cars, the Philippines on petrochemicals, the poorer countries on rice, and so on. Equally importantly, the member states did little to remove nontariff barriers to imports, especially when it came to formulating shared procedures and standards. This mixed performance record can be attributed to a combination of nonexistent enforcement mechanisms, economic instability in the region, and plain mistrust among the member states (Economist 2002a; Reyes 2000; Stubbs 2000).[21]

Africa has a large number of overlapping and varied free trade areas. A good example is the SADC Protocol on Trade. Signed in 1999 by fourteen members, it envisions a free trade area for goods and services by 2012 extending throughout Southern and portions of Eastern and Central Africa (Deutsche Presse-Agentur 1999). To attain those objectives, the protocol calls for the abolition of all tariffs and most nontariff barriers. Progress has been slow but again real. By August 2001, almost 47% of all goods traded in SADC (Southern African Development Community)

---

[21] We should note that, at the time of writing, the AFTA member states have agreed in a watershed agreement to form a common market by the year 2020. Under the name of ASEAN Economic Community, the common market is explicitly intended to emulate the European common market in comprehensiveness and success (Nusa Dua 2003).

were traded at zero tariffs (Xinhua General News Service 2003). At the time of writing, a proposal was on the table to accelerate the implementation of the protocol in order to achieve a full-fledged free trade area by 2008 (Agence France Presse 2003a). At the same time, the failure of three countries—Angola, the Democratic Republic of Congo, and Seychelles—to comply with the essential requirements of the agreement has undermined the viability of the overall project (AllAfrica 2001).

The EU, Mercosur, NAFTA, AFTA, and SADC are only five of the many RTAs that came into existence at the end of the twentieth century. We cannot consider the others in detail here. The most impressive, however, include the 1992 Central European Free Trade Area, the 1996 Andean Community, the 1996 Central African Customs Union, and the 1994 West African Economic and Monetary Union.

RTAs in Historical Perspective

RTAs constitute a new, aggressive, and so far quite successful attempt to create markets that extend beyond established geographical boundaries. Even a very brief overview of the history of trade can illustrate their significance.

Trade across human communities has existed for thousands of years. Archeological and written records show that spices, wool, silk, precious metals, teas, weapons, and a host of other goods have been exchanged across societies since the invention of agriculture and the first sedentary communities (Pomeranz and Topik 1999: 3). Much evidence exists to indicate, for instance, that in the third millennium B.C. trade flourished between Mesopotamia and the Harappan civilization of the Indus River valley. A thousand years later, donkey caravans were linking Mesopotamia and Asia Minor (Bentley 1993: 2001). Later, at the time of the Roman Empire, a number of trading routes collectively known as the Silk Road stretched across the Eurasian landmass. After the fall of that empire, trade boomed in much of Asia, the Middle East, and Africa for many centuries. Even in the pre-Colombian Americas, societies were actively exchanging many goods. In Europe, following a hiatus in the Middle Ages, trade exploded again in the fifteenth and sixteenth centuries (Abu-Lughod 1989; Curtin 1984; Frank 1998).

Though impressive, all of this trade did not amount to a planned integration of local economies. It was quite selective in terms of what was being traded (mostly a few types of goods). There were tariff barriers: taxes were imposed on trade between empires, city-states, nations, and other types of political organizations. There were also a number of non-tariff barriers—such as quotas and subsidies, but also language, mistrust, and distance—which limited what and how much could be exchanged. The doctrine of mercantilism, with its preference for heavy tariffs on imported manufactured goods and strict trade regulations, perhaps combined the most powerful mix of tariff and nontariff measures in history. Developed by the powerful colonial European nations of the sixteenth, seventeenth, and eighteenth centuries, it imposed some of the most severe restrictions on trade in history (Ekelund and Tollison 1997).

The great economists Adam Smith and David Ricardo in the eighteenth century launched a reevaluation of all protectionist tendencies. Their liberal ideas made some headway in the nineteenth century, most famously when Great Britain—partly driven by a desire to eliminate the illegal smuggling of goods into its territories—repealed its Corn Laws in 1846. The move unilaterally dismantled protectionist tariffs in place since the middle of the 1300s. Other areas in Europe, including France, embarked on similar changes (Cain 1999; Nye 1991).[22] Yet by the 1870s and under pressure to fund ever more costly militaries, most countries in Europe and elsewhere in the world were reverting back towards protectionism and began to impose very heavy tariffs on trade (Cain 1999: 2). By the end of World War I even those countries that had shown a preference for free trade had backtracked. The world was entering one of its most protectionist phases in history (Gibb 1994: 8–9).

The late 1940s ushered in a new, unprecedented era of market integration. World leaders began to view protectionism as having contributed to the rise of nationalism, belligerence, and ultimately World War II. They thus turned to free trade: they hoped that free trade would encourage specialization and reliance on international commerce, and that countries whose economies depended on each other were by necessity less likely to go to war. The signing of GATT in 1947 represented one of the first major achievements of the new economic philosophy.[23] Spearheaded by the United States, the original document involved twenty-three nations, in-

---

[22] Britain and France signed short-lived bilateral trade agreements with a number of other European countries in the 1860s (Cain 1999: 2). More committal and comprehensive agreements were also signed in what is Germany today: the Bavarian-Württemberg Customs Union of 1828–33, the German Zollverein of 1834, and the Tax Union between Hanover, Brunswick, Oldenburg, and Lippe Schaumburg of 1834–54. Also noteworthy were the Moldovian-Wallachian Customs Union of 1847 in today's Romania and the Swiss Confederation of 1948. See Mattli (1999: 1–5).

[23] In 1944, world leaders met at Bretton Woods, New Hampshire, to set up the institutional framework for the postwar economy. They gave birth to three major institutions: the International Monetary Fund (IMF), the World Bank, and the International Trade Organization. While the IMF was dedicated to macroeconomic stability and the World Bank to helping poorer nations develop, the International Trade Organization was designed specifically for trade regulation. The GATT incorporated the objectives of the International Trade Organization.

cluding Brazil, the United Kingdom, South Africa, Australia, and most countries in South Asia. The signatories committed themselves to a reduction in formal tariff barriers. The number of GATT members stayed more or less stable throughout the 1950s and 1960s, and then exploded to over one hundred in the 1970s. By the late 1980s, selected nontariff barriers were also included (Gibb 1994: 10–13).

The first three decades of the GATT proved to be a success. The value of trade subject to the new rules went from approximately US$10 billion in 1947 to US$160 billion by the end of 1980 (Gibb 1994: 12). In 1960, according to the World Bank, the ratio of foreign trade to gross domestic product stood at 25%; by 1999 it had become 52% (Urata 2002). Tariffs on manufactured goods dropped from a peak of almost 40% in 1947 to around 5% among the contracting parties in the 1980s (Gibb 1994: 13). In 1993, a new agreement was reached to replace the GATT with the WTO. Around 120 organizations participated in the negotiations. The WTO, a permanent organization based in Geneva, Switzerland, was given unprecedented conflict-resolution powers and a mandate that included not only goods but also services. Membership continued to increase until, by September 2003, the WTO boasted 148 members.

By the 1980s and 1990s, however, the GATT, the WTO, and the multilateral system of bargaining that they embodied began to be plagued by difficulties. The process relied on a cumbersome consensus system: a single small country could veto any given initiative of which it was a part. Though lofty in their aspiration to liberalize trade at the global level, most of the parties focused on goods and not on services, capital, or labor. The primary tool for liberalization, moreover, remained tariff barriers. Nontariff barriers could thus be used easily to limit trade, and most countries took advantage of this option to protect vulnerable industries and special interest groups. Rich countries from Europe and North America continued to offer their farmers and other players in a wide array of industries enormous subsidies. Exasperated, poor countries retaliated by making ample use of complex domestic regulatory schemes, collusion between the state and the private sectors, and other tools to keep imports from rich countries outside of their economies (Economist 2003a: 26–28). Most member states in any case showed great hesitation to comply with tariff reduction agreements and schedules. Tariffs were lowered often only when domestic players could withstand international competition. They were kept high if they could not.

RTAs offered an alternative. Impressive progress in the EU showed the viability of a different kind of market building: regional, rather than global, and more aggressive and deeper in terms of what would be subject to liberalization, how liberalization would be obtained, and what tools would be used to ensure compliance. A wave of RTAs followed.

Some of these efforts, such as those in South America, built from moribund agreements that had been put into place in the 1950s and 1960s but had never materialized into something concrete. Others, like those in North America, represented fresh departures. All espoused visions of integration that superseded the multilateral collaboration put forth by the GATT and the WTO, and sent warnings to GATT and WTO negotiators that slow and ineffective multilateral processes could no longer be accepted.[24]

The formation of all these RTAs took observers by surprise. This was an unprecedented reorganization of international economic activity. "The surge in regional trading arrangements over the last 10 years," noted the eminent economist Frankel, "constitutes a break with preceding postwar history. Previous regional agreements had been neither so numerous, nor so successful, as those of recent years" (1997: 4). The economic and political physiognomy of the world was quickly changing. The vision of a world with a single economic system was being replaced by a world with multiple, parallel systems of trade. As a group of economists put it in the late 1990s, RTAs, "and not the WTO, are the driving force in the international organization of economic activity. New regional trade organizations are continually being proposed and many are negotiated. . . . [T]he expansion and deepening of regional organizations dominates the international trade landscape at the start of the new millennium" (Yeung, Perdikis, and Kerr 1999: 2).

Our attention in this book turns to this remarkable effort at regional market building. Scholars have only begun its investigation and much remains to be discovered. The next section offers a brief overview of the following chapters.

The Organization of the Book

This book seeks to show that, and explain why, officials in the EU, Mercosur, and NAFTA have, in their pursuit of free trade, addressed differences in the worldviews of market participants quite differently from each other. It also seeks to document and explain the divergent evolution of societal organizations (interest groups, businesses, states) in the three RTAs. Throughout, special attention is given to the impact of legal traditions and powerful actors on the evolution of law and organizations. The next chap-

---

[24] See, for instance, Kerremans (2000: 144–45) and Vernon (1996). Vernon writes: "The emergence of a NAFTA possibility offered the Americans a splendid opportunity to send a signal to the negotiators in Geneva that, if those negotiations failed, the Unites States had an attractive option, namely to build its own block from a North American base" (625).

ter outlines the arguments of the book in detail after examining the limits of the existing literature on regional integration. Chapters 3 and 4 follow by offering empirical evidence on the different responses by RTA officials to the standardization challenges inherent to regional integration. In chapter 3, attention turns to their activities in the realms of economic life, public health, and the environment. In chapter 4, we turn to their activities in three key areas within the realm of economic life: women's rights in the workplace, dairy products, and labor rights. Chapter 5 explores the divergent evolution of women's interest groups, dairy companies, and state labor structures across the three RTAs. Chapter 6 summarizes and reflects on the findings. The book raises interesting questions about the desirability of different legal approaches to market integration, how trade agreements across RTAs might be structured, and the possibility of change in any given RTA. It also offers new evidence on the limits of globalization, the nature of markets, and the spread of neoliberalism. The chapter concludes with a discussion of promising venues for future research.

Chapter 2

INSTITUTIONS, POLITICS, AND THE MAKING

OF REGIONAL MARKETS

THE PROLIFERATION OF RTAs in the 1980s and 1990s raised a number of questions. Never before had the world witnessed so many countries enter into formal trade agreements with countries in their geographical proximity. Never before had there been such a collective and organized embrace of free trade principles across the globe. Startled by these events, a number of scholars confronted this wave of regional market building. Their responses varied, but most fell into one of three types. One group searched for the causes of this concurrent turn to free trade. A second wondered what the consequences of RTAs might be for the functioning of a global economy. A third asked what the implications of market building might be for the well-being of society. Together, these studies shared a common trait: a tendency to interpret the events of the 1980s and 1990s as constituting a fundamentally homogeneous turn in history—an embrace of free trade that would bring countries into regions designed to attain very similar economic objectives.

This chapter examines and then challenges these works. The RTAs of the 1980s and 1990s may have shared a similar commitment to free trade. Yet important and enduring differences set them apart. First, RTA officials have developed dramatically different legal systems to address disparities in the worldviews of market participants. In some RTAs, officials have developed extensive legal systems designed to standardize the world; in others, they have adopted a more minimalist approach. When we compare what, exactly, is subjected to standardization and the content of the standardizing principles, we discover crucial differences. Second, organizations—interest groups, businesses, state administrations—have responded quite differently to integration: which organizations have established regional-level operations varies from RTA to RTA, as do their specific structures and programs.

This chapter then offers an explanation for these differences, one that focuses on the institutional and political contexts in which RTAs are built. With the support of key groups in society, officials have shown a propensity to standardize when they have operated in RTAs where most or all of the member states share a tradition of civil law. They have adopted a more minimalist approach when they have operated within common-law traditions. They have then produced laws whose targets and content show continuity with existing national legal approaches and compliance with the preferences of powerful actors. Organizational developments, too, reflect national institutional and political contexts. At the same time, however, they also reflect a regional-level institution: regional law itself. The chapter concludes with an overview of the case studies of this book.

CREATED EQUAL? EXISTING APPROACHES TO RTAS

A number of academics, journalists, activists and other observers reacted to the wave of regional markets in the 1980s and 1990s. Assuming most RTAs to be *fundamentally similar projects*—parallel attempts to liberalize trade among neighboring countries—they proceeded to investigate the collective turn to regional markets from a variety of angles. Comparative questions were, accordingly, lost. This section examines the main claims and inherent limitations of these works.

Explaining the Wave of RTAs

Many of the earliest works on the new RTAs asked why so many countries felt compelled, in the space of a few years, to enter into such trade agreements. The focus was on the collective turn to regional markets. What factors could explain this general embrace of regional free trade? Could this phenomenon be elegantly explained by a theory focused on certain key variables, whether political, economic, or social? The key questions, applied in blanket fashion to all RTAs, became "Why the change, and why now?" (Frankel 1997: 4).

One of the most popular economic explanations for the new RTAs pointed to the growing ineffectiveness of the WTO and the GATT. The arrival of new members—mostly from the postcolonial and developing regions of Africa, Asia, and the Middle East—presented new needs and a diversity of economic philosophies. Talks became increasingly complex and time consuming. Compliance rates with timetables and tariff schedules worsened (Hormats 1994: 105). "The 120-nation World Trade Organization," wrote one journalist, "looks tired" (Terry 1996). At the Uruguay Round of negotiations in the 1990s, countries proved to be far less interested in opening their economies than gaining access to those of others (Economist 1996). The GATT's exclusive focus on goods and its limited capacity for liberalization proved frustrating, as did the WTO's failure to improve on both fronts. In this atmosphere, "regional trade organizations provided one alternative. Smaller groups were more manage-

able. They did not have to accommodate those with very different perspectives. Neighbors shared common problems" (Yeung, Perdikis, and
Kerr 1999: 4). Problems that were intractable at the global level had solutions at the local level (Hormats 1994: 99). "Regional groupings,"
wrote one observer, "are demonstrably willing to proceed more boldly:
many of them have decided to adopt totally free trade, whereas none of
the global conclaves to date has even considered such an ambitious goal"
(Bergsten 1996: 106).

Still, disillusionment with multilateral progress could have easily translated into a dismissal of free trade as a whole. Alternatively, it could have
led to the pursuit of free trade through less institutionalized venues, such
as ad hoc bilateral agreements. The new RTAs, as a whole, betrayed a
newly found determination and commitment to the principles of free
trade. Whence did that commitment come? Proclamations and public
statements from the period reveal a widespread conviction that RTAs
could generate unprecedented wealth for all countries involved through
increased competition and specialization (Gibb 1994: 6).[1] Thus, in the
case of NAFTA for instance, "the alliance" was expected to "promote
long-term efficiencies of production, expand opportunities for capital investment, and increase commodity trade," all of which would guarantee
"rising standards of living for all three countries" (McConnell and
MacPherson 1994: 169). The demise of Communism in the 1980s and
1990s, and the failure of import substitution experiments in Latin America and elsewhere, of course, fueled this optimism (Hormats 1994: 101;
Yeung, Perdikis, and Kerr 1999: 5).

A third, economic explanation for the general rush to form RTAs focused on their function as the formal acknowledgment of the de facto rise
of regional economies all over the world. New technological advancements
and lower costs of transportation and communication had made it possible for companies to reach beyond national borders, market-wise and organizationally, years before RTAs were signed (Yeung, Perdikis, and Kerr
1999: 5). A complex international division of labor had already been
evolving. RTAs merely crystallized an economic reality already in place
(Ohmae 1993: 78): they "supplied" the institutional structures demanded
by the steep increases in trade across nations (Jayasuriya 2003a: 200).[2]

---

[1] Ricardo elegantly articulated these ideas in his famous chapter 7 of *Principles of Political Economy and Taxation* (Ricardo 1984 [1817]). See the *Economist* (1990) for a simple
rendition of Ricardo's already clear prose on why this would occur.

[2] This line of argument builds from works from the 1950s and 1960s intent on explaining the earlier, but far less impressive, post–World War II wave of RTAs. Functionalists and
neofunctionalists argued then that an "expansion of economic activity creates incentives for
states to further liberalize and standardize economic exchange" (Mansfield and Milner
1997a: 6).

Thus, analysts were able to write, "the growth in, and strength of, intra-regional trade is a key contributing factor of NAFTA, Mercosur" and other RTAs (Yeung, Perdikis, and Kerr 1999: 11; Stubbs 2000).[3]

Economic explanations of the spread of RTAs did not convince all observers. For some, they shared "an assumption that, as the demand for regional co-operation increases because of deepening economic integration or the opening of markets, it will be matched with a 'supply' of regional institutions" (Jayasuriya 2003a: 200). In fact, increases in trade or simply an interest in free trade need not necessarily lead to formal, long-term agreements among sovereign nations. What role did politics play in all of this? For some, RTAs were most directly the creation of political leaders everywhere eager to remain in power (Milner 1998: 20; Mattli 1999; Moravcsik 1998). More specifically, "international economic co-operation result[ed] from the calculations of political leaders," who have had to juggle at once the desire to be reelected, weak domestic economies, and the allure of international economic cooperation (Milner 1998: 20). Thus, in Mexico, for instance, the leaders of the Partido Revolucionario Institucional supported the creation of NAFTA in the hope that it would revitalize the national economy and ensure their reelection (Milner 1998). Moravcsik (1998), Mattli (1999), Milner (1998), and others offered similar accounts for the EU. Other scholars would do the same for countries in Asia, Latin America, and elsewhere (Jayasuriya 2003a: 202, 2003b: 339; Carranza 2003; Mecham 2003: 376).

Geopolitics also played an important role. For many observers, RTAs helped stabilize countries that had just emerged from dictatorial or communist regimes. Mercosur certainly reflected a desire to safeguard the newly established democracies of its four member states. Two military coups in Paraguay in 1998 and 2000 were hence averted because Argentina and Brazil stated their unwillingness to tolerate a dictatorship in

---

[3] To be sure, not all proponents of economics-driven accounts of RTAs were willing to view RTAs as outgrowths of a commitment to liberal economics or as reflections of a de facto international economy. To some, the RTA phenomenon represented something quite different: a calibrated compromise between liberalization and protectionism (Gardels 1993). As Michalak put it, "regional trading blocs" reconcile "two contradictory aims: extending the benefits of the international division of labor and flexible specialisation, and protecting domestic and regional based enterprises from outside competition" (1994: 61). Thus, in Latin America "regional integration [is] a halfway house that possesses intrinsic merits and is preferable to existing alternatives" (Castañeda 1994: 313). The EU's push for internal liberalization was not matched by a reduction of subsidies for farmers and other ailing industries. Internal liberalization in NAFTA did not lead to the removal of protective measures for steel, textiles, or timber (Gordon 2003: 117). And in Asia, AFTA officials continued to extend favorable national treatments to vulnerable industries. This interpretation of RTAs was rooted in recent, and quite revolutionary, developments in theories of free trade (Krugman 1990; Prestowitz 1992; Economist 1993a; Thurow 1992).

the bloc. The entry of ten countries mostly from Central and Eastern Europe into the EU in 2004 "locked" those countries into a permanent partnership founded on democracy and capitalism, much as had been done with Germany earlier (Milward 1992). Similar arguments were made for NAFTA and Mexico (McConnell and MacPherson 1994: 170).

If security considerations made RTAs appealing, so did the arrival of a new set of transnational problems, such as cross-border pollution, illegal immigration, and cross-national crime. To some observers, RTAs offered institutional mechanisms for dealing with those problems: RTAs provided stable channels of communication, cooperation, and accountability. RTAs offered regional-level solutions for regional-level problems. They were also expected to increase wealth and make cooperation in key policy areas easier. Thus, a key impetus behind NAFTA was the hope that stronger links with Mexico and a wealthier Mexican population would make illegal migration to the United States less desirable (McConnell and MacPherson 1994: 171). At the same time, RTAs offered advantages for dealing with *interregional* problems as well, above all the rise of an integrated and protectionist EU. RTAs became a "defensive mechanism" that put the governments of the member states "in a more favourable position to bargain against threats of increased protectionism that might be put forth by trading blocs" elsewhere (McConnell and MacPherson 1994: 167). Such reasoning applied to Asia, North America, and other areas (McConnell and MacPherson 1994: 167; Mattli 1999: 166).[4]

Sociological accounts quickly complemented economic and political accounts for the spread of RTAs. Higgott, for instance, proposed an "ideational, as opposed to a material" or "economistic" approach (1998: 44). A new culture of cosmopolitanism, openness, and progress was ultimately the driver towards regional integration (Inglehart et al. 1996). The "conversion" of the United States "to travel the regional route" was in this regard critical for inspiring countries throughout the world to do the same (Bhagwati 1993a: 29). Sociological accounts also focused on emulation. The successes of the EU in the late 1980s instigated changes in North America. Officials in South America, Asia, and elsewhere, eager to demonstrate both an understanding of world events and their progressive

---

[4] There developed additional, though perhaps less important, political explanations for the rapid formation of RTAs at the end of the twentieth century. Some scholars argued that some member states formed regional blocs in order to gain access to more successful RTAs elsewhere. This is posited to have occurred in Latin America and Eastern Europe (Switky 2000: 18). Others proposed that countries formed RTAs as a way of signaling to GATT and WTO officials their dissatisfaction with stalling progress (Gordon 2003: 105; Hormats 1994; Switky 2000: 18). Yet another school of thought proposed that a presumed decline of the United States as a hegemonic power at the end of the Cold War pressured nation states to form protectionist economic blocs (Mansfield and Milner 1997a: 10; Tussie 1998: 82).

attitudes, mobilized quickly with plans of their own (Baldwin 1997: 884; Hormats 1994: 101). Regionalism spread rapidly, fueled by a "domino effect" (Baldwin 1997: 871) driven by legitimacy and a quest for prestige. Countries joined regional projects as a way to "to enhance [their] political or economic credibility" both within and outside of their geographical areas (Yeung, Perdikis, and Kerr 1999: 20).

There were many other, more daring, reactions to the remarkable events of the 1980s and 1990s. Urging a "spatial" analysis, Niemann insisted that RTAs were attempts by nation states to fight off the diluting effects of globalization on national identity and citizenship. "Regionalization," he wrote, constitutes a "space created by the competing trajectories of globalization, the desires of imagined communities and the efforts of states to maintain the legitimacy of their spatial form against pressure from above and below" (2000: 16; Golob 2003). Others argued that smaller or otherwise weaker countries were especially powerful forces of integration. These countries were using integration to protect themselves from the forces of global competition (Yeung, Perdikis, and Kerr 1999: 20). Yet others suggested that RTAs allowed member states to experiment with new policies and ideas (22).

RTAs and the Global Economy

The rapid spread of RTAs in the 1980s and 1990s shook the advocates of multilateral trade and the global economy. The unit of analysis was, again, RTAs *as a whole*: the critical question was whether "regional arrangements" should overall be seen as "stumbling blocks or building blocks for a more integrated and successful economy" (Lawrence 1996: 2; De Melo and Panagariya 1993; Kerremans and Switky 2000: 1; Krueger 1999). Could RTAs coexist with the GATT, or would RTAs "supplant the WTO"? (Yeung, Perdikis, and Kerr 1999: 27).[5]

Cogent arguments concerning the destructive impact of RTAs on the world economy were quickly produced (Bhagwati and Krueger 1995). Perhaps the most powerful focused on the protection of vulnerable industries from global competition. This "special interests" thesis argued that "negotiators frequently seek to exclude from regional FTAs [free trade agreements] precisely those sectors that would be most threatened by welfare-enhancing trade creation" (Frankel 1997: 212). RTA officials every-

---

[5] One of the primary concerns behind these questions focused on global welfare. If regionalism did hurt global trade, and if global trade would be the most beneficial arrangement from the point of view of wealth creations for all countries—as traditional economics suggested—then regionalism presented serious problems that needed to be addressed (Bhagwati 1993a). See De Melo and Panagariya (1993) for an introduction to this topic and Viner (1950) for a classic rendition.

where had introduced substantial measures to protect "less-competitive or inefficient domestic industries from the rigours of wide open global competition" (Yeung, Perdikis, and Kerr 1999: 19; Michalak 1994: 64). Pundits pointed to a long list of discriminatory measures. The measures included voluntary export restraint agreements, dumping, subsidies, rules of origin, and complex regulatory regimes (Frankel 1997: 212; Hormats 1994: 103).[6] The spread of RTAs thus dealt a serious blow to a multi-lateral world economy. "The GATT is not dead," wrote one observer, but "it seems unlikely that it will regain its one-time vitality" (Michalak 1994: 64). The prominent economist Lester Thurow was less equivocal and simply announced that the GATT was dead (1992). Others adopted similar stances. "These agreements," wrote Henderson, "are . . . dis-criminatory . . . and can be viewed as a factor making for disintegration, rather than integration, within the world economy as a whole" (1992: 644).[7]

Protectionism, however, was only one of several ways in which RTAs undermined the global economy. A second was "trade diversion": the in-evitable increase in regional trade at the expense of trade formerly con-ducted with third countries (Gordon 2003; Krueger 1999: 107). Regional trade would increase for a number of reasons. One reason was the ab-sence of tariff and nontariff barriers to trade among the member states. A second was the use of the rule of origins in a free trade area. With this rule, market officials allowed a member state to impose a special tax on goods coming from another member state if these had components orig-inating from countries outside the bloc that had been subject to compar-atively lower tariffs. Manufacturers in an RTA now had an incentive to

---

[6] Additional reasons were given for how and why RTA officials would act in a protec-tionist manner. One focused on problems of coordination among blocs, where a harmful prisoners dilemma would push RTAs to raise tariffs against each other (Frankel 1997: 210).

[7] Real-life examples in support of these claims abounded. The AFTA member states of-fered perhaps the clearest evidence of protectionism. In one amusing example, Indonesia early on "excluded major sectors [from free trade] but offered to liberalize imports of snow ploughs" (Frankel 1997: 213). NAFTA officials showed similar tendencies in agriculture and the manufacturing sector. They decreed that Mexican-made apparel, for instance, could only enter the United States duty-free if produced with textiles and yarn originating from North America (Hormats 1994: 104). Perhaps the most striking examples, however, came from what many called "Fortress Europe." A long list of industries in the EU had benefited from protectionism, but perhaps none as much as agriculture. The EEC Treaty (Article 115) ex-plicitly acknowledged that the EC could take actions to protect vulnerable industries. The Common Agricultural Policy (CAP), with its mix of direct subsidies to farmers, inflated prices, and quotas, was the most obvious instance (Gardner 1996). Other sectors benefiting from the EU included high technology and the automotive industry (Wise 1994: 88), much to the consternation of some politicians and public figures (Financial Times 1990; Goldsmith 1990; Thurow 1992).

utilize regional products even if products from outside, prior to the imposition of a tax, would have cost less (Frankel 1997: 14, 215; Hormats 1994: 103).[8]

RTAs as a whole presented a third challenge to the global economy. Bhagwati and others stressed that the process of regional integration—preparation, ratification, and so on—was requiring enormous effort and political capital. In a world of limited time and resources, all this diverted resources away from multilateral efforts. Bhagwati wrote: "Lobbying support and political energies can readily be diverted to preferential trading arrangements such as FTAs [free trade agreements]. . . . That deprives the multilateral system of the support it needs to survive, let alone be conducive to further liberalization" (Bhagwati 1993b: 162). Frankel echoed this sentiment: "If a US trade representative spends all his or her time and political capital with Congress on a regional agreement, then there might be less time or capital left over for multilateral negotiations. As with the incentive-to-protect argument, regional trading arrangements may set back the negotiation of worldwide trade liberalization under the WTO" (Frankel 1997: 214).

These pessimistic arguments about the incompatibility of RTAs with the global economic system were opposed by a vocal group of economists and other analysts (Kono 2002; Panagariya 2000). They argued that trade blocs were in fact increasing trade within but also across regions. RTAs made it easier for representatives of distant countries to strike trade agreements, increased regional specialization and therefore interdependencies, and pressured officials from countries with relatively high tariffs in a free trade area to lower their tariffs (Krueger 1999: 118). Of course, intraregional trade was likely to grow more than interregional trade. Yet, in terms of absolute levels, the formation of RTAs was sure to affect global trade positively. Frankel and his colleagues presented empirical evidence in support of this view after examining trade data from the 1960s, 1970s, 1980s, and 1990s. "The tentative conclusion," they wrote, "is that regionalism has in recent experience been politically consistent with more general liberalization, in the sense that members of trade blocs have tended to increase their trade with nonmembers as they intensify their trade (even more) with each other" (Frankel 1997: 209–10). These findings were supported by a number of empirical studies of particular RTAs as well as by countless politicians.[9]

[8] In common markets, where a CET exists, rules of origins are obviously not an issue. The economic literature on trade diversion is rich and complex. For more details, see Bhagwati, Greenaway, and Panagaraiya (1998), Krueger (1999), and Bagwell and Staiger (1998).

[9] Reuveny and Thompson turned, for instance, to NAFTA and considered the extent to which the United States' exports to Canada and Mexico as a percentage of all exports had increased since NAFTA's founding. They concluded that the "North American trading bloc

Proponents then argued that RTAs should be seen as "building blocks," "stepping-stones," or even "apprenticeships" towards the formation of a truly integrated global economy (Summers 1991; Thapanachai 1999). They noted that RTAs were allowing member states to test trade liberalization on a smaller scale while not exposing themselves to the rigors of global competition. RTAs were thus preparing member states for participation in the global economy. Following an initial period of adjustment for sensitive industries, officials from those RTAs would pursue trade liberalization with the outside world, including other RTAs.[10] A number of prominent officials and politicians shared this view, such as United States Trade Representative Robert Zoellick for the George W. Bush administration, who systematically maintained that RTAs represent the "building blocks" of a global economy (Gordon 2003: 112),[11] Mexican president Carlos Salinas (Salinas 1995: 38), and others.[12]

A third argument centered on the experimenting and learning that RTAs made possible. RTAs were serving as grounds for testing and evaluating various approaches to liberalization. What proved successful at the regional level could be translated to the global level. Unsuccessful schemes and solutions could be disregarded. Regional integration served as a "useful laboratory for new approaches to deeper integration which can be applied multilaterally," which could produce lessons "in relation to, for example, market standards, services, government procurement, state subsidies, competition policy and dispute settlement" (Cable 1994: 12). Useful lessons were already available from across the globe. Hormats, for instance, suggested that "future multilateral negotiations could adopt as prototypes NAFTA's investment protection codes, dispute settlement arrangements and environmental provisions. The EU's harmonization of

---

has not led to noticeable . . . decrease in trade openness. . . . The unqualified equation of greater trade regionalization and less trade openness does not appear to be particularly valid" (Reuveny and Thomson 2000: 5). The words of Carlos Salinas, former president of Mexico, are also representative: "If regional blocs comply with the strengthened rules of the World Trade Organization (WTO), that is, if they do not create or increase trade barriers to third parties, then they will have a positive effect on world trade. This is because, in addition to eliminating obstacles to trade among their members, regional blocs tend to create, rather than divert, trade" (Salinas 1995: 38).

[10] This, according to Scollay, was possibly more likely to happen in a world composed of three "mega-blocs": Europe, the Americas, and the East Asian blocs (Scollay 2001: 1155–56).

[11] Zoellick, along with a number of other officials, also maintained that RTAs made multilateral bargaining at the WTO easier, as countries reacted to mutual fear of regional protectionism (See Gordon 2003: 112).

[12] Hence, for instance, Pongsak Asakul, president of the Thai Textile Manufacturing Association, would state: "AFTA is the trial period because there is only one potential rival—Indonesia. We are anxious about global liberalisation of the textile and garment trade in the WTO as there will be many players" (Thapanachai: 1999).

competition policy and product standards are also appropriate as models" (1994: 100–101). Teague (2003), in turn, noted that NAFTA's labor regulations could inform "global" agreements. And, turning to capital flows, Atkinson observed that EU and other regional integration officials have devised flow and control schemes that can inform the design of a global regime for capital markets. In that context, he noted, "we have much to learn from attempts to create regional institutions at all levels that could instruct us on means to create global institutions" (1999: 338).[13]

The Local Implications of RTAs

A variety of activists, scholars, and journalists reacted with unease to the spread of RTAs. What impact would free trade have, they wondered, on the welfare of a set of countries or a particular region? The focus was typically on one RTA—understood, however, as the local manifestation of the new ideology of trade. Thus, there was again little interest in comparative questions. A few key topics proved particularly important: economic well-being, the environment, and social issues such as workers' health and safety. Had NAFTA, for instance, benefited powerful corporations and the rich, while bringing about major job losses, poverty, and weaker protection for the environment (Cavanagh and Anderson 2002)? Or did it lead to a better use of resources, lower costs, higher environmental and labor standards, and, ultimately, more wealth for all involved (Serra and Espinosa 2002)? The majority of the critics belonged to the left of the political spectrum or had populist inclinations, but a number of conservative critics also voiced concerns.

Left-leaning critics put forth mostly functionalist arguments: tariff and nontariff barriers to trade served at least two purposes, and their removal was likely to have negative effects. First, barriers helped companies in key industries to survive. Their abrupt removal would generate higher unemployment rates, depressed wages, and poverty. Barriers also protected companies operating in very demanding regulatory constraints from companies functioning in more deregulated countries. Removal of those barriers would generate pressures to deregulate, with adverse consequences for the environment, workers' rights, safety and hygiene, and so on. Con-

---

[13] There were, of course, additional arguments about the positive impact of RTAs on global trade, such as the notion that RTAs could be used as "bargaining threats" to encourage multilateral talks (Krueger 1999: 118). Taken together, all these arguments pointed to a single conclusion: "Contrary to what is often asserted, regional arrangements do not do not necessarily, or even probably, involve a move away from closer integration in the world as a whole" (Henderson 1992: 648). Indeed, the opposite seemed true: RTAs bring the world closer to having a single, truly international global economy.

servatives raised different sorts of criticisms. They found RTAs to have
too many protectionist measures and unnecessarily complex and bureaucratic regulatory regimes. Inefficient companies could thus survive but at
a huge cost for society's welfare. RTAs also limited access to the resources
and technologies of nonmember states, with adverse consequences for
growth.

NAFTA, possibly because of its size, generated the strongest reactions.
Trade unions, civil society groups, and some industry associations pointed
to the differences in wages and regulatory standards between the United
States and Canada on the one hand, and Mexico on the other. Those disparities, they argued, would promote the relocation of investments, fac-
tories, and jobs south to Mexico (McConnell and MacPherson 1994: 175;
Reuveny and Thompson 2000: 64). Even without the relocation of productive forces in Mexico, those disparities were expected to lead directly
to increases in poverty. The logic was that Mexican producers, who enjoyed lower costs, would flood the American and Canadian markets with
cheap goods. This would create pressures for competitors in those two
countries to lower costs by cutting wages, reducing the workforce, and
lowering product quality. Thus, during a memorable debate in the 1992
United States presidential race, Ross Perot famously predicted that with
NAFTA "you're going to hear a giant sucking sound of jobs being pulled
out of this country" (quoted in Griswold 2002: 1). A number of empirical studies were then produced to support all of these claims.[14] The following passage is representative:

> [T]he employment effects on the United States have been consistently nega-
> tive, with NAFTA's structure responsible for employment losses of approxi-
> mately 315,939 in 1999 due to both trade effects and investment shift ef-
> fects. . . . Further, NAFTA works to adversely impact labor through the
> threat effect to move operations to Mexico. (Cypher 2001: 6–7)

Importantly, the negative consequences of NAFTA were argued to affect
not only the United States and Canada but also Mexico. Critics pointed
out that, though investments and production might move to Mexico, such
a shift would perhaps benefit the rich in Mexico but certainly not the poor
(Cavanagh and Anderson 2002: 58–59). Moreover, it seemed questionable whether Mexican productivity and employment would, in the first

---

[14] For a review of these and other related studies, see MacDonald (2003: 176–79). Interestingly, some extended the presumed negative impact of NAFTA on Mexico not only to
wages, employment, and other labor issues but also to a different side of the economy: cultural products. Here the argument was that movies, food, clothing, and other products from
the United States would gradually replace Mexican products, thus depriving the country of
an important element of its national economy as well as identity (McAnany and Wilkinson
1996).

place, improve (Ramirez 2003: 863; Larudee 1998).[15] Such arguments and data compelled activists and others to challenge NAFTA in every possible way, including arguing before courts that the treaty was not constitutional (Harvard Law Review 2000).

NAFTA attracted the ire of environmentalists as well. Critics charged that NAFTA simply lacked sufficient environmental provisions (Cavanagh and Anderson 2002: 59). Competitors from the United States and Canada were therefore competing at a cost disadvantage against companies from Mexico, a country with a more permissive regulatory regime and, more importantly, weak enforcement mechanisms. The new competitive dynamics were pressuring politicians in both the United States and Canada to dismantle whatever regulatory regime might be in place domestically, starting a "race to the bottom" in environmental regulation. At the same time, firms from the United States and Canada were moving to Mexico to lower their production costs. The relocation would inevitably damage Mexico's environment, with little that politicians from the United States and Canada would or could say (McConnell and MacPherson 1994: 177; Reuveny and Thompson 2000: 64). A number of reports, articles, and books offered evidence in support of those claims (Ecologist 2002: 16).[16]

Mercosur generated much concern as well. Situated in a region mired by stark class differences and underperforming economies, it was inevitably judged to be a scheme by the powerful to further enrich their own ranks. Mercosur had structures designed to perpetuate social economic inequalities within the member states, and destined Argentina and Brazil to remain "underdeveloped" nations unable to achieve genuine macroeconomic growth (Mecham 2003: 378). In a representative passage, for instance, Richards argued that Mercosur, rather than "creating the conditions for balanced and equitable development," would in fact serve "the function of more thoroughly incorporating [the member states] within the world capitalist system while preserving their subordinate status in that system" (1999: 133, 144–45).

On the other hand, Mercosur disappointed certain conservatives as well. In their view, officials had insulated the member states by not having sufficiently liberalized trade with the outside world. Reliance on a CET and strict rules of origin was at the heart of the problem:

[15] Much attention was also given to the negative impact of NAFTA on working women. See, for example, Quintero-Ramírez (2002).

[16] One report, for instance, would conclude "that 8 years after NAFTA's passage there are generally diminished expectations that the agreement's environmental provisions and institutional frameworks will help control the negative environmental consequences of increased trade between Canada, Mexico, and the United States. This brings into question NAFTA's reputation as a 'green' trade agreement" (Sanchez 2002: 1369).

In forgoing freer trade relations with the rest of the world, the Mercosur countries lost one important means of achieving dynamic gains—the technological diffusion that occurs through trade between developed and developing countries. Because Mercosur includes only developing countries, its members are less likely to be exposed to the advanced technology embodied in imports from developed countries. Indeed, the external tariff that Mercosur applies to the rest of the world heightens the union's isolation from developed countries. (Connolly 1999: 5)

Environmentalists and others voiced their own worries as well. They accused Mercosur officials of dealing with environmental matters only as obstacles for the completion of a single market. Serious initiatives to safeguard the environment were missing. As a critic would write in an analysis of the Treaty of Asuncion: "The negotiators of this treaty were concerned about the environment only to the extent that environmental regulations had the potential to restrict trade in the form of non-tariff barriers" (Blum 2000: 444). Later adjustments, such as the formation of a working group for the environment, were deemed of limited relevance (Hochstetler 2003: 12–16).

The EU too, as it progressed towards the completion of a common market, generated criticism. Environmental concerns were again at center stage. Observers recognized that EU officials were passing numerous environmental laws and programs as they strove for the completion of the single market. Yet they noted that those initiatives were difficult to enforce (Jordan 1999; Skjaerseth and Wettestad 2002)[17] and, moreover, had centered on subject areas (such as air pollution, for instance) where shared regulatory principles were necessary for the creation of a single marketplace. Those were also areas of high public visibility (Grant, Matthews, and Newell 2000; McCormick 2001). The EU had instead neglected forests, marine life, soil, and other aspects of the environment. In the case of the EU, however, a series of other issues—many of which are only now beginning to receive attention in other RTAs—proved also to be quite salient. They included questions related to national sovereignty, the evolution of national administrations, civic and popular representation, public health, and many more.[18]

Not all agreed with this barrage of criticisms against RTAs. Many scholars and politicians called for a more balanced perspective. Knowing with any degree of accuracy what impact RTAs were actually having was

[17] Studies of specific EU laws and their implementation abound. See, for example, Diaz (2001) and Duina (1999) on directives on natural habitats and air pollution.

[18] On these topics, there has been a deluge of writings. Some representative works include Costa (2003), Duina and Kurzer (2004), Knill (2001), Moravcsik (1998), Thatcher (1998), and Zweifel (2002).

impossible. They noted that most signs pointed to rather small consequences. In a representative article, Krugman asserted that NAFTA was
likely to have a negligible impact on the United States. It was to have "no
impact on the number of jobs" and a slight impact on wages: overall income was to rise somewhat though the real wages of unskilled workers
might experience a slight decrease (1993: 14). Data from later years
seemed to confirm his arguments (Serra and Espinosa 2002). NAFTA, he
also noted, would as well "not hurt and may even help the environment"
(Krugman 1993: 14). A similar neutral stance was taken by a number of
policymakers and academics concerning NAFTA and AFTA (Deere and
Esty 2002; Malaysia General News 2002).

Other observers simply praised RTAs. They pointed to increased foreign direct investments and the rationalization of existing investments.
Firms in AFTA, two analysts wrote, "are likely to consolidate some production processes while at the same time geographically distributing these
activities to reap the best from members' comparative advantages" (Heinrich and Konan 2001: 143). The restructuring process did not entail the
relocation of firms away from AFTA, but only their improvement (143),
as data from Vietnam and Laos clearly showed (156–57). RTA officials
had also instituted unprecedented mechanisms for cooperation and
progress with regards to the environment, health, peace, and many other
areas. Observers praised NAFTA's NAAEC (Blum 2000). They pointed to
the EU and the impact of its rich and complex environmental laws on the
policies and practices of the member states (McCormick 2001; Cichowski
1998).

Several supporters also emphasized that RTAs had had positive geopolitical effects. NAFTA had contributed to democratic stability and peace
in Mexico, and had improved the relationship between Mexico and the
United States (Griswold 2002). The Mercosur member states had successfully averted two coups in Paraguay. AFTA had welcomed Vietnam,
Cambodia, and Laos—three countries with very unstable political histories. AFTA had also augmented the diplomatic clout of its member states
on the world scene. Similarly, the enlargement of the EU successfully pressured formerly communist Eastern and Central European countries to de-
mocratize and stabilize.

THE COMPARATIVE QUESTION

The most visible responses to the proliferation of RTAs in the 1980s and
1990s did not involve close comparative investigations of those RTAs. On
the contrary, their premise was that officials and politicians everywhere
had embarked on rather similar trade liberalization projects and that *this*

very phenomenon had to be analyzed. This view of RTAs was an assumption—one based above all on a simple reading of the objectives of RTAs. Some years after the explosion of RTAs, we are now in a position to revisit that assumption. What we find may alter drastically our understanding of RTAs.

With regard to the basic objectives of RTAs, few could indeed argue that profound differences exist among RTAs. Yet, these objectives are often worded with loose and ambiguous language, representing only the starting point—or, perhaps, a rather remote finishing point—for regional integration projects. The philosophy of free trade specifies goals, not means. It does not provide guidelines for how officials should mobilize to achieve their stated goals, how they should address the multiple challenges raised by regional integration, or what venues, structures, and strategies they should put into place. Nor does that philosophy specify how societies will respond to integration.

In the late 1990s, a handful of scholars began to wonder about the nature of RTAs. It is too early for the resulting body of works to constitute a coherent body of literature on the subject. Still, two thematic strands are emerging: one concerned with the basic structural design of RTAs, the other with examining the basic breadth and content of RTA laws and regulatory frameworks across selected policy realms. Together, the two strands offer some of the earliest evidence of systematic differences in the architecture of RTAs (Atksinon 1999; Mansfield and Milner 1997a: 14; Mattli 1999). They thus provide us with a first, important step in the comparative analysis of RTAs.

One key dimension of structural variation is the difference between the supranational versus the intergovernmental character of RTAs (Grieco 1997; Mansfield and Milner 1997a). In supranational RTAs, the member states have agreed to relinquish some of their decision-making authority. This may not happen in matters related to the general direction of integration. But it can happen in committees, for instance, where officials are given the mission to advance the cause of the RTA rather than the interests of the respective countries whence they come. It might also happen with the use of qualified or simple majority voting for legal and other decisional processes. In intergovernmental RTAs, by contrast, member states retain most, if not full, control over the process of regional integration. This applies to grand decision making but also to more operational and day-to-day activities. Committees are composed of representatives of the member states and work by unanimous consensus, for instance. Similarly, regulations are taken with the approval of all national representatives.

From this perspective, the EU is clearly the most supranational RTA. Grieco notes that its member states "have invested substantial responsi-

bility in the Commission"; those countries "have also accepted that the
European Court of Justice may have an important voice in both Community and therefore national economic regulatory policy" (Grieco 1997:
169). Yarbrough and Yarbrough reach a similar conclusion about the
supranational character of the EU when they investigate dispute-settle-
ment mechanisms: decision-making processes, incentives, enforcement
tools, and so on (1997: 139). The EU has obviously created some of the
most supranational mechanisms. In that sense the EU—note Mansfield
and Milner in their own chapter—is "highly institutionalized, whereas
NAFTA is far less so" (1997b: 14).

The same could not be said of RTAs in the Americas, where the member states have intergovernmental structures that, at any given point, any
one member state can control. As Grieco states:

> The level of regional authority associated with cooperative arrangements in
> the Americas is much more modest than in Western Europe. . . . NAFTA and
> Mercosur envision the establishment of similar dispute settlement arrange-
> ments. However, these arrangements are strictly intergovernmental accords
> with little aspiration to significant forms of supranational authority as in the
> EC case. (Grieco 1997: 169)

RTAs in Asia, in turn, exhibit even less supranationalism. There, most
RTAs are purely intergovernmental, with member states retaining control
over most, if not all, aspects of integration.

Additional dimensions of structural variation concern the rigidity, efficiency, and precision of policymaking and decision-making bodies and
mechanisms. For instance, Blum (2000) examines how NAFTA and Mercosur officials approach environmental problems: working groups, dis-
pute-resolution procedures, decision-making processes, and so on. The
general conclusion is that NAFTA has more formal structures than Mercosur and that Mercosur has a more flexible but less stable and ad hoc
system. Dubal et al. describe NAFTA as having serious "flaws in procedures and programs" at all levels while commending the EU's far more
solid review and enforcement mechanisms (2001–2: 47). Teague compares NAFTA's labor-standard setting processes (as set out in the NAALC)
and the EU's own mechanisms. He describes NAFTA's process as "a tri-
national institutional arrangement that grafts formal international procedures onto domestic labor market regimes," which can at times be
"cumbersome and convoluted" but which nonetheless may have certain
advantages because of its decentralized and horizontal character (2003:
428). The EU is quite different from that: a deliberative governance
arrangement that can prove very hierarchical. Abbott (2000) in turn an-
alyzes how precisely the founding treaties of RTAs specify objectives and
mandates. Interestingly, NAFTA's founding treaty and its corollary agree-

ments are very precise. The EU treaties adopt far more ambiguous language. In his view, each approach both limits and empowers officials.

The second emergent field of comparative analysis focuses on the laws and regulations that RTA officials have produced. For some, the central question concerns the presence or absence of laws across policy realms. Grieco again observes, for instance, significant variation in the number of issues covered by regional arrangements. EU officials have over time gained the right to legislate and make policies in a variety of topical areas. Mercosur, by contrast, "is concerned almost exclusively with the reduction of barriers to trade, and in particular the reduction of tariffs" (165). He then points out that NAFTA addresses subtle questions related to intellectual property rights and the environment. In a similar study, Milner explores the degree to which RTAs have liberalized various sectors of the economy. She notes: "For instance, NAFTA treats the textile and apparel industry differently than the telecommunications one. Trade liberalization . . . is very substantial and rapid in the latter and much more moderate in the former" (1997: 78). The same could not be observed in other RTAs, which have their own idiosyncratic arrangements. What could explain the fact, she asks, that "these agreements, although all free trade areas or customs unions, are shaped differently?" (77).[19]

A number of studies have focused on policy-specific analysis of the quality and nature of laws and rules in particular subject areas. The environment is again a favorite subject. Dubal et al. observe that, "in marked contrast to NAFTA's tacked-on environmental protections, the EU's trade-environment rules are well developed and environment-friendly," exhibiting an "upward harmonization" rather than a "race-to-the-bottom" tendency (2002: 47). They then focus on the specific measures in place in both RTAs on toxic disposal. In a parallel comparative study, Stevis and Mumme (2000) suggest that despite such differences there exist important similarities in regulatory approaches in the two RTAs: in both NAFTA and the EU, environmental protection is treated as a burden to economic growth. Steinberg (1997) offers a parallel analysis of environmental laws in the EU and NAFTA.

Going beyond the environment, Hoekman and Sauvé (1994) compare EU and NAFTA initiatives in the area of services. They find that EU officials have devised one of the most far-reaching liberalization frameworks. NAFTA officials too, though, have taken initiatives that go beyond those imposed by the GATT's General Agreement on Trade in Services. Melnik

---

[19] In my investigations of the reach of EU and Mercosur, I too found important differences in what officials from the two regions subject to legislative regulation. The EU has proven more aggressive than Mercosur at targeting labor, capital, and services. Interestingly, though, most of the EU efforts still center on the movement of goods (Duina 2003).

compares NAFTA and EU initiatives on the legal protection of databases
(1994). Galperin (1999) focuses on cultural industries (audiovisual products, etc.) policy in NAFTA, the EU, and Mercosur. Gittermnan (2003)
examines labor regulation in those three RTAs and AFTA. Other scholars
have examined agricultural policies, capital movement, mutual recognition of educational degrees, and other such topics.

Taken together, the new comparative studies of RTAs all point to variation.[20] The evidence concerns mostly the architecture of RTAs, rather
than analyses of the practical impact of RTAs on societies. Nonetheless,
the findings send a powerful message about the dangers of assuming that
the proliferation of RTAs in the 1980s and 1990s constituted the first step
towards the creation of a world of broadly comparable regions. This book
contributes to this emergent field of regional studies in two related ways.
First, it builds on the architectural theme: how have RTA officials responded to the subtle, but crucial, challenge of standardization for market participants? It then departs from existing studies by posing a new
type of comparative question: how have societal organizations adapted to
regional integration? The answers to these questions point to significant
variation across RTAs. An integral part of the book is therefore an explanation of the observed differences.

The Making of RTAs

All markets may be defined as physical and virtual spaces where buyers
and sellers meet to exchange valuable tangible and intangible items. They
are characterized by a certain degree of permanence: they are spaces
where participants meet time and time again to trade. The participants
need not be the same in every transaction, of course; similarly, the items
being exchanged need not be of the same type each time. Markets are also
functional environments: exchanges happen more easily than in ad hoc
situations because participants share a set of guiding viewpoints about reality. Participants need not spend time and resources specifying what they
may be searching for, the desired terms of exchange, and so on.[21] Of
course, these shared viewpoints emerge slowly over time as interactions
intensify and participants learn to communicate, express their preferences, and adjust and readjust themselves to interacting with each other.

---

[20] We should note that there is a third strand of comparative works on RTAs: those focused on measuring and accounting for the success of regional integration efforts. These
works are not concerned with questions of convergence or difference across RTAs and are
thus not discussed here. Illustrative works include Mattli (1999) and Lecuona (1999).

[21] Markets, in other words, offer a predictable environment for transactions to take place
(Collins 1980: 927–28: Fligstein 2001). See as well Seabright (2004).

Once in place, however, they are essential for the efficient working of any market.

We may classify these viewpoints as *definitional* and *normative* notions about reality. Definitional notions are concepts that participants hold about the essential characteristics of objects (e.g., apples, cars, computers), activities (e.g., weighing a good, paying, consulting), and agents (e.g., buyer, doctor, a firm) in the world. What is an "apple"? What does it mean to "pay" for something? What is a "firm"? These notions are generally not available in an articulate or otherwise explicit fashion in some public venue. They reside primarily in the minds of participants and cannot be easily described: they combine images, ideas about physical qualities (such as taste, feel, components, etc.), expectations about functions and abilities (for instance, a doctor cures people, a car travels), and so on. Despite being amorphous, however, these notions are very real and specific. For instance, when asking for wine and a receipt, customers at a restaurant have something fairly precise in mind, as will the waiter who will respond to that request (whose own version will more or less be aligned with that of the customer). The same may be said of patients in a medical center requesting to see a doctor for a routine physical examination, or of litigants in a courtroom requesting to call witnesses to the stand.

Normative notions, by contrast, are concepts that participants have about the desirability of certain situations, practices, behaviors, procedures, conditions, and countless other aspects of reality. Unlike definitional notions, they say nothing about the way the world is; instead, they specify something about how the world should be. Examples of normative notions include ideas about the proper handling of merchandise, safety requirements for particular goods, the availability of information about a product, discriminatory practices, how much pollution should be allowed, minimum quality standards, expected levels of professionalism, the depletion of fish populations, and so on. Normative notions are visions of an ideal reality that participants wish would materialize but at times does not materialize or, at the very least, has the potential of not materializing.

Unlike definitional notions, normative notions in most markets are often explicitly articulated in the form of contracts, laws, and other types of written documentation. This is probably a function of two facts. On the one hand, normative notions depict a reality that does not exist and hence requires active definition; on the other hand, market participants have a tendency not to comply with these normative notions.[22] Their ex-

---

[22] As to why individuals are tempted to go against normative notions even when compliance is ultimately a collective good, see Williamson (1985). In the view of Williamson and others, individuals have limited knowledge about themselves, others, and the world and have a limited ability to make optimal decisions over time.

plicit articulation serves then as a constant reference available to participants for consultation and as a tool to judge behavior and, if necessary, punish transgressors. The articulation of normative notions, then, ultimately makes market life fall more in line with the ideal, and hence safer and more predictable (Hall 1986; Powell 1991: 185; Weber 1978: 314, 1992: 277).

In any market, both definitional and normative notions about reality are not fixed: they can evolve, but often slowly and gradually. In Europe, for instance, labor and land came to be seen as commodities (i.e., as something that could be sold for money) gradually during the fourteenth and fifteenth centuries (DiMaggio 1994: 36; Polanyi 1944). The role of a "father" in the family context changed during the last decades of the late nineteenth century in the United States (Zelizer 1992). So did ideas about risk and death (Douglas and Wildavsky 1983). At any given point, then, markets depend for their functioning on broadly accepted, stable views about the world.

Markets can develop within a culture but, importantly, also across cultures. When they occur within a culture, the process of definitional and normative alignment is relatively smooth. There is certainly some conflict and struggle (Campbell and Lindberg 1990; Fligstein 1996), but participants already share countless interpretations of the world around them and thus have the basis to arrive at acceptable definitional and normative notions about their economic activity. Matters are quite different in the case of cross-cultural trade. There, parties interested in trading face the problem of misalignment and, moreover, ignorance of what each other may or may not know. Countless questions plague the participants. What goods are actually available? How are prices set? What counts as high quality? How are exchanges to be performed? Economic historian Curtin describes the challenges as follows:

> Cross-cultural trade and communication present special problems. People with a different way of life are strangers by definition; their ways seem unpredictable, and the unpredictable is probably dangerous as well. Communication itself is difficult. Even after an appropriate medium comes into existence, like a second language in common, understanding is hard to come by. Strangers may appear not to be hostile, but they are still not to be trusted in the same full sense that neighbors and kinfolk can be trusted. (1984: 1)

History is, of course, replete with instances of cross-cultural trade and, therefore, with examples of how human beings solved the problems of disparate worldviews. In all cases, they devised and built processes, institutions, and structures to improve communication, mutual knowledge, and ultimately trust. As Curtin writes: "These problems in cross-cultural understanding in general have meant that cross-trade has almost always

been carried out through special institutional arrangements to help guarantee the mutual security of the two sides" (1984: 1). One of the most
common of these arrangements, developed with the invention of agriculture and in place until the industrial revolution, was "trade settlement."
Commercial merchants would leave their hometowns and begin living in
foreign cities. They would then serve as "cross-cultural brokers, helping
and encouraging trade between their host society and people of their own
origin" (2). Such arrangements took place all over the world, but the
strongest evidence concerns Africa in the sixteenth and seventeenth centuries, ancient Greece, early modern Europe, and North America at the
time of the French and British explorations.

The formation of an RTA presents truly unprecedented challenges. Previous solutions to cross-cultural trade were gradual and paralleled the intensity of trade itself. As the worldviews of market participants became
more and more aligned, more and more trade could take place. As trade
increased, the worldviews of market participants grew closer and closer,
fostering more trade and thus more cognitive alignment. RTAs, by contrast, envision the creation of a marketplace comprising participants who,
until that point in time, have largely operated in distinct cultural traditions. Now thousands of new tangible and intangible products are to be
exchanged, capital investments are to flow across borders, services are
offered across borders, and—in the deepest instances of integration—
trained and untrained workers are to move freely across national boundaries. This artificial push for a single marketplace naturally raises a fundamental question: *how are the disparate definitional and normative
outlooks of market participants to be aligned*?

The existing literature on regional integration does not directly address
this question. European Union scholars have certainly noted the tendency
of EU officials to set specifications for numberless objects, activities, and
agents (Duina 2001; Nugent 1994: figs. 10.1 and 10.2). Scholars of
NAFTA have in turn noted the tendency of officials to avoid such a task
(Atkinson 1998; H. P. Glenn 2001; Kahler 1995). Yet these scholars have
not engaged in systematic comparative investigations. Scholarship on
Mercosur and other RTAs offers limited insights. The next few pages offer
a conceptual framework to answer this important question.

RTA officials have responded to the question of disparate definitional
and normative worldviews among market participants in fundamentally
different ways.[23] The first difference concerns whether RTA officials have

---

[23] As discussed earlier in this chapter, some RTAs (especially the EU) have supranational
characteristics while others are mostly intergovernmental (such as NAFTA and Mercosur).
Throughout the book, the term "RTA officials" refers to those individuals charged with the
responsibility of making RTA law. In the case of the EU, these are a combination of supranational and intergovernmental actors; in the case of NAFTA and Mercosur, these are in-

sought to resolve actively and directly those differences themselves by producing what we might call a cognitive guidebook to reality or, by contrast, whether they have sought alternative means to bridge the cognitive gaps among participants.

In some RTAs, officials have engaged in massive projects of cognitive standardization. Through the medium of regional law, they have articulated thousands of definitional and normative definitions about the world. On the definitional front, they have produced countless regional laws specifying the essential characteristics of numberless objects, activities, and agents. They have generally done so by stating something about the constitution, function, form, or origin of those objects. On the normative front, they have produced similarly countless regional laws specifying their view on the desirability of countless aspects of reality. Typically, they have done so by making (direct or indirect) reference to some a priori principles of justice or ethics or, by contrast, to some utilitarian ideas. The definitional component of this massive standardization effort has had no precedent in human history. While national and international systems of law are full of normative principles about social (including economic) life, they cannot be said to contain many definitional notions.

In other RTAs, the solution to disparate definitional and normative viewpoints has been to produce only a small number of basic definitional and normative notions and then to rely on alternative mechanisms for further definition. Those mechanisms are varied. Participants are asked to comply with industry standards set by international associations. They are also asked to begin trading without having sorted out their differences beforehand: in case of conflict, they are provided with resolution mechanisms to sort out those differences. Yet in other instances, participants are simply provided with very little help. We may describe these approaches as minimalist, focused far less on activism and preemptive standardization on the part of RTA officials and more on gradualism, trial and error, and reaction.

The two approaches have profoundly shaped the design of RTAs. In the interventionist type, we notice the evolution of a rich and very intrusive system of laws rich with standardizing principles, one that attempts to provide a comprehensive guidebook to reality. In the minimalist type, we observe an altogether smaller legal system, one reflecting a more laissez-faire approach to integration.

The second difference concerns the nature of the definitional and normative notions that RTA officials produce (in both interventionist and, in more limited fashion, in minimalist RTAs). On the one hand, RTA offi-

---

tergovermental actors (i.e., members of national governments or national legislatures charged with making Mercosur laws). This distinction is not very consequential for the main arguments of this book, but the terms should nonetheless be clarified. See the appendix for a more detailed elaboration.

cials vary in what, specifically, they deem should be subject to standardization. For example, though apples may be traded in two different RTAs, only in one are they subject to definitional and normative standardization. In another RTA, however, we observe that cars' heating systems are subject to standardization, something that is not observable in the first RTA. These variations are pervasive rather than occasional and, as such, set RTAs apart from each other in important ways. On the other hand, even when RTA officials subject identical aspects of reality to definitional and normative standardization, the actual content of what they produce varies across RTAs. In one RTA, for instance, child labor might be defined as work done by a human being under the age of ten years old; in another, it is defined as forced work imposed onto children under the age of twelve. The two RTAs may then differ on whether and how they make such practice illegal.

We may combine the first and second type of difference to formulate the *first* major claim of this book. It is a general statement about how RTA officials have dealt with the problem of cognitive standardization: *Officials have created remarkably different cognitive guidebooks to reality. Some RTAs boast thick guidebooks, others thinner ones. When we open those guidebooks, we discover differences in the nature of the notions being produced.*

We are now pressed to ask, What can explain such differences? I propose an explanation centered on institutional and political contexts: the approach may be called *political-institutional.* Institutionalists explain the evolution of policies, programs, organizations, and other social phenomena by emphasizing the influence of existing institutions on actors' choices and actions (Pierson 2000; Thelen 1999: 388). Depending on their specific theoretical inclinations, proponents identify different types of institutions as important (Campbell and Pedersen 2001c: 9; Torfing 2001: 283–84). For some, institutions include less tangible factors such as practices, traditions, habits, and so on. For others, they include more structural factors such as legal traditions, formal organizational structures, the distribution of resources among players, and so on. In almost all cases, however, institutionalists argue that institutions constrain, channel, or enable actors and choices. Change reflects institutional contexts and seldom represents an abrupt departure from the past. Institutionalists hence underplay the unmediated influence of individual actors or groups (as rational choice or group theorists might propose), the objective requirements of systems and organizations (as functionalists might propose), popular pressure (as public choice theorists might argue), and other factors (Thelen 1999).[24]

---

[24] There are, of course, a variety of institutionalist approaches; for those familiar with the literature, the one of primary concern here is historical institutionalism (Campbell and Pedersen 2001c: 11).

Politics-centered explanations focus, in turn, on the role of powerful actors in society as they strive to influence societal processes and outcomes. As group theory teaches us (Hall 1986), these actors can be collectivities—such as trade unions, business associations, interest associations, political parties, and so on. In line with rational choice theory (Coleman 1990; Becker 1986), they can also be individuals—such as political leaders, business entrepreneurs, bureaucrats, intellectuals, and so on. In all cases, proponents argue that these actors mobilize in the face of opportunities to advance their visions and improve their positions. The attention is far less on cultural, institutional, or other types of variables, and much more on the desires of key actors.

Despite the apparent tension between the two approaches, institutionalist and political theories can, in some cases, be combined. This is especially appropriate when the preferences of powerful actors are aligned with institutional contexts: when those actors wish and take action to maintain existing conditions. Both institutions and powerful actors then help ensure that future changes in a given system replicate in some form existing conditions. This, I argue, is precisely what has taken place in the three RTAs in consideration. In the case of regional law, I propose that preexisting legal contexts and the preferences of key powerful actors in each region together have pressured market planners in a given RTA towards creating legal systems that replicate, at the regional level, legal approaches prevalent throughout the member states.[25]

More specifically, with regard to minimalism versus interventionism, I suggest that we consider whether common-law or civil-law traditions are in place throughout the member states. Common law is a legislative system that avoids the codification of the world and the promulgation of rigid, a priori principles for the regulation of social life. It favors instead court precedents: courts generate law on an ongoing basis as they rule on individual cases. The system is reactive, self-adjusting, and perennially evolving; it seeks to respect the particular and to avoid imposing the universal onto it. Civil law, by contrast, is a legal regime centered on the a priori articulation of regulatory principles that are to regulate social life. Though these principles can change over time, they are intended to be definitive in spirit. The system favors extensive codification of the world that applies universally everywhere: definitions, categorizations, ordering, and so on. Only in civil-law countries, then, are we likely to observe extensive books of law.[26]

Economic integration in regions where most countries share a common-

---

[25] This political-institutional approach is thus quite similar to a currently fashionable approach in political science, economics, and sociology: path dependency. Path dependency theorists stress that changes in society typically occur within a specific range of possibilities that is predetermined by past conditions and events (Mahoney 2000).

[26] See Merryman (1985) for a thorough discussion of civil- and common-law traditions.

law tradition is unlikely to lead to the articulation of a complex cognitive guidebook to reality. Why? Officials—accustomed to a reactive approach to conflict resolution—are unlikely to engage in a massive effort to impose upon themselves and all other parties unprecedented definitions for, and viewpoints about, the world. The effort would not only represent a dramatic departure from the past, but also force all involved to have to accept an entirely new system for the regulation of life. Officials are hence much more likely to adopt a more minimalist approach—one that replicates at the regional level the reactive approach that has been operational at the national levels. Thus, in this minimalist solution, there is no effort to deal with conflict preemptively. Instead, actors are asked to interact with each other: as problems arise, resolution systems are put into place. It follows that RTA officials from member states with common-law traditions are very likely to devise mechanisms to deal with conflicts as they arise: dispute settlement mechanisms, reference to standards set by external organizations, and so on.

The preference, on the part of market officials, for a minimalist approach is very likely to receive the support of key actors in society: industrialists, employers, various types of associations and interest groups, and national government representatives. For many of them—especially those in industry—a new and extensive system of regulation would impose new constraints and costs: they much prefer an agreement that liberalizes trade by removing tariffs and only some types of nontariff barriers. The support of these actors for minimalism is of course quite important. Without it, officials would face a much more difficult choice.

Officials in RTAs where the member states share a civil-law tradition are, by contrast, naturally more inclined toward standardization. Each member state brings to the table a heavy set of established and openly articulated views about the world. Inevitably, there exist important and consequential differences across systems. Such differences must be resolved. The most natural and obvious way to address the problem is to develop a transcendental codification system for the entire region. This codification system replicates at the regional level what has happened at the national level: it attempts to sort out differences in outlooks by preemptively articulating countless definitional and normative notions about the world. In such a system, of course, courts exist, but their job is not to make law but rather to ensure compliance with the established code.

Most powerful actors in society, especially those in industry, are likely to support, if not pressure for, this type of regional effort. Rich but also different, and therefore conflicting, national systems create product compatibility problems and regulatory compliance hurdles. Import and export costs are therefore high, especially when trade occurs with more than one member state. The harmonization of differences will necessitate an initial investment to comply with the new regulatory environment: it will,

however, be a worthy investment. Representatives of national governments, too, favor harmonization: they recognize it as necessary for a truly
free trade area to take place.

With regard to differences in the targets and content of regional law in
a given area of social life, powerful actors play perhaps an even more important role. After all, those actors are most affected by specific laws.
They thus mobilize and oppose significant deviations from their preferences. They instead support laws that further solidify their positions in society. Through their pressure, they ultimately give regional law its specific
character. Importantly, in most cases, this will mean that they ensure some
form of continuity between national and regional law: after all, such continuity will replicate at the regional level the legal environment in which
they have flourished.[27] In pushing for such replication, they are supported
by national legislators and state officials, for whom challenges to the status quo represent direct challenges to their positions and functions in their
respective societies.

By and large, market officials themselves exhibit their own natural
propensity towards ensuring continuity with existing national legal traditions. Themselves accustomed to operating in those traditions, they hesitate to introduce novel principles that impose major adjustments on the
member states. Thus, often, national legal traditions and powerful actors
pressure RTA officials in the same direction with regard to the target and
content of regional law.

This explanatory framework for the overall nature and specific targets
and content of regional law, we should emphasize, does not assume the
complete absence of any conflict among national legal traditions or powerful actors in society. In some cases, when regional law provides much
continuity with existing conditions on the ground, it also challenges some
national traditions and the preferences of some powerful actors. For that
reason, there is some struggle over the direction of regional law. Moreover, specific pieces of regional legislation can take on many forms while
providing continuity with most existing national traditions: this can ig-
nite competition among national representatives and powerful actors over
the details of regional law. In all cases, however, the ultimate result is one
and the same. Regional law reflects what is dominant in a given region:
what is shared by most, if not all, of the member states. Conversely, regional law rarely imposes major departures on most of its member states.
Quite often, in fact, it reflects rather faithfully existing realities in all those
countries.

---

[27] I have explored extensively the close relationship between legal traditions and powerful interest groups in my previous book (Duina 1999) and two related articles (Duina 1997
and Duina and Blythe 1999).

Disparities in the legal architectures of RTAs constitute one dimension of variance across RTAs. There is a second dimension of variance: how societal organizations react and adjust to the process of integration. Consider in particular three types of organizations: interest groups, businesses, and national state administrations. Prior to integration, many of these organizations operate at purely or mostly national levels. Interest groups concentrate their efforts in national capitals, where lawmaking and policies happen. Their membership bases are national. Businesses import and export, but a significant number have their production capacities within national territories. State administrative units are occupied with overseeing the implementation of domestic laws and policies. They only occasionally deal with international matters, and they rarely collaborate with their counterparts from other countries.

Regional integration induces organizational changes. In the case of interest groups, membership bases are expanded as people and other groups from abroad join. Lobbying no longer occurs only in national capitals but also in regional seats of power, such as Brussels or Montevideo. In the case of businesses, as the market expands, new production facilities are established in foreign territories.[28] Acquisitions, mergers, and other forms of collaboration increase. In the case of state administrations, new units busy with overseeing the implementation of regional regulation are created. Departments in similar policy fields collaborate across national borders in informal or formal fashion. In the latter case, new transnational coordinating and educational bodies, commissions, and conferences are set up.

Yet not all organizations change in the same way in all RTAs. We can observe differences in two important respects. First, which organizations develop regional characteristics differs from one RTA to the next. Different interest groups (e.g., environmentalists vs. anti-tobacco groups), businesses (e.g., textile vs. television manufacturers), and state units (e.g., food safety vs. transportation departments) expand regionally in different RTAs. Second, when similar organizations do develop regional characteristics, the specific programs (i.e., activities, objectives, products, and so on) and structures (i.e., membership bases, production plants, working committees, and so on) of those organizations often vary across regions. We may thus say that the organizational landscapes of RTAs are different across geographies.

We are now in a position to articulate the *second* general claim of this book about RTAs. The claim concerns the evolution of organizations: *Organizational fields vary dramatically across RTAs. Which interest groups,*

---

[28] The focus here is on manufacturing companies but could also be extended to service-oriented companies, in whose case expansion entails the opening of new offices in foreign territories with professionals ready to serve the local market.

businesses, and state administrative units develop regional programs and structures varies from one RTA to the next, as does the specific nature of those programs and structures.

As with regional law, we must ask what can explain such variation. And, as with regional law, I suggest that national legal systems and power configurations in the member states influence if and how organizations expand at the regional level. Resourceful, well-established, and internationally minded organizations are the most likely to expand once regional integration is under way. Underfunded, marginal, and nationally minded organizations, by contrast, are less likely to capitalize on the opportunities presented by regional integration. Domestic legal contexts and power dynamics greatly influence which organizations develop these characteristics—for they ultimately control the allocation of numerous types of resources and the type of mindset that organizations develop.

Yet in the case of organizations, one additional institutional variable is crucial for shaping organizational developments: regional law itself. Regional law creates and shapes new, broad spaces in which organizations can operate. Regional law—standardizing processes, terms, constraints, opportunities, and so on—creates the opportunity, if not the pressure, for organizations to expand their programs and structures beyond national borders. How, exactly, regional law stimulates the internationalization of organizations depends on the type of organization itself.

Standard definitions and norms about a given aspect of social life encourage interest groups active in that realm to develop transnational agendas and membership bases aimed at supporting or challenging those definitions and norms (Greenwood 2003; Greenwood and Aspinwall 1998; Imig and Tarrow 2001; MacDonald 2003; Mazey and Richardson 2001). The standardization of selected products and processes lowers the cost of expanding production infrastructures for firms, as international markets become more accessible (and thus generate more revenues) and gaps in technical requirements diminish (Nikolaïdis and Egan 2001). And the need to enforce certain definitions and visions for selected aspects of social life, in turn, pressures selected state departments to be active in permanent transnational forums and to develop domestic arms that oversee the implementation of the specific laws in question (Mény, Muller, and Quermonne 1996; Knill 2001). The content of definitional and normative principles, in turn, affects the particular nature of those programs and structures. Interest groups develop agendas and membership bases designed to support or challenge regional definitions. Firms have incentives to engage in the production of goods and services that conform to the available regional definitions for those goods and services. And states are pressured to create administrative units that specialize in the implementation of regional principles.

We can now summarize the main argument of this chapter. Figure 2.1

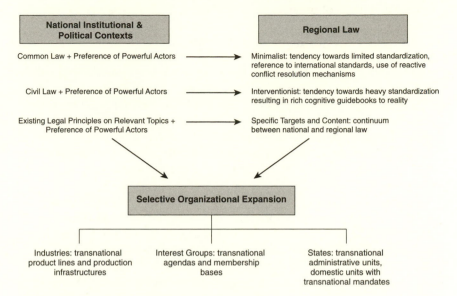

Figure 2.1. Law and Organizations in Regional Trade Agreements

summarizes the relationship between preexisting legal and political contexts, regional law, and organizations in RTAs. Note that figure 2.1 points to a *parallelism* or *coherence* between the evolution of regional law and the evolution of organizations. They are shaped by similar variables and, in addition, regional law itself influences how organizations evolve. Law and organizations thus evolve in a manner that is often complementary.

Note that figure 2.1 could be refined in several ways. It could suggest that organizations with regional reach, once in place, influence regional law. This link seems logical and further intensifies the relationship between law and organizations. EU scholars have noted how rules and collective actors live in "symbiotic" relationships in the EU space and elsewhere (Fligstein and Stone Sweet 2001: 37, 2002; Stryker 2003). We can expect companies with transnational operations to have a vested interest in shaping the standardizing principles of regional law. In the words of an expert observer of the European Union, "once shunned by European Commission officials . . . multi-national firms and key industry groups now enjoy strong working relationships, particularly during the drafting stage of European Union (EU) legislation" (Cowles 2001: 159). Regional interest groups lobby RTA legislators directly to produce legislative principles in line with their objectives (Greenwood 1997). National administrations, in turn, participate regularly in consultative forums with market legislators (Börzel 2001).

Figure 2.1 could also indicate that a number of additional factors affect the evolution of organizations. To begin, the very absence of regional law may serve as a catalyst for the regional development of organizations. This may be especially so for interest groups. Transnational alliances may develop to protest the absence of regional law on topics of importance to those groups. Yet we should also note that the absence of law is generally indicative of either organizational weakness or disinterest in regional affairs on the part of interest groups. Thus, the absence of law as such is not very likely to serve as a powerful stimulant for regional mobilization. Other variables might prove important: the vision of particular leaders, dominant values and norms, economic and political events outside of the RTA in question, economic calculations (especially in the case of companies), a desire to emulate the example of others, and so on.

Figure 2.1 could suggest as well that the nature of regional law is from the start not solely a reflection of institutional and political conditions in particular RTAs. In fact, a number of factors influence both the targets and content of such law (Greenwood 1997; Zeff and Pirro 2001). These include the vision and the leadership of key individuals, the relationship between regional legislators and other organs of RTAs, the relative balance of power among the member states, the impetus behind integration (Mansfield and Milner 1997b; Mattli 1999), and the relationship between new and existing regional laws (Majone 1996; Ross 1995). We shall consider some of these variables in the last chapter of the book.

Clearly, then, figure 2.1 is not comprehensive. It does focus, however, on a critical and thus far *much neglected* set of dynamics associated with the establishment of regional integration areas. It is to these dynamics that the rest of the book now turns.

THE CASE STUDIES

The following chapters investigate empirically these theoretical claims. I chose to focus on three RTAs: the EU, Mercosur, and NAFTA. As seen in chapter 1, these are some of the most important and best functioning integration projects in the world. They are at the same time representative of RTAs in general. NAFTA is an area where only goods, capital, and some selected services should in theory circulate free from tariffs and some nontariff barriers; Mercosur is a common market in formation; and the EU is an advanced common market. The EU is comprised of developed nations. NAFTA includes a developing economy and two of the most sophisticated economies in existence. Mercosur has only developing countries as member states.

I examined the entire NAFTA treaty and its two corollary agreements on labor and the environment to determine the extent to which officials have embarked on a project of cognitive standardization. As I explain in chapter 3 in detail, the EU and Mercosur have an enormous quantity of legal texts. I thus focused on three representative topical realms to assess the cognitive strategy of officials in those RTAs: economic life, the environment, and public health.

To investigate differences in the targets and content of the cognitive notions being produced in all three RTAs, and to examine related differences in the evolution of interest groups, businesses, and states, I focused on three subject areas within the realm of economic life: women and work, dairy products, and labor rights. A number of different subject areas could have been selected, of course. Yet these three areas present certain advantages: they are quite diverse, they affect significant portions of the population, and they exhibit rather clearly some of the most striking variation across RTAs that one can possibly find.

I relied on a wide array of data collection tools throughout the book. Much of the analysis of the definitional and normative nature of regional law was done through coding of legal texts. I explain how the coding proceeded in chapters 3 and 4 before presenting the findings. For all the empirical chapters (chapters 3, 4, and 5), I conducted extensive reviews of local newspapers, magazines, press releases, brochures, Internet sites, secondary sources, official reports, and other sources. I also drew heavily from personal interviews with officials, professionals, and people from various walks of life in Europe, North America, and South America. I collected most of the data between the years 2001 and 2004.

## PART II

The Evolution of Law and Society in the EU, Mercosur, and NAFTA

Chapter 3

THE USE OF REGIONAL LAW TO

STANDARDIZE REALITY

THE EU, MERCOSUR, AND NAFTA bring together countries with remarkably different cultural backgrounds and traditions. By the time of the major push for the completion of the common market in the late 1980s, the EU had member states as disparate as Greece, Denmark, Belgium, and Ireland. Mercosur combines three Spanish-speaking and ethnically homogenous countries with Brazil, a Portuguese-speaking country with a rich mixture of races and cultural traditions. NAFTA connects Canada, with its anglophone and francophone populations, with the diverse United States and predominantly Catholic, racially mixed, poorer and Spanish-speaking Mexico. The history of trade teaches us that cross-cultural exchanges depend, for their survival, on market participants developing shared definitional and normative viewpoints about the world. How have officials from the EU, Mercosur, and NAFTA addressed the problem of "cognitive dissonance" that they inevitably created with the rapid imposition of markets onto their very diverse populations?

In this chapter, I show that RTA officials have approached this problem in two rather different ways. In NAFTA, they have adopted a minimalist approach: they have produced a small number of definitional and normative notions about the world, and have then relied on a creative two-pronged approach that combines reliance on industry associations standards and a reactive conflict-resolution system. In both the EU and Mercosur officials have, by contrast, adopted a more proactive approach: the articulation of complex webs of secondary laws rich with definitional and normative notions applicable to a large variety of subject matters. The empirical data for the EU and Mercosur concerns the realms of economics, the environment, and public health.

I offer an explanation for NAFTA's miminalism and the more interventionist tendencies of the EU and Mercosur. In line with the political-institutional theory outlined in chapter 2, I propose that market planners have pursued—with the approval of key societal actors—cognitive strategies that build upon preexisting legal traditions in the various regions. Specifically, NAFTA's minimalist approach has been in line with the prevalence of common law in the United States and Canada, while the inter-

ventionism of the EU and Mercosur has reflected the prevalence of national civil-law traditions in their member states. Officials have thus opted
for continuity, replicating at the regional level fundamental approaches to
the regulation of the social world already present at the national level.

THE LEGAL TEXTS OF RTAS: METHODOLOGY FOR INVESTIGATION

All RTAs are grounded in some form of law: treaties, agreements, and so
on. Most, if not all RTAs, also have additional protocols, frameworks,
secondary legal systems, and other legal tools. These documents specify
procedures, concepts, and structures that permit the attainment of the
broad goals set out in the foundational documents. It is to these foundational and supporting documents that we must turn if we wish to learn
how RTA officials in the EU, Mercosur, and NAFTA have chosen to address the question of cognitive standardization in their respective regions.

In the case of NAFTA, our attentions should turn to its long and fairly
detailed (over a thousand pages long, with an additional two thousand
pages of annexes) founding agreement: the North American Free Trade
Agreement. NAFTA officials have used this agreement to specify nearly
everything of relevance for the functioning of their free trade area. We
should also examine NAFTA's two corollary agreements signed by the
member states to address labor and environmental matters: the NAALC
and the NAAEC.

The founding treaties of the EU and Mercosur are more generic and
provide only limited insights into the question of cognitive standardization. In both RTAs, however, there exist complex systems of "secondary"
laws (most importantly, *directives* and *regulations* for the EU, and *decisions* and *resolutions* for Mercosur): specific measures designed to attain
in practice the broader goals specified in the founding treaties. EU officials have produced over eighty thousand pages of such laws. Mercosur
officials have produced a smaller but nonetheless impressive volume of
laws—around fifteen hundred laws. The size of the secondary legal systems of the EU and Mercosur made a complete investigation nearly impossible. I thus elected three important but also rather different realms
with the hope (later confirmed) that the results would make further coding unnecessary: economic life, the environment, and public health.

The appendix explains in detail how I identified laws related to each of
these three realms. The total number of relevant laws exceeded three thousand. All were examined to determine if they had definitional or normative passages. A representative subset was then taken to estimate the exact
number of passages for the entire set. The appendix details how that representative subset was selected. At a more general level, the appendix also

discusses the overall character of NAFTA, EU, and Mercosur law: Does it constitute international versus supranational law? Who is responsible for drafting laws? What makes them obligatory?

How, then, were the legal texts of NAFTA, the EU, and Mercosur coded for definitional and normative content? Recall that we are concerned with market planners *affecting market participants' basic perceptions of reality*. I coded an EU, Mercosur, and NAFTA passage as *definitional* when, as its primary function or as part of its mandate, that passage spelled out, for all market participants, the essential characteristics of an object, activity, or agent. Objects include tangible items, such as vision glasses or a valve, and intangible items, such as a computer code or a song. Activities include series of steps taken through time and for a specific purpose, such as telemarketing, donating blood, driving, and hunting. Agents include living beings, such as a pilot or a fish, but also inanimate entities such as not-for-profit organizations, banks, and so on.[1]

I considered a passage as spelling out the essential characteristics of an entity if that passage stated something about its constitution (e.g., ingredients, components), function (e.g., intended use, purpose), form (e.g., liquid, solid, color, appearance), or origin (e.g., steps required for its creation, natural sources). A constitution-focused passage would, for instance, list the ingredients of "dark chocolate." A function-focused passage would define "an accounting audit" as an action taken to verify the accuracy of a company's financial reporting. A form-focused passage would define "fresh fish" as shiny, vivid in color, with bright, clear, and transparent eyes. And an origin-focused passage would define "honey" as a substance produced by the *Apis mellifera* bee and obtained from the honeycombs it produces for storage.

Note that two rather different types of passages were hence coded as definitional: those truly designed to impose on market participants standard definitions *and* those which, though intended for altogether different purposes, set out to define the meaning of key terms used throughout the passage.[2] The former are obviously more consequential for the worldview of market participants, but the latter can also be quite important, for they provide those participants with definitions that, though formally not

---

[1] Some things defied simple classification as an object, activity or agent. Though such ambiguity cannot be resolved, it can be addressed by way of close examination and then consistency in the coding procedure going forward.

[2] An example of the first type would be a passage stating: "food producers shall call chocolate only that food which complies with the following characteristics." An example of the second type would be a passage stating: "for the purposes of regulating how many hours an employer can ask an employee to work, we shall define a 'workday' as a time period of eight hours where the employee works for at least seven hours."

imposed upon them, cannot be ignored. We shall call the former *first-order* and the latter *second-order* definitional passages.

I coded a passage as *normative* when it made a statement about the desirability of particular situations, practices, behaviors, procedures, or any other aspect of the world. Situations include actual or potential conditions in society or nature, such as the presence of toxic ingredients in food or the existence of high tariffs on trade. Practices refer to habitual or repeated ways of doing something, such as certain storing techniques for food products or the use of gender to determine hiring decisions. Behaviors refer to specific actions or reactions of persons or groups, such as the act of breaching a contract or operating equipment in a dangerous fashion. And procedures include a set of established forms or methods for conducting a task, such as the steps taken to gut a fish at a food processing plant or the steps required for a mortgage application.[3]

I considered a passage as making a statement about the desirability of something when it either banned its occurrence or, on the contrary, asked market participants to ensure the opposite: that it in fact occurs at all times. Such passages often made ample use of terms such as "must," "shall," and "will." They also made implicit or explicit reference to either a priori principles of justice and ethics (e.g., animal rights, the sanctity of human life, etc.) or to more utilitarian calculations (higher productivity, lower prices, healthier food) to infuse their claim with legitimacy.

Note that normative passages were more difficult to identify than definitional passages. The latter were generally short, contained, stand-alone, and expressly presented as definitions. Normative passages, by contrast, were often long, complex, and embedded in other types of passages. There were also a large number of passages that, though normative in the common sense of the word, did not alter the basic worldview of market participants and were, therefore, not coded as such. These included passages specifying short-lived requirements[4] and affecting very specific people, groups or entities,[5] future RTA objectives,[6] or trade agreements with other economic blocs. They also included passages listing exceptions to stated normative principles, specifying the basic institutions and operat-

---

[3] This list is by no means intended to be comprehensive of all the types of passages that I coded as normative. Unlike definitional statements—which almost always can be said to apply to an object, activity, or agent—normative statements may apply to countless aspects of reality.

[4] E.g., "sugar growers in Brazil will not receive aid from the government for the year 1997," "the tariff reduction schedule for apples shall be x and y," etc.

[5] Such as a law stating that Ford France is to allow its dealerships to carry competitor brands.

[6] E.g., Mercosur officials express a desire for a future immigration policy.

ing procedures of RTAs, or articulating in a more refined fashion normative principles already stated by broader passages.[7]

The overall coding procedure had certain limitations. Above all, it did
not take into account how important to the life of market participants the
subject matter undergoing standardization might have been. For instance,
a passage in the legal texts of one RTA defining the essential characteristics of "fresh North Atlantic salmon" was classified as definitional much
like a passage in a second RTA defining the essential characteristics of
"drinkable water." Yet, it would be reasonable to assert that the life of
market participants in the second RTA had undergone wider-reaching
standardization than in the first. This and other limitations made the results of the coding offer an *approximate*, rather than precise, overview of
the approaches taken in different RTAs.

NAFTA's Minimalist Approach

NAFTA officials have avoided producing an extensive cognitive guidebook to reality. As one observer noted when contrasting NAFTA to the
EU, "there is no Brussels in North America, and there are no North American directives bringing about uniformization or harmonization of North
American" law (H. P. Glenn 2001: 1793). This is most evident in the case
of definitional notions: there are relatively few definitional passages and
all of them, moreover, are *second-order*.[8] There are more normative notions. As we shall see, however, these are also relatively few when compared to other RTAs. Table 3.1 reports the number of definitional and
normative notions in the NAFTA legal documents.

There are a total of 282 second-order definitional notions in the
NAFTA agreement, the NAALC, and the NAAEC. The majority of these
notions (over 50%) concern a few topical areas, all related to the trade of

[7] Consider, for instance, a broad law stating that the production of certain pharmaceuti-
cal products should follow certain hygienic steps that are then described in a second law. We
can say that the two laws together comprise the normative statement. Note as well that passages that asked market participants to accept each others' products, professionals, etc. (i.e.,
that stated the principle of mutual recognition) were coded as having normative content.
Passages that required market participants to refer to specific definitions found in other
agreements or organizations (such as the IMF) were coded as having definitional or normative content too, since these passages essentially adopted, without actually transcribing,
those definitions.

[8] As discussed in the previous section, second-order definitional passages do not have, as
their primary purpose, the objective of defining for market participants the essential characteristic of an entity. They have instead other objectives (often normative ones) which, for
their proper realization, require a definition of a number of aspects of reality.

Table 3.1

Number of Standardizing Notions in NAFTA (1993–2003)

Chapter	2: General Definitions	3: National Treatment and Market Access for Goods	4. Rules of Origin	5. Customs Procedures	6. Energy, Basic Petrochemicals	7. Agriculture, Sanitary and Phytosanitary Measures	8. Emergency Action	9. Standards-Related Measures	10. Government Procurement	11. Investment
# Definitional Notions	11	74	31	7	6	27	7	14	9	14
# Normative Notions	0	134	23	51	15	89	8	43	73	32

Chapter (or Corollary Agreement)	12: Cross-Border Trade in Services	13. Telecommunications	14. Financial Services	15. Competition, Monopolies, State Enterprises	16. Temporary Entry for Business Persons	17. Intellectual Property	19. Anti-dumping, Countervailing Duty Matters	Annex 1	NAALC	NAAEC
# Definitional Notions	6	12	9	6	4	8	5	5	8	7
# Normative Notions	12	27	23	10	15	56	2	0	11	8

TOTAL DEFINITIONAL NOTIONS: 282

TOTAL NORMATIVE NOTIONS: 628

Note: Annexes are included in their relevant chapters, unless they are stand alone annexes.

goods: national treatment and market access for goods (Chapter 3), rules of origins (Chapter 4), agriculture, sanitary and phytosanitary measures (Chapter 7), and standards-related measures (Chapter 9). The remaining notions are thinly spread across all remaining chapters, providing only a handful of definitions for a very few aspects of the world. Consider, for instance, the six notions related to competition, monopolies, and state enterprises (Chapter 15), all provided only "for the purposes of this Chapter" (Article 1505). Of all that could be targeted in this realm, only the following are subject to definition: "government monopoly," "monopoly," "market," "non-discriminatory treatment," "state enterprise," and activities executed "in accordance with commercial considerations."

The definitional notions found in Chapters 3, 4, 7, and 9 are more numerous. Yet here too there are no rich webs of definitional notions surrounding given subject areas, as will obviously be the case for the EU and Mercosur. Rather, we observe sets of fairly unrelated notions concerned only with the most basic aspects of reality. Consider, for instance, two representative sets of definitional notions from the two richest sections of the agreement: Chapters 3 and 7. Chapter 3 is central to NAFTA, for it establishes that no discrimination of goods can take place on the grounds of being produced in one of the member states. It thus covers a large number of goods. Yet very few definitions in any given area are provided. Consider the case of textiles and apparel, which are given an entire appendix. Appendix 300-B has definitions for a small constellation of objects, activities, and agents. These include "average yarn number," "wool apparel," "categories of textile and apparel goods," "exporting" and "importing" parties, "square meter equivalent," "specific export limits," "tariff preference level," "consultation export level," and "flexibility provisions." There are no additional definitions. What is a skirt? What is a sweater? What are stain-resistant garments? What are wrinkle-free shirts? What is natural leather? Are there different qualities of wool? What counts as handmade? Hundreds of potential aspects of reality related to textiles and apparel are thus left undefined.

Consider now the all-important Chapter 7, which has two sections: Section A on agriculture and Section B on sanitary and phytosanitary measures. Section A has a disarmingly short list of definitions: "agricultural good," "fish or fish product," a handful of definitions related to sugar ("sugar," "plantation white sugar," "sugar-containing product") and a few tariff- and custom-related definitions. All other aspects of agriculture (different types of fruits and vegetables, various production processes, industry players, and so on) are left untouched. Section B is equally limited in coverage. Basic definitions are provided for "animal," "contaminant," "plant," "pest," "sanitary or phytosanitary measure," and "scientific basis." There are no additional definitions for all else that could be targeted: different types of animals, contaminants, plants, pests, various harmful practices, and so on. Without question, this is truly a very limited approach to standardization.

On the normative side, we note a total of 628 passages. This is not a small number, though it will seem so when compared to those of the EU and Mercosur, and when one develops an understanding of how many stipulations are needed to accomplish the most simple tasks associated with trade liberalization. As with the definitional notions, here too we observe a certain clustering of normative notions in a few topical areas. Most of these, understandably, are directly related to the trade of goods. Chapter 3—again the richest chapter—has seventy-five normative notions that deal directly with the national treatment and market access of goods: tariff elimination, the illegality of discriminating against goods from a member state, and so on. Article 309 is in this sense very representative of the overall flavor of these passages:

> Except as otherwise provided in this Agreement, no Party may adopt or maintain any prohibition or restriction on the importation of any good of another Party or on the exportation or sale for export of any good destined for the territory of another Party, except in accordance with Article XI of the GATT, including its interpretative notes.

A large set of passages also standardizes custom procedures (Chapter 5). The relatively large number of normative notions related to agriculture and phytosanitary measures (Chapter 7) may suggest that NAFTA officials have promulgated numerous principles related to how farmers and others operate. In fact, NAFTA officials allow each member state to set such principles independently (see Article 712) and have dedicated the vast majority of the normative notions to matters related to trade. These include principles on discrimination based on origins, modalities for inspection of goods (see, for example, Article 717), the subsidization of farmers (Article 705), and so on. Smaller articles broadly repeat this pattern. Article 607, for instance, on energy and basic petrochemicals, states: "No Party may adopt or maintain a measure restricting imports of an energy or basic petrochemical good from, or exports of an energy or basic petrochemical good to, another Party."

To be sure, not all normative principles concern themselves with the trade of goods as such. In the case of intellectual property, much attention was given to matters of copyrights, ownership, protection, and so on. These represent an important extension of NAFTA's reach into sensitive and very important aspects of social life. Article 1708 for instance states:

> Each Party shall provide to the owner of a registered trademark the right to prevent all persons not having the owner's consent from using in commerce

identical or similar signs for goods or services that are identical or similar to those goods or services in respect of which the owner's trademark is registered, where such use would result in a likelihood of confusion.

In addition, a number of normative notions are altogether not concerned with goods. Some attention has gone to services, again in a way that does not strictly focus on trade. Chapter 10 on government procurement, for instance, is fairly rich with normative principles related to how governments should go about announcing their need for services and selecting candidates from across NAFTA.[9] Topics addressed include invitations to participate, nondiscrimination, negotiation principles, contract submission and handling, bid challenges, and so on.

Overall, we may thus state without hesitation that NAFTA officials have avoided the cognitive standardization of the world. This is a conclusion implicitly shared by all those observers who conclude that the NAFTA legal texts do not have the objective of harmonizing legal texts (Condon 1997). The focus of whatever standardization exists has been above all on streamlining the trade of goods, and much less on defining those goods or, even less, anything a bit removed from such trade. Interestingly, a close reading of the agreement reveals that officials have in fact been rather explicit about their desire *not to codify the world*. In a number of important cases, officials openly opt not to pursue standardization and instead rely on the principle of mutual recognition: participants are openly asked to treat the goods, investments, and selected services originating from other member states as if they originated from domestic providers. Protectionist behavior, unless allowed by formal exemptions, is thus deemed illegitimate and unacceptable. Chapter 3 (Article 301) covers goods, Chapter 11 investments, and Chapter 12 services. This passage from Chapter 12 is representative of the overall spirit:

> Each Party shall accord to investors of another Party treatment no less favorable than that it accords, in like circumstances, to its own investors with respect to the establishment, acquisition, expansion, management, conduct, operation, and sale or other disposition of investments (Article 1102).

At the same time, officials have also recognized the limitations of such a minimalist approach. Market participants are bound to have cognitive conflict. The solution, in keeping with the overall intention not to codify the world, has involved two separate initiatives (Rojo 1992). First, especially in the case of complex products, officials repeatedly ask participants

---

[9] Though, according to some accounts, "ninety per cent of the government purchasing market in all three countries, a market worth hundreds of billions, is not covered by the agreement" (Hadekel 1994).

to comply with standards set by other organizations. These are typically technical standards formulated by international industry associations and trade organizations such as the General Agreement on Tariffs and Trade (Atkinson 1998; Martin 1998). In Chapter 9 of the treaty, officials ask that those standards be used for simple goods (such as food, textiles, apparel, etc.) as well as more complex products (such as automobiles, land transportation vehicles, telecommunications, etc.). In Chapter 7, they address sanitary measures in agriculture. The language there is typical of the treaty in general:

> Without reducing the level of protection of human, animal or plant life or health, each Party shall use, as a basis for its sanitary and phytosanitary measures, relevant international standards, guidelines or recommendations with the objective, among others, of making its sanitary and phytosanitary measures equivalent or, where appropriate, identical to those of the other Parties. (Article 713)

Second, NAFTA officials have chosen to address cognitive conflicts reactively as they arise. The conflict-resolution process, which of course addresses more than just cognitive disputes as defined in this article, is spelled out in Chapters 11 (for investments), 14 (for financial services), 19 (for antidumping and countervailing duty matters), and 20 (for most trade issues) of NAFTA. For labor-related matters, the process is addressed in the NAALC and for the environment in the NAAEC.

The steps laid out in Chapter 20 are among the most commonly used ones and can serve as an example. Chapter 20 asks that representatives of the member states first attempt to solve their differences by means of "consultation," or essentially dialogue. Article 2006 (5) states: "The consulting Parties shall make every attempt to arrive at a mutually satisfactory resolution of any matter through consultations under this Article or other consultative provisions of this Agreement." If consultation fails, the parties can then turn to the NAFTA Commission, a group of cabinet-level government representatives whose primary mission is to ensure a "mutually amiable effectuation of the agreement" (Byrne 2000: 418). The Commission has the power to call on experts and create panels and working groups, again all for the purposes of mediation and resolution (Article 2007). If the Commission's efforts fail, the parties can then turn to an arbitration panel (composed of individuals from the member states who are expected to serve the interest of NAFTA and not that of their country of origin). Again, NAFTA officials urge participants to avail themselves of this venue: "Each Party shall, to the maximum extent possible, encourage and facilitate the use of arbitration and other means of alternative dispute resolution for the settlement of international commercial disputes between private parties in the free trade area" (Article 2022). The opinion of the panel will have binding nature: it shall be respected by the member states (Article 2018).

Importantly, we should note that governments only are allowed to participate in arbitration procedures: private individuals or organizations must rely on those governments to represent their interests. Only Chapter 11, the NAALC, and the NAAEC allow individual investors or groups to take issue with a government (Chew and Posthuma 2002: 38). This limits the number of grievances that are likely to find a solution within the NAFTA context (Byrne 2000).[10]

Whether, in fact, reliance on international standards and reactive conflict resolution mechanisms will prove sufficient to overcome the different worldviews of the participants from the three member states remains to be seen. There is certainly much evidence to suggest that private sector companies have—with the support of the three governments—not only complied with international standards but have also met to develop regional-level standards for their various industries. One of the most relevant examples is the North American Trilateral Standardization Forum.[11] There is also much evidence of the proliferation of national industry agencies determined to develop standards that conform with international ones.[12] Arbitration, in turn, has been widely used in NAFTA as well, with the most frequent cases focusing on normative questions of product safety and product dumping.[13]

Yet several observers insist that economic integration in North America, as elsewhere, simply cannot take place without some form of comprehensive legal harmonization (Condon 1997). They then add that use of international standards or arbitration procedures may simply not be enough to overcome differences.[14] Something additional, they believe,

[10] For an excellent analysis of the various dispute resolution mechanisms in NAFTA, see Hansen (2003).

[11] The Forum is sponsored by the Standards Council of Canada, the American National Standards Institute, Dirección General de Normas (General Directorate for Standards) of the Mexican government, and the Cámara Nacional de la Industria de Transformación (Mexican National Chamber of the Transformation Industry).

[12] See, for example, the creation in 1993 in Mexico of the Asociación de Normalización y Certificación del Sector Eléctrico (Association for the Normalization and Certification of the Electric Sector) (ANCE). A journalist has observed: "The certification entity ANCE and other privately-owned, non-profit organizations that now are actively being promoted by the Mexican government are by-products of NAFTA and the general opening of Mexico's economy. The agencies help ensure that products sold in Mexico, both imported and domestic, conform to quality standards in the United States and Canada" (Delgado 1994). Indeed, ANCE has permanent contacts with Underwriters Laboratories, Inc., the equivalent agency in the United States, to facilitate cooperation.

[13] Publicly available information on all cases is available on the Internet homepage of the NAFTA Secretariat: http://www.nafta-sec-alena.org.

[14] On this point, see Condon (1997), who reviews examples of how arbitration panels in

needs to take place. This could be a planned intervention or, in the absence of that, a natural process of harmonization. According to Glenn, such a "spontaneous and voluntary . . . informal process" has already been happening in NAFTA (H. P. Glenn 2001: 1801). Glenn notes: "NAFTA has created, as it were, a legal slipstream, a draft, the effect of which is arguably larger than that of NAFTA's specific provisions" (1793). These adjustments have occurred because of court decisions, new laws, amendments to existing laws, and other measures taken by national judges and lawmakers. Courts in all three member states now recognize the validity of decisions reached by courts in other member states on matters of relevance to the functioning of a single market (as well as other matters). Cooperation between legislators of the three member states on new laws is now commonplace, as is the adoption by the legislatures of all three member states of international covenants (such as the Vienna Convention on the International Sale of Goods).

COGNITIVE GUIDEBOOKS IN THE EU AND MERCOSUR

In contrast to their NAFTA counterparts, officials in the EU and Mercosur have adopted a very aggressive approach to cognitive standardization. Table 3.2 reports the number of EU and Mercosur laws affecting economic life, the environment, and public health. It identifies the number of laws with definitional and normative content and, as discussed in the methodology section of this chapter, specifies the number of definitional and normative notions in each realm.

Both EU and Mercosur officials have developed a truly large number of laws with cognitive content in the realms of economics, public health, and the environment. EU officials have produced approximately 2,504 definitional notions and 14,465 normative notions in those three realms, for a total of nearly seventeen thousand cognitive notions: this represents a volume *eighteen times* that of the entire NAFTA output. Note as well that a good share of the definitional notions is first-order: those notions have, as their primary mission, the objective of standardizing the world for participants.

Most of the EU laws with cognitive content concern the realm of economic life. Such a realm, however, is very extensive in coverage, stretching well beyond the trade of goods. Services, capital, and labor receive much attention. Especially in the 1980s and 1990s, EU officials worked hard to categorize and regulate financial services, though much remains

---

NAFTA simply failed to reach their objectives because of engrained differences in the worldviews of panel judges and major differences in the legal cultures from which they emerged.

TABLE 3.2

Number of Standardizing Notions in the EU (1959–2000) and Mercosur (1991–2000) in Selected Realms

	Economics			Environment			Public Health			Total Laws	Total Notions (estimated)
EU	Directives	Regulations	Notions (estimated)	Directives	Regulations	Notions	Directives	Regulations	Notions		
# with definitional content	228	256	2,137	31	4	283	13	3	84	535	2,504
# with normative content	517	863	13,217	48	13	687	18	11	561	1,470	14,465
MERCOSUR	Decisions	Reso-lutions	Notions (estimated)	Decisions	Reso-lutions	Notions	Decisions	Reso-lutions	Notions (estimated)		
# with definitional content	37	313	6,638	2	5	56	2	114	1,550	473	8,244
# with normative content	79	314	11,813	4	10	140	4	174	8,793	585	20,746

Note: When a law has both definitional and normative content, it is counted twice on the table (once as a law with definitional content, once as a law with normative content).

to be done. Various forms of investment are also targeted, as are various types of employment and matters associated with work (health, safety, information, and much more).

We note as well a fairly high number of cognitive notions related to the environment. Here a direct comparison with NAFTA is possible: the NAAEC has a total of fifteen cognitive notions (seven definitional and eight normative). The EU has a total of 970 cognitive notions (283 definitional and 687 normative). Topics covered by EU laws are truly diverse: water, air, soil, nuclear activities, fauna and flora, waste management, and much more.

The numbers from Mercosur are also impressive. Officials there have produced an estimated total of 8,244 definitional and 20,746 normative notions in the three selected realms, for a total of almost twenty-nine thousand cognitive notions. This subset of all notions produced for Mercosur is nearly *thirty-two times* the entire number of cognitive notions found in the NAFTA text. Mercosur officials have clearly been very busy standardizing the world for market participants. Indeed, at least in the three realms considered, they have outdone their EU counterparts. Their efforts are especially remarkable in the case of definitional notions, where they have produced over three times the number of notions found in the EU. When we consider that a very large proportion of these definitional notions are first-order, the output of Mercosur officials becomes all the more impressive. The Mercosur legal system is both very rich with cognitive content and relatively well-balanced in definitional and normative terms.

As with the EU, we notice that in Mercosur much attention has been given to the realm of economics. Again, here too the range of topics is remarkably diverse. A truly astounding number of products have been subject to first-order definitional standardization. Mercosur officials exhibit a strong preoccupation with specifying the essential characteristics of a huge number of products: food, consumer goods, durable goods, and much more. But much attention is also paid to a number of processes, procedures, safety requirements, and so on.[15]

A clear difference between Mercosur and the EU is the high number of public health cognitive notions in the former. The EU had a total of 645, compared to a total for Mercosur of 10,343. While certainly Mercosur

---

[15] Even in these cases, however, the overarching concern of officials has been the liberalization of the trade of goods, and much less with that of services, capital, or labor (Haines-Ferrari 1993). In this regard, we see a noticeable and general difference with the EU. We should also note, however, that the EU itself targeted the world of goods much more comprehensively early on in its existence (Duina 2003).

officials have gone to great lengths in specifying health measures for production processes, illnesses, food, and so on, a possible explanation for this difference lies in the categorization schemes used in the EU and Mercosur legal databases. As noted in the appendix, the EU has a section dedicated to public health. Mercosur does not have a categorization scheme. EU officials categorized under "economics" a number of laws that, had they been manually coded for this book, would have been categorized as public health measures.

The next sections offer a closer view of the complex and rich webs of cognitive notions that EU and Mercosur officials have produced for their market participants. The focus is on representative subsets of notions in each of the three realms that were coded. In the case of economics, I discuss definitional and normative notions found in the EU related to working conditions. For the environment, I turn again to the EU (where the number of laws is rather high) and consider notions related to flora and fauna. In the case of public health, I turn to Mercosur and select a number of laws that are broadly representative of the scope and character of the initiatives taken by officials in that area.

A Close View of the Cognitive Guidebooks of the EU and Mercosur

EU officials have subjected countless aspects of economic life to definitional and normative standardization. Tables 3.3 and 3.4 offer insights into one of those many aspects: working conditions. They identify key definitional and normative notions, and also specify the basic technique (constitution, function, form, origin for definitional notions; right vs. wrong or practical consequences for normative notions) used by market officials to develop those notions.

Officials have heavily targeted the world of employees with definitional passages. Aspects covered include the organization of time, varieties of occupations, categories of workers, and workplace risks. Time is divided into day and night, hours, weeks, months, and time spent working and resting. For example, "night time" is defined as at least a seven-hour period including the five hours between midnight and five o'clock, and "weekly rest" is defined as a continuous twenty-four-hour period of resting from work each week. Types of occupations include "seafarer," defined as a worker on board a commercial maritime ship. Categories of workers include "mobile worker," or one who travels via road, air, or inland during work. Risks include "asbestos," "radiation," and "biological agents." Note that most definitional notions rely on constitution and function.

Normative assertions then build on these definitional definitions to in-

TABLE 3.3
Working Conditions in the EU: Definitional Notions

Constitution	"Night time'" as not less than seven hours including the hours from midnight to 5 a.m.; "daily rest" as a period of 11 consecutive hours per every 24-hour period; "weekly rest" as a period of 24 consecutive hours per every 7-day period; and "annual leave" as four weeks paid leave per year (93/104).
	"Equal treatment" as the absence of discrimination directly or indirectly (75/117; 97/80).
	"Pregnant workers" as pregnant, recent birthing, and breast-feeding workers whose condition is a specific safety and health risk (92/85).
	"Maternity leave" as a minimum of 14 weeks continuous leave offered to pregnant workers, including a mandatory 2-week leave period near the time of birth (92/85).
	"Parental leave" as leave spent taking care of a born or adopted child, for at least three months, until a given age up to 8 years (96/34).
	"Explosive atmosphere" as flammable gases, vapors, mists or dusts mixed with air (1999/92).
	"Asbestos" as one or more of six fibrous silicates (80/1107).
	"Radioactive contamination" as the exposure of any person (externally or internally), material, surface or environment to radioactive substances (96/29).
Function	"Worker" as someone given tasks by an employer (excluding domestic servants); and "employer" as any natural or legal person who has an employment relationship with the worker and is responsible for the workplace (89/391).
	"Working time" as any period during which a worker works at an employer's disposal (2000/79).
	"Seafarer" as any person employed on a seagoing ship, publicly or privately owned, engaged in commercial maritime activities (Dir 1999/63); and "skipper" as any worker who has command and responsibility of a seagoing vessel (93/103).
	"Radiation" as a particularly harmful workplace health and safety risk (96/29).

TABLE 3.3
Continued

	"Mobile worker" as any worker who travels via road, air or inland waterway (94/103).
	"Adequate rest" as sufficiently long and continuous to prevent injury to themselves or fellow workers in the short or long term (2000/34).
	"Employers' obligations" as activities to encourage and protect the safety and health of workers including supervision, provision of first aid, provision of drills and information, prevention of fire, and assignment of specialized or dangerous work to competent workers (89/391; 92/104).
	"Asbestos" as a harmful agent found in many workplaces (83/477).
	"Biological agents" as things capable of provoking an infection, allergy, or toxicity (2000/54).
	"Radiological emergency" as a situation involving the release of radioactive agents and posing an immediate threat to the health and safety of workers (96/29).
Origin	"Radiation" as a product of radioactive objects originating naturally, terrestrially, and cosmically (96/29).

Note: Numbers in parentheses refer to EU directives.

troduce principles protecting employees and, far less often, employers. Time is organized so as to prevent overworking and to grant the worker adequate periodic rest (daily, weekly, etc.). All workers taking part in the various occupations and categories of work are granted the principle of equal treatment. Furthermore, employers have the burden of proof in all cases of discrimination. Workplace risks are controlled to protect the worker: maximum levels of exposure to dangerous substances are, for instance, specified and employers are called upon to protect and inform the worker against any such risk. The grounding principles of protection for employees are evenly distributed between notions of right and wrong and practical consequences. An abstract sense of fairness or equality pervades laws related to matters such as equal treatment for men and women and the placement of the burden of proof on employers. But the maintenance of worker health and safety and a functional worker-employer relationship are obviously concerns. Hence, workers and employers should in-

TABLE 3.4
Working Conditions in the EU: Normative Notions

	Vision	Grounding Principle
Right and Wrong	Pay discrepancies between workers of equal stature should be systematically investigated (Reg 530/1999).	Equal treatment
	Workers should be treated without discrimination regardless of nationality (Reg 1612/68 and Dir 92/51), biological sex (Dir 75/117; 76/207), racial or ethnic origin (Dir 2000/43), and religion, belief, disability, age, and sexual orientation (Dir 2000/78).	Equal treatment
	The living and working conditions of workers should be maintained and improved whenever possible (Dir 93/104).	Worker rights
	Workers should not be overworked (Dir 1999/63).	Worker rights
	Seafarers (Dir 93/104) and air travel workers (Dir 2000/79) who have abnormal and long hours should not be overworked.	Worker rights
	Workers' movement and pursuit of employment should not be inhibited in any way (Reg 1612/68) and workers shall also have the right to remain in a location after having been employed there (Reg 1251/70).	Freedom of movement
	Pregnant or recent birthing mothers must take a 2-week maternity leave from work (Dir 92/85).	Integrity of mother-child relationship
	In employment discrimination disputes, the burden of proof is on the employer (Dir 97/80).	Structural fairness

Practical Consequences	Migrant workers shall receive free tuition for any language schooling (Dir 77/486).	Maximization of human resources
	Workers should not be exposed to certain levels of asbestos (Dir 80/1107), noise (Dir 86/188), carcinogens (Dir 90/394; 97/42), radiation (Dir 96/29), biological agents (Dir 2000/54), chemical agents (Dir 98/24) and explosive atmospheres (Dir 1999/92).	Worker health and safety
	Workplace buildings and equipment must be kept clean and safe (Dir 80/1107).	Worker health and safety
	Workers must be informed in a comprehensible way of relevant dangers, work equipment in the work area, and any changes affecting them even if not directly (Dir 89/30).	Worker health and safety
	Daily and weekly rest, and annual paid leave must be granted to all workers (Dir 93/104).	Maximization of human resources
	The safety and health of workers must be promoted in every aspect of their work (Dir 89/391).	Maximization of human resources
	Seafarers may be overworked any number of hours in the necessary case of giving assistance to other ships/persons in distress at sea (Dir 1999/63).	Prevent loss of goods, rescue human life
	Workers and employers should not take legal action against one another without prior notification (Dir 91/533).	Maintain production, prevent disputes over work

Note: Numbers in parentheses refer to EU directives (if preceded by Dir) and regulations (if preceded by Reg).

form each other before undertaking legal action and workplace buildings and equipment must be kept clean and safe.

In the realm of the environment, definitional and normative topics range from the protection of pristine areas to harmful agricultural and industrial activities. We consider here those related to flora and fauna. Tables 3.5 and 3.6 summarize the results of the coding in detail. In the case of flora and fauna, definitional notions again apply to entities deemed in

TABLE 3.5
Flora and Fauna in the EU: Definitional Notions

Constitution	"Natural habitat" as a terrestrial or aquatic area distinguished by geographic, abiotic, and biotic features, whether entirely natural or semi-natural (Dir 92/43).
	"Genetically modified organism" as an organism having genetic material that has been altered in an unnatural way (Dir 2001/18).
	"Environment" as water, air, land, wild species of fauna and flora, and interrelationships between them and/or humans (Dir 91/414).
	"Controlled environment" as having controlled boundaries and any of the following: artificial housing, waste removal, health care, protection from predators, and an artificial supply of food (Reg 1808/2001).
	"Plant protection product" as having one or more active substances (a list is given) (Dir 91/414).
	"Information relating to the environment" as any available information on the state of water, air, soil, fauna, flora, land, and natural sites, and on activities that impact these (Dir 90/313).
	"Plants" as living plants, living parts of plants, and seeds (Dir 2000/29).
	"Pig" as any member of the Suidae family, including those in and out of holdings (Dir 2001/89).
	"Forests" as natural or sub-natural woodland vegetation of native species forming forests of tall trees with undergrowth (Dir 92/43).
	"Case of classical swine fever" as any pig or pig carcass having clinical symptoms, post-mortem lesions, and/or reactions to laboratory tests (Dir 2001/89).

TABLE 3.5
Continued

Function	"Holding" as an agricultural establishment or supervised dealership where animals for breeding, production, or slaughter are regularly kept or bred (Dir 64/423; 2001/89).
	"Organism" as any biological actor capable of replication (Dir 2001/18).
	"Harmful organism" as an organism that can have a detrimental effect for humans, animals, or the environment (Dir 98/8).
	"Zoo" as a location with the function of displaying animals for seven or more days at a time (Dir 1999/22).
	"Plant protection products" as substances that destroy or prevent harmful things (Dir 91/414).
	"Pollution" as anything that harms humans, resources and/or the ecosystem (Dir 78/176) or harms outdoor public air (Dir 96/62).
	"Conservation" as activities intended to restore natural habitats and populations (Dir 92/43).
	"Breeding stock" as all the animals in an operation used for reproduction (Reg 1808/2001).
	"Controlled environment" as an environment manipulated for the purpose of producing a certain species of animals that prevents animals, eggs, or gametes from entering or leaving (Reg 1808/2001).
Form	"Zebrafish" as an aquatic actor similar to a carp, rarely exceeding 45mm in length, having a cylindrical body with 7–9 dark-blue horizontal silvery stripes, having an olive-green back, males being slimmer than females, and eggs that are transparent and non-adhesive (Dir 2001/59).
	"Genetically modified organism" as having a specific phenotype, description, physiology, and differences vis-à-vis naturally occurring forms of the organism (Dir 2001/18).
Origin	"Pollution" as harmful discharge derived from humans (Dir 78/176; 96/62).

Note: Numbers in parentheses refer to EU directives (if preceded by Dir) and regulations (if preceded by Reg).

TABLE 3.6
Flora and Fauna in the EU: Normative Notions

	Vision	Grounding Principle
Right and Wrong	Environmental information should be made available to the public (Dir 90/313).	Free public access to information
	Animals subject to experiments shall be protected from avoidable suffering, granted freedom of movement, housing, food, care, etc. (Dir 86/609).	Animal rights
	Wild animals in zoos will be housed in adequate facilities (Dir 1999/22).	Animal rights
	Birds shall not be hunted during migration and mating periods, endangered bird species shall not be hunted, traded, or sold, and nests and eggs cannot be destroyed (Dir 79/409).	Sanctity of bird species
	Products from harp and hooded seal pups will not be imported into the EU (unless obtained from traditional hunting by the Inuit people) (Dir 83/129).	Sanctity of seal species
	Standing and running water capable of supporting fish shall be protected from dangerous levels of pollution (Dir 78/659).	Sanctity of fish species
	Animals shall not suffer during or as a result of trade (Dir 91/628).	Animal rights
	Live decoys, tape recordings, explosives, crossbows, and other non-selective techniques shall not be used to hunt mammals (Dir 92/43).	Procedural fairness, integrity of biodiversity
	Natural habitats in danger of disappearance or covering small geographical areas shall be protected and, whenever possible, restored (Dir 92/43).	Integrity of biodiversity
	Waste disposal should not harm water, air, soil, plants and animals (Dir 75/442).	Integrity of biodiversity

Practical Consequences	
Forests shall be safeguarded from fires (Reg 2158/92; 1727/99).	Economic exploitation of forests
The diversity, productivity, and vitality of forests shall be protected (Reg 2494/2000).	Economic exploitation of forests
Action should be taken to monitor and remedy the situation if discharge, dumping, storage, tipping, or injection procedures produce a deleterious effect on leisure activities, the extraction of raw materials, desalination, plants, animals, or regions of scientific importance (Dir 338/97).	Human health, conservation of natural resources
The discharge, dumping, storage, tipping, and injection of titanium dioxide waste in the natural environment or elsewhere should be prohibited (Dir 78/176)	Human health
The release of genetically modified organisms into the environment must follow rigorous testing (Dir 90/220; 2001/18).	Sustainability of environmental resources
Unhealthy animals (diseased, malnourished, etc.) shall not be traded (Dir 64/432; 92/65).	Farmer protection
Plant propagation material for sale to the public must be free of defects in propagation capacity, diseases, and harmful organisms (Dir 98/56).	Plant health
Trade of selected wild flora and fauna shall not exceed specified limits (Reg 338/97).	Economic exploitation of wild flora and fauna

Note: Numbers in parentheses refer to EU directives (if preceded by Dir) and regulations (if preceded by Reg).

need of protection and to those capable of improving conservation. Specific animals, such as "zebrafish" and "pig," and broader categories of beings, such as "organisms," "breeding stock," "plants" and "forests," all undergo definition. Habitats, including "environment," "controlled environment," "natural habitat," and "zoo," are also defined. Entities that directly affect conservation are targeted. We note "pollution" (anything that harms humans or the ecosystem), "plant protection products" (active substances that protect plants against harm), and "conservation" (a set of activities that maintain and improve the status of plants and animals). Again, constitution and function drive most definitions.

As with working conditions, normative notions build on definitional notions to promote protection. Many demand preemptive measures in areas such as hunting, forests, natural habitats, diseases, water bodies, and even zoos. Polluting and wasteful activities, for instance, are prohibited. Other normative notions demand that constructive actions, such as maximizing the number of natural habitat areas, be taken. Both an abstract sense of right and wrong and a concern with practical consequences drive these normative notions. The EU clearly believes in the sanctity of animal and plant species. On the other hand, it recognizes the usefulness of plants and animals to human life.

Mercosur officials have targeted rather extensively the world of public health. Laws cover medical care, public spaces (airports, marine terminals, etc.), beauty products, illegal drugs, prophylactics, epidemics, and much more. Perhaps the most intensively targeted topic is food, however. Tables 3.7 and 3.8 review a representative set of passages from Mercosur resolutions (and one decision). Much definitional attention has been given to hygiene problems associated with processed and unprocessed foods. Definitions are given for terms such as "plague," "contaminant," "food additives," and "processing agents." At the same time, officials have shown a preoccupation with establishing clear definitions for measures and tools that can address those problems. Hence, we observe definitions for terms such as "fermentation," "sterilization," "eradication," and "pasteurization." Most definitions are given in functional terms—a logical approach when one considers the focus on solutions.

On the normative side, officials go to great lengths to limit and guide the actions of food producers (modalities for the use of additives, packaging requirements, etc.), impose precautionary steps for importing goods (especially quarantine), and provide the public with product information (most often through informative product labels). We should note that a large variety of products are regulated, from fruits to vegetables and semiprocessed and processed goods. The driving normative principles are by and large utilitarian: the protection of consumers. Importantly, how-

TABLE 3.7
Public Health in Mercosur: Definitional Notions

Constitution	"Pasteurization" as the heating of a liquid for 30 minutes at temperatures of 638C—658C (with some variance) followed by a rapid chilling to 108C or less, without altering the nutritional qualities or taste of the liquid (52/02).
	"Harmonization" of phytosanitary measures as the developments, adoption, and implementation—across countries—of phytosanitary measures based on common standards (52/02).
	"Plague-free area" as an area in which scientific evidence points to the absence of a given plague or where a given plague is under control (59/94).
Function	"Quarantine" as official confinement of a given article to allow for observation, investigation, and inspection (50/92).
	"Plague needing quarantine" as any plague in vegetable products capable of having consequences for the national economy of any member state (66/93).
	"Inspection" as a official visual examination of plants, vegetable products, or other substances for the purposes of determining the presence of a plague and/or assessing compliance with agreed-upon standards (50/92).
	"Phytosanitary measure" as any law, standard, procedure or recommendation aimed at the prevention or elimination of plagues (59/94).
	"Sterilization" as the destruction of harmful germs so as to disinfect foods, obtained either through heat (steam, dry, water), cold, or dehydration (52/02).
	"Food additive" as any ingredient added during the production, conditioning, packaging, or transportation of a food product in order to modify the physical, chemical, biological, or sensory characteristics of that product (31/92).
	"Processing agent" as any substance or element (excluding equipment and utensils) that is used intentionally to alter the raw materials or ingredients of a given food product, and which may or may not leave a residue (31/92).
	"Eradication" as the application of phytosanitary measures to eliminate a plague in a given area (59/94).

continued

TABLE 3.7
Continued

Form	Phytosanitary certificate as a document specifying time, hygienic treatment, transportation history, and other data relative to a given product (44/92).
Origin	"Fermentation" as the slow process of change or decomposition of substances produced by the catalytic action of a fermenting agent (and often accompanied by effervescence or release of heat) (52/02).
	"Contaminant" as an undesirable substance present in a food coming from agricultural processes, animal rearing, or from the machinery or equipment used for processing and conservation (31/92).

Note: Numbers in parentheses refer to Mercosur resolutions.

ever, one also encounters passages where officials use more moralistic language, especially when discussing public health as a fundamental good that cannot be sacrificed to market considerations.

EXPLAINING THE OBSERVED DIFFERENCES

The observed differences between NAFTA on the one hand and the EU and Mercosur on the other are significant. NAFTA officials have adopted a minimalist approach, relying explicitly on mutual recognition, standards set by other organizations, and a reactive conflict-resolution system. Officials in the EU and Mercosur have clearly developed extensive cognitive guidebooks to reality, rich with many (first- and second-order) definitional notions and normative notions. How are we to explain such variation in approaches?

Recall our discussion from chapter 2. I suggested there that a minimalist approach is likely to occur in RTAs where most, if not all, member states share common law traditions. Common law is a reactive, case-by-case, and thus gradual approach to regulation. It is pragmatic and flexible, relying on a few a priori general legislative principles and courts (and thus precedent setting) to settle conflicts as they arise. Officials operating in RTAs with common-law traditions tend to replicate at the regional level the principles found at the national level. I then suggested that a more in-

TABLE 3.8
Public Health in Mercosur: Normative Notions

	Vision	Grounding Principle
Right and Wrong	Market integration cannot come at the cost of public health: economic and political actors shall prioritize the health of consumers and the population (Dec 23/93).	Public health as a fundamental good
	No product or service may be put in the marketplace if it presents health risks to consumers or dangers to their physical integrity (Res 125/95).	Public health as a fundamental good
	Chemically modified amidos shall be listed as ingredients on food labels (Res 106/94).	Consumer's right to information
Practical Consequences	Inorganic contaminants (e.g. mercury, arsenic) can appear in different types of drinks and foods (e.g. milk, coffee, fish, chocolate) only in certain quantities (Res 102/94).	Poisonous effects of contaminant
	Chemically modified amidos for use in the food industry shall conform to certain specifications (Res 106/94).	Consumer health
	Food producers can utilize generic names for ingredients (such as fish, sugar, and cheese) without further specification when these constitute only one of several ingredients and a number of other conditions are met (Res 6/94).	Limiting producers' obligations
	Vegetable food products considered at risk of spreading plague shall be quarantined according to specific requirements (Res 66/93).	Protection of crops and food chain, consumer health

continued

TABLE 3.8
Continued

Additives in chocolate and selected candies shall be subject to strict quantitative limits (Res 54/98).	Consumer health
Pineapples traded within Mercosur shall conform to certain sanitary measures (Res 37/03).	Consumer health
Rice traded within Mercosur shall conform to certain sanitary measures (Res 40/03).	Consumer health
Tomatoes traded within Mercosur shall conform to certain sanitary requirements (Res 92/96).	Consumer health
Potatoes traded within Mercosur shall conform to certain sanitary requirements (Res 113/96).	Consumer health
The use of food additives must be justified by sanitary, technological, or sensorial reasons and must always comply with a specific set of requirements (Res 31/92).	Hygienic considerations
Plastic materials for packaging which come into contact with foods must comply with strict temperature, timing, cleanliness, and other types of requirements (Res 36/92).	Hygienic considerations
Recycled cellulose materials which come into contact with foods must comply with strict temperature, timing, cleanliness, and other types of requirements (Res 55/97).	Hygienic considerations

Note: Numbers in parentheses refer to Mercosur resolutions (if preceded by Res) and decisions (if preceded by Dec).

trusive approach is likely to occur instead in those RTAs where most, if not all, member states have established traditions of civil law. Those traditions exhibit a propensity for a comprehensive and definitive codification of reality. In those RTAs, officials at once have a natural tendency to engage in extensive, a priori regulation of reality and, equally importantly, view extensive regional-level regulation as the logical solution to the presence of conflicting sets of rich national-level legal systems.

I added as well that the choice of legislative approach must be largely supported by key players, especially commercial ones most directly affected by integration. In minimalist RTAs, key groups support what is essentially a deregulated approach to market creation. In more intrusive RTAs, those groups eagerly support the elimination of widespread regulatory differences across the member states.

Let us now examine the legal traditions of the member states of the three RTAs in question. Consider first the case of NAFTA. The United States and Canada are common-law countries. They have traditionally avoided codification through law, relying instead on court precedents and case law for the regulation of society (Nikolaïdis and Egan 2001: 465). Characteristically, the two governments have directly supported standard setting by industry associations,[16] rather than undertaking extensive programs themselves. Importantly, but for two exceptions, the common-law systems of the countries themselves preside over state-level (the United States) or province-level (Canada) common-law systems.[17] Regulators at the federal level in both countries are accustomed to resolving conflict between states and provinces though negotiation, litigation, and arbitration (H. P. Glenn 2001: 1791). Mexico alone is a civil-law country. Interestingly, however, Mexico is also a federation of states with strong traditions of legislative independence. The government has traditionally relied on

---

[16] In 1970, for instance, the Standards Council of Canada was established. Reporting to Parliament through the Ministry of Industry, by the early 1990s it was working with over two hundred organizations and thousands of representatives from industry, the government, consumer groups, and labor. In the United States, government has funded, collaborated with, and adopted thousands of standards set by the American National Standards Institute—perhaps the most important standard associations in the country since 1918. Note, however, that such support was more irregular than in Canada. The institute itself was not given the right to develop standards and its accreditation was merely optional for industry players—all indications of an overall broad disinterest in standardization on the part of the government (Tate 2001: 464).

[17] Louisiana and Quebec have civil-law traditions. Of course, it should be made clear that there are, in fact, no pure common- or civil-law countries (or states, provinces, etc.). The United States, for example, has more legislation than a truly common-law country would have, while a country such as France does depend, to some extent, on precedent setting through court interpretations. The focus in this chapter is on the predominant system in each country.

arbitration to resolve conflict among states—thus developing some elements of a common-law tradition.

Given the legal contexts in place in the United States and Canada, it would have been rather difficult for the proponents of NAFTA in the early 1990s to present the public and industry with a project that would have entailed an unprecedented definitional and normative codification of the world. Politicians and the public alike in those two countries would not have tolerated such an initiative. The hegemonic United States, with its traditional dislike of foreign interference with its legislative system, would have been especially opposed to it. Indeed, the two countries had already demonstrated their preferences for a minimalist RTA when they formed CUSFTA, the minimalist precursor agreement to NAFTA.

A much more minimalist system, then, that could replicate at the regional level a common-law approach was likely the only option. As Glenn, a legal scholar of trade law, observed, most of North America "adheres to the common law tradition. . . . [T]here would be no need, because of North American circumstances, for a central policy of uniformization or harmonization of laws. . . . [T]he design principle of NAFTA would really be that of subsidiarity" (H. P. Glenn 2001: 1791–92). In NAFTA, Glenn continues, it was therefore "necessary" for officials to ensure that the law would allow for a "dynamic between the general and the particular," much as was occurring in the United States, Canada, and to some extent in federal Mexico. The texts would in this way embody a "much older idea" present in those countries that "people are governed both by law that is particular to them and by law that is common to humanity" (1792).

From the outset, therefore, officials made clear that they would not deviate from established traditions: they would craft an organ that would make use of, and depend on, domestic law (Fried 1994). NAFTA, they pointed out, could only be a simple, minimally regulated trade agreement, and not a version of European interventionism (Baer 1991: 148). Despite pressure from some politicians and activists, who did ask for uniformity in health, safety, and environmental regulations, "officials in all three countries" working on drafts of the texts were thus "insist[ent] on the limited nature of NAFTA" (Baer 1991: 148). The words of an attorney working in the United States Trade Representative's Office during the NAFTA negotiations put it as follows in an interview with the author:

> It would have been unrealistic for us to achieve anything like the EU legal
> structure in North America. . . . We did not think about it much because it
> was not a possibility in North America. . . . It wasn't in the cards; it wasn't
> even a choice. . . . The noninterventionist nature of the NAFTA text made it

a lot easier for the U.S. government to proceed—it implied that the U.S. did not have to make too many legal changes. . . . That was a positive thing: that NAFTA did not require much changing of U.S. law.[18]

As such, this minimalist approach suited a large number of export-oriented constituencies. NAFTA would at once expand their markets while requiring few to no changes in how they operated: the supply and demand for given goods and services at the regional level would finally dictate levels of trade. In the United States, large businesses eager to increase their interactions with Mexico and Canada proved especially supportive. The limited nature of the NAFTA legal system appealed to them especially. Most, if not all, had operated in a domestic environment characterized by a "liberal, uncoordinated approach to standards," where multiple and diverse industry associations ensured "heterogeneity" in approaches (Tate 2001: 464–65). Thus, as the attorney from the United States Trade Representative's Office active during the NAFTA negotiations explained to the author, "business quite liked the fact NAFTA opened markets without demanding changes": NAFTA replicated at the regional level the laissez-faire approach that was so familiar to them.[19] Quickly, they formed USA-NAFTA, a loose alliance of twenty-seven hundred companies, including most of the Fortune 500 companies (Economist 1993b). Though admittedly off to a slow start as a result of having underestimated the opposition, they mobilized rapidly to lobby Congress (Smith 1993). Support from large Canadian business, also off to a slow start because of the relative unimportance of the Mexican market for them, became increasingly determined over time (Profit 1993). By 1993, the Business Council on National Issues, the Canadian Chamber of Commerce, the Alliance of Canadian Manufacturers and Exporters, and other export-oriented organizations were voicing their strong support for NAFTA (Toronto Star 1992, 1993, 1998).[20]

[18] Telephone interview with the author, February 2004. The attorney requested that his name not be used.

[19] See previous note.

[20] Environmental organizations and especially labor unions proved much more ambivalent about NAFTA's minimalism (Walker 1993). They would have preferred a regional-level harmonization of laws, particularly in areas of interest to them. Nonetheless, many ultimately accepted the NAAEC and NAALC. These agreements committed the three governments to enforcing existing national legislation on both labor and the environment. This proved appealing because the issue, especially in Mexico, was not a lack of national laws but a lack of enforcement. In Mexico, the largest labor association (the Confederación de Trabajadores de México, or Mexican Workers' Association) thus "extended its unconditional support to the free trade agenda, publicly expressing its hope that workers' rights would be insured under such an agreement" (Poitras and Robinson 1994: 23). The Congreso de Trabajo (Labor Congress) assumed a similar position. In the United States, many

In Mexico, too, where a number of players relied on the market of the United States, several business groups perceived that they stood to gain a great deal from liberalization at a minimal cost:

> A powerful alliance of interests within the business community set the tone of *support* for *NAFTA*. The devoted core . . . was composed of large Mexican manufacturing firms (especially those with the potential to find a large US market for their exports, like Cementos de Mexico and Cerveceria Cuauhtemoc, a leading brewer), medium-sized manufacturers who may be able to find niches in the export market, some agricultural producers (e.g. growers of fruit and vegetables), capital-intensive foreign businesses, the international financial community, and domestic suppliers of foreign businesses in Mexico. (Poitras and Robinson 1994: 14)

Support came from business associations, such as the Confederación Patronal de la República Mexicana (Mexican Employer Association), the Confederación de Cámaras Industriales (National Association of Industrialists), and the Confederación de Cámaras Nacionales de Comercio (Association of National Chambers of Commerce). A special state-business association was even set up to coordinate efforts: the Coordinadora de Organismos Empresariales de Comercio Exterior (Coordination for Entrepreneurs and External Commerce).

In the case of the EU, all of the original member states followed a civil-law tradition for centuries. The only common-law countries are two late entrants, who joined the EU with little power to alter its basic mold: the United Kingdom and Ireland. All four Mercosur member states, in turn, rely on civil law.[21] All these countries hence engaged in an extensive codification of much of social life throughout the nineteenth and twentieth centuries—a process that in Europe was closely related to the creation of a national sense of identity (H. P. Glenn 2003). Relatively rich national legislative regimes developed. Importantly, most EU countries are also, on the whole, unitary states: they have strong national-level legal traditions and generally very limited subnational legislative units.[22] In those coun-

---

trade unions, with the exception of the AFL-CIO, eventually gave their support once the NAALC was included. In the area of the environment, the biggest support came from six of the United States' most important environmental organizations: the Environmental Defense Fund, the World Wildlife Fund, the Nature Conservancy, the National Resource Defense Council, and the National Audobon Society (Earth Island Journal 1993).

[21] See Merryman (1985) for a thorough overview of the civil-law traditions of Europe and South America.

[22] This applies to Germany as well, where the federal government has a very broad range of exclusive legislative powers, though the sixteen states (Länders) retain the power of veto over legislation affecting them (through their representation in the Bundesrat, the second chamber of the federal legislative branch).

tries, there is no tradition of judicial arbitration between semi-independent legislative units.

In both the EU and Mercosur, the existence of extensive codified legal systems in the member states thus presented a problem. As Glenn notes in the case of Europe, "formal differences in codification [were] readily seen as conflict of laws" (H. P. Glenn 2001: 1791) and, as such, required a solution. The same may be safely asserted for Mercosur. The solution in both cases was naturally a legal one. Glenn observes the following for the EU:

> So the common market of Europe is one in which the need for pan-European institutions could be seen as evident, given the absence of any other means of reconciling national legislative wills. Given conflict, uniformization or harmonization had to be imposed. . . . The law of the European Union would therefore represent nineteenth century thought cast forward into the twentieth and twenty-first centuries. Uniform national laws, which had replaced local customs, must in their turn be replaced by uniform European laws. (1792, 1793)

"European harmonization," Glenn writes in a later essay, was "consistent with historical European concepts of national legislative unity and [was] arguably necessary, given the underlying European concept of disunity or conflict of European national laws" (2003: 32).

From the very first impetus to create a common market in 1957, therefore, EU officials never doubted that extensive legislation would be needed to remove differences in the regulatory regimes of the member states. The clearest sign was the TEEC itself, in which they explicitly recognized the presence of rich, but also conflicting, national traditions. In the original text, they asserted that the Commission had the right to issue legislation "when it finds that a *difference* between the provisions laid down by law, regulation, or administrative action in Member States is distorting the conditions of competition in the common markets and that the resultant distortion needs to be *eliminated*" (Article 101 of the TEEC, italics added). The natural solution that they prescribed was "the approximation of the laws of Member States to the extent required for the proper functioning of the common market" (Article 3 of the TEEC). Throughout the decades, the same officials pointed to legislative differences across the member states as detrimental to the functioning of a common market.

This aggressive approach softened somewhat in the 1980s, when detailed harmonization came under criticism as impractical, especially with regard to the technical regulation of products (Mattli 2001; Nikolaïdis and Egan 2001; Egan 1998). Officials opted to delegate such standardization matters to specialized and private European organizations.[23] This,

[23] These were the European Committee for Standardization, the European Committee

however, did not necessarily translate into a reduction in regional legislative output. The number of new directives and regulations skyrocketed during the 1980s and 1990s, following the Single European Act and the push for the completion of a single market. In the 1960s, legislative output (including decisions) totaled around twenty-five a year. That figure would become two hundred during the period 1970–85 and six hundred for 1986–96, covering ever more policy spheres (Duina 2003; Fligstein and McNichol 1998: 77; Fligstein and Stone Sweet 2001: 44). These, we should stress, were mostly not mutual recognition laws; rather, they were serious regulatory initiatives rich with definitional and normative notions. As two analysts observed in 2001, "positive integration—the replacement of national rules by supranational ones—now clearly constitutes the major activity of the EC" (Fligstein and Stone Sweet 2001: 44).

Faced with a similar cacophony of rich national legislative traditions, Mercosur officials also spoke of "legal harmonization" and "convergence" in a very large number of spheres as a necessary precondition for the creation of a single market (Agence France Presse 2001a). In an interview, Manuel Olarreaga—a central player in the evolution of law in Mercosur—stressed the inevitability of the imposing character of Mercosur law.[24] As he put it, somewhat baffled by the fact that the author was even raising the question:

> It was necessary for us to have laws at the Mercosur level. It was not a question. If you have a single economic market, you need to introduce uniformity, to harmonize; you must have laws to coordinate and regulate the action of participants. . . . Otherwise there is chaos, and the will of the stronger prevails. It would be absurd not to have laws for us, simply absurd.

María Juana Rivera—an important player in shaping laws in a large number of industrial and agricultural sectors—reflected on the nature of Mercosur's rich legal system.[25] In her view, integration has highlighted differences in quality, safety, health, environmental, and other standards across the three member states, with Argentina typically sporting the most stringent approaches. "Those differences have posed problems; they have acted as obstacles to commerce among the member states," she noted, "and we must continue to work towards their elimination." To that end, she continued, "we look around, especially with the Internet, and study

---

for Electrotechnical Standardization, and the European Telecommunications Standards Institute (Mattli 2001: 329).

[24] Olarreaga is Director of the Departamento de Normativa (Law Department), Secretaría del Mercosur. Interview with the author, Montevideo, Uruguay, July 2003.

[25] Rivera is National Coordinator for Argentina for Mercosur's Subgrupo de Trabajo N°3 (Technical Regulation and Evaluation of Conformity). Mercosur's various subgroups aid the Grupo Mercado Común in drafting resolutions.

different regulatory approaches in different parts of the world; we then borrow from the EU but also other international organizations, adapt them to our own circumstances, and then use them."[26]

It seems that from the very early phases of planning officials thus never questioned that the harmonization of rich but quite different legal systems would be necessary. They made sure to assert in Article 1 of the founding Treaty of Asuncion their position: "The Member States commit themselves to the harmonization of their laws in the pertinent areas, so as to strengthen the process of integration." The same treaty sought the establishment of several specialized working groups (Subgrupos de Trabajo) whose mission was to help the Grupo Mercado Común devise regional-level legislation. Then, throughout the years, officials repeatedly reiterated their view on the necessity of harmonization. In the 1990s, pressure for harmonization was especially strong for agriculture, manufacturing health and safety standards, industrial products, mining, and other related areas (Duina 2003). While pressure continued in these areas in the new century (Agence France Presse 2001b), attention also turned to services and investments. Interestingly, throughout officials collaborated with European representatives and advisors on matters of legal harmonization (Agence France Presse 2003b).

As with NAFTA, but for obviously different reasons, business leaders and other key elements of society proved to be largely supportive of the regulatory strategies taken in both the EU and Mercosur. Indeed, in many instances, they pushed officials down the road of standardization. The reason for their position was generally the same: for many, differences in national legal systems represented an obstacle to market expansion, since compliance with those rich systems—a necessity for exchanges with those countries—imposed heavy costs. Importantly, in a number of cases the creation of a single competitive space would also mean increased market potential due to the elimination of public monopolies in certain industries.

The large numbers of newly founded lobbying groups every year in Brussels since 1957, and especially during periods of intense legislative output, might serve as an indication of the active interest on the part of various actors in promoting and shaping EU law (Fligstein and Stone Sweet 2001: 43). The most striking examples of direct support in the case of the EU are found in the 1980s, however, a time when EU Commission President Jacques Delors began planning and executing the major drive to complete the common market with the push for the Single European Act. Ross (1995) and others have described in detail the close collaboration between Delors and industry representatives. "Delors," he notes, "was frequently visited by the captains and generals of European indus-

[26] Interview with the author, Buenos Aires, Argentina, August 2003.

try" (115). Some actually feared the implications of broader competition in a European space. Yet many were very interested in ensuring that legal standardization would take place and, most importantly, in shaping its direction.

Among the many, telecommunications companies proved to be especially interested in standardization. The presence of different national technological standards had stifled private business growth in the region. Technologies of scale, moreover, made a European market a necessity for European players struggling to compete against players from Japan and the United States. Yet a "European market," noted Sandholtz, "could only be achieved on the basis of common technological standards for future networks" (1998: 150). When the Commission mobilized with a set of initiatives, all the major industry groups "responded enthusiastically" (151). The Roundtable of European Industrialists, which included many telecommunications equipment firms, "strongly supported the Commission's plans;" so did the service providers as well as the International Telecommunications Users' Group, a body representing European national users' groups, including large firms (149, 150).

Air transportation companies also proved particularly interested in the harmonization of rules during the 1980s. Major businesses joined the International Chamber of Commerce, the Roundtable of European Industrialists, and consumer interest groups (such as the Federation of Air Transport User Representatives) to lobby the Commission intensely for transnational regulation (O'Reilly and Stone Sweet 1998). Here, standardization not only meant the elimination of compliance costs with foreign regulatory regimes but also the opening of certain industries to private players. The Association of Air Carriers in the European Community would thus argue that the industry should "be allowed to evolve commercially in step with the changing pattern of demand for air transport services and . . . governments [should] refrain from obstructing that natural process" (quoted in O'Reilly and Stone Sweet 1998: 172). Similar arguments were advanced in a number of other industries, such as banking, postal services, and pharmaceuticals (Cowles 1998: 116; Smith 2001).

Many of Mercosur's business leaders proved similarly interested in regional harmonization. With the cessation of domestic protectionism in the 1980s and the introduction—on the part of government in all four member states—of incentive measures to export (Haines-Ferrari 1993), these actors quickly learned that differences in national regulatory systems represented one of the most serious obstacles to their growth.[27] The position taken by representatives of the mining industry offers a good example. In

----

[27] There were some exceptions, of course, most notably in the automotive and sugar sectors.

1997, negotiations for the harmonization of laws in the industry (including matters related to the protection of the environment) were progressing in earnest. At the first major meeting of all interested parties (the Primera Cumbre Minera del Mercosur, or Mercosur's First Mining Summit) government representatives, mining companies, and lawyers came from all four member states. Pressuring the group was the Foro de Empresarios Mineros del Mercosur (Mercosur's Mining Enterprises Forum). The forum made clear its keen interest in harmonization. In the minds of its participants, there continued to be regulatory "asymmetries [within Mercosur] that cause distortions . . . as in the case of environmental and transport laws" (Notimex 1997). The organization thus "asked the four governments that there be clear rules for the circulation of machinery, team, and supplies for its activities, with in mind the improvement of competitiveness" (Notimex 1997). It continued its pressure for harmonization for years thereafter.

A number of other business groups similarly asked for regulatory convergence in their spheres of activity. In the middle of the economic crisis of 2000 and 2001, for instance, the Cámara de Exportadores de la República Argentina (Argentina's Exporters' Chamber) declared itself interested in even deeper regional integration. It asked for further "positive integration," deeper regulatory cooperation, and new laws more in tune with reality on the ground (Spanish Newswire Services 2000a). It also asked for the establishment of a permanent organ for the resolution of disputes over compliance. Other similar organizations, such as financial companies (Nepomuceno 1995), the Cámara de Industrias de Uruguay (Uruguay's Industry Chamber) (Agence France Presse 2001c), and the Grupo Brasil (Brazil Group)—an organization of 190 Brazilian companies with investments in Argentina (Spanish Newswire Services 2003a)— also expressed their strong support for the Mercosur project.[28]

CONCLUSION

Officials from the EU, Mercosur, and NAFTA have responded quite differently to the challenges of cognitive standardization inherent to regional market building. In NAFTA, they have opted for a minimalist approach. There exists a small quantity of laws with standardizing content. In some

---

[28] As with NAFTA, though again for different reasons, a number of labor and environmental organizations through time supported integration in the EU—see for example Johansson (1999: 92–94), Greenwood (2003), Cullen (1999), and McCormick (2001)— though less so in Mercosur—see La Jornada (1996a) and Spanish Newswire Services (1998). In the EU especially, regional law over time became seen as offering an opportunity for "raising the bar" uniformly across the member states.

cases (especially those related to the manufacturing of goods), market participants are asked to refer to standards set by international associations. In all cases, they are asked to trade first and, if problems arise, to make use of reactive conflict-resolution mechanisms. Officials from the EU and Mercosur have chosen a different path. They have sought to standardize much of the world. Market participants are given countless definitions for, and normative stances towards, the world. Those officials have developed rich cognitive guidebooks to reality.

This chapter accounted for the differences between NAFTA on the one hand and the EU and Mercosur on the other by pointing us towards the legal foundations upon which these RTAs are built. The majority of NAFTA officials come from the United States and Canada: countries with strong common-law traditions. Mexico alone has civil law. Imposing a rich and intrusive regional legal system on the United States and Canada would have entailed a major transformation of those systems. The choice of market officials was widely supported by key powerful businesses and other groups in the region. For them, NAFTA expanded their marketplace without requiring significant adjustments to their practices. Officials in the EU and Mercosur have operated instead within rich civil-law traditions. Rich national legal systems presented serious barriers to trade. Those barriers could be removed through the harmonization of legal systems. The choice for a rich regional legal system—both pragmatic and in line with tradition—was also supported by a variety of key groups in both regions.

One major lesson emerges from this chapter: the basic legal architecture of RTAs varies significantly, in ways that provide continuity with existing realities in the member states. This observation generates a number of questions. We wonder about the advantages and disadvantages of minimalism and interventionism. We wonder how minimalism and interventionism affect trade *among* RTAs. We are also curious to know more about the possibility of change within a given RTA, and more broadly about the key topics that future research should address. Chapter 6 will discuss these important questions. We must now proceed further in our comparative analysis of RTAs: the targets and content of regional law.

## Chapter 4

THE TARGETS AND CONTENT OF REGIONAL LAW

WE HAVE SEEN that officials in the EU, Mercosur, and NAFTA have pursued rather different strategies to address the difficulties associated with cross-cultural trade. NAFTA officials have engaged in only minimal standardization of the world. Officials in the EU and Mercosur have instead developed rich guidebooks to reality. In this chapter, I offer evidence of further differences across the three RTAs. When we compare standardizing notions across RTAs, are the targets and content of those notions similar? The evidence presented here suggests that important differences exist across RTAs.

The focus is on three specific areas from the realm of economics: women in the workplace, dairy products, and labor rights. In all three RTAs, women are active members of the workforce and society, dairy products are traded across borders, and the majority of adults are active workers. Yet differences in the targets and content of standardizing notions abound. In the case of women in the workplace, EU officials have been quite active whereas Mercosur and NAFTA officials have, by contrast, done very little. On the other hand, Mercosur officials have heavily standardized the world of dairy products, but the same cannot be said of EU and NAFTA officials. Finally, officials in all three areas have endowed workers with impressive rights; yet they have differed in their understanding of what those rights are.

I explain these differences in the targets and content of standardizing notions in political-institutional terms. In the EU, powerful interest groups pressured officials to replicate, at the regional level, domestic progressive laws on women and labor rights. EU officials could not touch dairy products, however: longstanding partnerships between producers and governments protected a large number of products and processes from widespread standardization. In Mercosur, very weak national legislative traditions on women and women's groups made it unlikely that officials would engage in regional activism. A powerful dairy sector, strong labor unions, and favorable domestic regulatory environments ensured, on the other hand, that officials would promulgate rich laws on dairy and labor rights. In NAFTA, despite favorable domestic legal legacies, key women's groups did not mobilize to pressure officials to produce regional-level principles. Protectionist legacies, especially in Canada, pre-

cluded in turn any regional standardization in the dairy sector. Matters
followed a different course in the realm of labor, where trade unions heavily pressured NAFTA officials to replicate at the regional level labor rights
already present at the national level.

Exploring the Targets and Content Regional Law

Women in the Workplace

In the EU, Mercosur, and NAFTA, women have increased their participation in the labor force steadily in the last fifty years (van Doorne-
Huiskes, van Hoof, and Roelofs 1995; Gabriel and Macdonald 1994:
537; Ulshoefer 1998). RTA officials, however, have responded to the ever-
increasing participation of women in the workplace in quite different
ways. In the EU, officials have undertaken an aggressive approach to
women and work, one that has not escaped the eye of EU scholars, who
have described it as a "crucial component" of European policymaking
(Liebert 1999: 197–98). Table 4.1 identifies the key EU legislation on
working women. There exists an extensive literature on the topic (Liebert
1999). Overall scholars have described two fundamental phases in the
evolution of EU law. In the first phase, during the 1970s and 1980s, planners focused on promoting equality at the workplace between the genders
(Mazey 1995). Directive 75/117 introduced the principle of equal pay for
work of equal value (and not only for equal work, thus prohibiting such
indirect discrimination as might exist in prejudicial job classification
schemes). Directive 76/207 ruled out direct and indirect discrimination
on the grounds of sex and marital status with regard to access to and conditions at work. And Directive 79/7 targeted direct and indirect discrimination in the scope of statutory social security schemes in the areas of
sickness, disability, redundancy, old age, and so on. Those safeguards
were extended by Directive 86/378 for private occupational pension
schemes.

In the second phase, during the 1990s, planners focused less on erasing
differences between the sexes and more on recognizing the needs and requirements of women as distinct from men. Two important measures
granted pregnant women rights at the workplace (Directive 86/613) and
guaranteed the safety and well-being of pregnant or breast-feeding mothers at the workplace (Directive 92/85).[1] These and other measures had,

---

[1] Interestingly, all laws on women's rights prior to the adoption of the Amsterdam Treaty
of 1997 built directly from Article 117 of the 1957 TEEC, which provided a rather narrow
legal basis for action: equal pay. Revisions made in 1997 included a direct mandate (Articles 2, 3[2], 13, 141) for the Council of Ministers to take action to combat various forms of
discrimination, including gender-driven ones (Rossilli 1999: 171–72).

TABLE 4.1
Law and Women in the EU

General Area	Target
Pay	Equal pay for equal work or work of equal value (Dir 75/117)
Workplace Treatment	Equal treatment in employment, occupation, vocational training, promotion, and working conditions (Dir 76/207, 2000/78)
Social Security Benefits	Women's ability to contribute and benefit from social security schemes at the workplace (Dir 79/7)
Occupational Security Schemes	Equal treatment with regards to scope, obligations, and benefits vis-à-vis social security schemes (Dir 86/378)
Pregnancy and Motherhood	Pregnant women's rights at the workplace (Dir 86/613), parental leave benefits for men and women (Dir 96/34), safety and well-being of pregnant or breast-feeding mothers at the workplace (Dir 92/85)
Mainstreaming	Gender perspective for EU international development policies and interventions (Reg 2836/1998), and for EU regional development programs (Reg 2836/98)

Note: Numbers in parentheses refer to EU directives (if preceded by Dir) and regulations (if preceded by Reg).

as their objectives, to increase the employability of women. Some scholars identify a third phase: "mainstreaming" (Pollack and Hafner-Burton 2001). This is an effort to ensure that women's issues and female representatives are shaping policy making in a variety of areas related to the workplace but also beyond (European Commission 1996: chap. 5, 1998: 22).[2]

---

[2] Positive Action Programs constitute yet another set of initiatives. These are practical initiatives to advance those equality concepts already found in the law. The initiatives include in-service training for women, the appointment of equal-opportunity advisers in companies and local authorities, and information campaigns for women (Mazey 1998: 141). None are mandatory laws or initiatives that are rich with definitional and normative content; as such, they are not discussed in this book. Note as well that EU legal initiatives have been both widely praised and severely criticized by feminists, women's supporters, and other observers. To some, they represent an impressive effort to help women; see, for instance, the various contributions in Rossilli (2000). To others, they embrace traditional notions of gen-

The approach of Mercosur officials to working women differs drastically from that of EU officials. They have stated on various occasions their commitment to pursue policies on behalf of women and to ensure the right institutional environment to achieve that end. For instance, government officials from the member states in charge of policies for women in their respective countries issued a joint Mercosur Declaration following their meeting in Rio de Janeiro on December 3–5, 1997. In it, they stated in rather vague terms a commitment to ensure that both men and women have an opportunity to participate in Mercosur negotiations and law-making (Espino 2000: 21). In Article 3 of the 1998 Declaración Socio-laboral del Mercosur—a document that, unlike any other joint declaration, became legally binding—the governments asserted their general support for equality of opportunity and treatment.[3] Yet to date, the only concrete measure in place is Resolution 84/2000, which asks Mercosur working forums and groups to incorporate a gender perspective into their deliberations.

NAFTA officials, too, have not subjected the world of working women to standardization. They have produced only one major normative principle in favor of women's rights. It can be found in the NAALC, a document that committed Canada, Mexico, and the United States to the promotion of eleven "labor principles." The eighth principle requires member states to commit themselves to equal pay for men and women. More specifically, the member states are to ensure "equal wages for women and men by applying the principle of equal pay for equal work in the same establishment" (NAALC, Annex 1).

The principle has important limitations. It is fundamentally a single normative pronouncement. There is no definition of pay (does pay include benefits, such as contributions to retirement plans? does it include social security? etc.). There is no definition of equal work—a notoriously difficult concept to define and, moreover, to measure. The passage also does not assert the principle of equal pay for work of equal value, a fundamental clause for any labor market in which there exists occupational segregation.[4] The most important limitation is perhaps the "same establish-

---

der differences and gender roles; see, for instance, Guerrina (2002) and Shaw (2000). In my view, these laws are on the whole progressive, at least in spirit and intention, and that is how I refer to them throughout the book.

[3] The member states agreed to adopt the declaration without translating it into a decision or resolution. This was an unprecedented adoption of a binding text (Ferreira 2001: 34). Decisions and resolutions normally require formal transposition by all member states before becoming actual law.

[4] "Equal pay for equal work" makes possible only comparisons of very similar jobs. Yet, in most labor markets, women tend to work in certain occupations and men in others. Cross-occupational comparisons are therefore necessary if real progress in the elimination of wage discrimination is to be made.

ment" constraint, whereby comparisons can only be made within the same place of work. Yet the inclusion of this principle in the NAALC was of significance. It set a precedent upon which further legislation might one day be built.

Dairy Products

In sharp contrast to their approach to women, EU officials hesitated to target dairy products until the 1990s, and then only sparingly did so.[5] They have instead relied on Regulation 2081/92 to claim that production in many instances *cannot be subject* to standardization. Often applied to cheeses but also to creams and butters, the regulation recognizes small geographical regions (typically areas with a radius of thirty or fewer miles) as having the exclusive right to manufacture certain products.[6] As a result, in a country such as Italy, the EU recognizes over thirty cheeses as protected from standardization. In France, over forty cheeses in addition to butters and creams enjoy protection.[7] Other countries, such as Spain, Ireland, and Germany, have followed suit, also with butters, cheeses, and other products (Europe Agri 2003; Rapid 1996; Spicers Centre for Europe 1998). In support of this regulation, EU officials in 1996 even embarked on a public campaign costing almost ECU 9 million (the Product with a History Campaign) to promote protected denominations (European Report 1996).

Table 4.2 reports the few laws with definitional and normative content in the EU. Only milk and butter have been subject to definitional and normative principles. Thus, Regulation 2597/97 describes various types of drinking milk (raw, whole, skimmed, etc.) on the basis of content, weight, and production processes. Directive 42/96 specifies in normative fashion the production and handling requirements of raw, heated, and pasteurized milk, keeping in mind hygiene and the consumption of milk as well as more complex products, such as cheeses. Caseins and caseinates are

[5] As discussed later in this chapter, agriculture in general has, of course, been the subject of much regulation since the birth of the EU (and, with it, the CAP initiatives). Yet most of this regulation, especially in the early phases, has not concerned definitional and normative standardization as defined in this book. Rather, it has focused mostly on temporary interventions in the market, such as setting prices, limiting production quantities, etc. For excellent analyses of the EU's early agricultural policies, see Snyder (1985 and 1996).

[6] Applicants for a protected denomination must specify a special link between the geographical environment of origin and the raw materials, production methods, and principal physical, chemical, microbiological, and/or organoleptic characteristics of the product in question.

[7] To date, a total of over six hundred products (dairy and other types) enjoy special denomination status (European Report 2003). For exact figures on cheeses, see the EU's Internet site: http://europa.eu.int/comm/agriculture/qual/en/1bbab_en.htm.

TABLE 4.2
Law and Dairy Products in the EU

General Area	Target
Milk	Partly or wholly dehydrated milk (Dir 2001/114), drinking milk (Reg 2597/97), production hygienic measures (Dir 89/362; 46/1992)
Milk Derivatives	Butter (Reg 577/97), use of caseins & caseinates in cheeses (Reg 2204/90)

Note: Numbers in parentheses refer to EU directives (if preceded by Dir) and regulations (if preceded by Reg).

targeted with normative principles only regarding their use in cheeses. The remaining eighty or so regulations and directives categorized in the EU's legal database as related to milk products (3.60.56) concern themselves with financial aid to farmers, setting production quotas, granting licenses, and other administrative matters of no definitional relevance and of very limited, if any, normative relevance.

Matters have developed quite differently in South America. Early on, Mercosur officials embarked on a comprehensive effort to standardize at the regional level the essential characteristics of a variety of dairy products. Starting as early as 1993 (i.e., only two years after the birth of Mercosur), they held, in the words of a local observer, "exhaustive meetings" with "technicians and specialists from all the Mercosur countries" (Gazeta Mercantil 1997a). The result was a comprehensive set of laws rich in cognitive principles. Figure 4.1 outlines the extent of legislative intervention in Mercosur.

All laws in Figure 4.1 are rich with standardizing principles. They typically state that their objective is to "fix the *identity* and quality characteristics" of the product at hand (emphasis added). The most impressive (in terms of departure from the EU) are those related to cheese. For instance, when addressing Tybo cheese with Resolution 42/96, Mercosur officials specify in Article 5 requirements for ingredients, appeals to the senses (texture, color, flavor, smell), shape and weight, physical and chemical composition, and production process. On the normative side, the law specifies in Article 7 handling, hygienic, and other requirements. A number of cheeses are thus targeted, but milk, creams and fats, and various derivatives are also subject to definitional and normative definition in ways that are significantly more expansive than in the EU.[8]

[8] Note that, until 1998, standardization applied only to products intended for trade

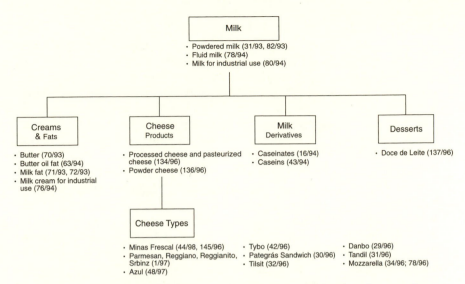

Figure 4.1. Law and Dairy Products in Mercosur. Note: Numbers in parentheses refer to Mercosur resolutions.

NAFTA officials, much like their EU counterparts, have by contrast adopted a very limited approach. Indeed, only with Article 713 of the treaty do they ask that member states use relevant international standards, guidelines, or recommendations for sanitary purposes.

Labor Rights

Officials in the EU, Mercosur, and NAFTA have agreed on the need to endow workers with rights. Thus, in all three RTAs we observe a number of important pronouncements in this area of social life. Interestingly, however, there exist very important differences in the content of the relevant legal passages. Officials have articulated very different ideas about what the rights of workers should be.

EU officials have hesitated to grant workers the rights to form labor associations and to strike. Indeed, the TEC excludes both rights explicitly from the domain of EU activities (Article 137). The 2000 Treaty of Nice presented an opportunity to amend the TEC with the introduction of the European Charter of Fundamental Rights, which recognizes the right to form trade unions and strike (Articles 12 and 28). But the European Council, despite great pressure from labor associations and others, rec-

---

across the member states. After 1998, many products intended for domestic consumption also became covered by Mercosur law.

ognized but refused to adopt the charter as legal or binding (Declaration No. 23 of the Treaty of Nice).[9] The proposed Constitution for the European Union includes the right to association and strike. Even if the Constitution is ever ratified by all the member states, however, the Charter comes with highly ambiguous language about its scope and binding character. It appears that its application will only be limited to the institutions of the EU and not to workers elsewhere. The Charter also says that its principles must be applied within the context of national customs and law, which would imply that countries without the right to strike would not be expected to comply (García 2002; Economist 2003b).

Mercosur and NAFTA officials, by contrast, understand labor rights to include the rights to association and to strike. Mercosur officials recognize those rights in the Declaración Sociolaboral of December 10, 1998, which became a binding and legal text with immediate application upon promulgation.[10] In a passage that has attracted much attention (Ferreira 2001: 34), the declaration states: "All workers and trade union organizations are guaranteed the right to strike" (Article 11). The right must be exercised in conformity with existing national laws (Articles 10 and 11), but it cannot be denied by member states. The right of association is stated in Article 8.

NAFTA's NAALC makes impressive statements on labor rights. Indeed, it was praised by Human Rights Watch: "The NAALC, for all its deficiencies in practice, remains the most ambitious link between labor rights and trade ever implemented" (Human Rights Watch 2001). Its very first principle is the "freedom of association and protection of the right to organize"; the third principle is "the right of workers to strike in order to defend their interests" (Annex 1). Such impressive rights are subject to the particular stipulations of each member state,[11] but they are nonetheless considered inalienable.

EU, Mercosur, and NAFTA officials recognize that migrant workers have certain social-security rights. Yet what those rights are varies in important ways across the three regions. We will focus here on unemployment benefits. Only in the EU are migrant workers given in explicit terms

---

[9] The Community Charter of Fundamental Social Rights for Workers of 1989 did include the right to strike but was only a "solemn commitment" by the member states to a set of fundamental rights. It served as a reference point (or a document of political intent) for later directives and regulations, but was never made part of any treaty or made legally binding.

[10] See note 3 for a discussion of the binding nature of the declaration.

[11] For instance, in Canada strikes are prohibited during the term of a collective bargaining agreement, in Mexico workers may be forced to return to work or lose their jobs if certain legal requirements are not fulfilled, and in the United States employers are permitted to replace striking workers permanently.

the right to collect unemployment benefits. EU Regulation 1408/71 of June 1971 grants migrant workers originating from one of the member states, and their families, social security benefits identical to those enjoyed by native workers. Article 3.1 specifies what those rights are. Chapters 1 through 6 identify sickness and maternity leaves, as well as invalidity, old age, work accidents, occupational diseases, death, and unemployment benefits.[12] The primary requirement for collecting unemployment benefits is to have resided in the country for at least one year.[13] With Decision 19/97, Mercosur officials recognize that migrant workers should be entitled to the same rights as native workers. They also specify a minimum period of one year of residence (Article 48 and Title VI respectively). However, Mercosur officials offer a significantly less comprehensive list of what those rights include. Titles V, VI, and VII of Annex I include sickness, old age, invalidity, and death benefits. But the decision does not discuss maternity rights, work accidents, occupational diseases, or, crucially, unemployment rights. Moreover, at the time of writing, the Paraguayan government still had to notify the Secretaría del Mercosur of ratification of the law. Without ratification by all member states, a Mercosur law cannot enter into force. In NAFTA, officials demand with the NAALC that migrant workers should be given the "same legal protection as . . . nationals in respect of *working conditions*" (Annex 1, emphasis added). Working conditions include, above all, safety, wages, and access to unions. At the same time, they are also likely to cover certain social-security rights, such as health insurance but also access to unemployment benefit programs,[14] though only through court cases and additional clarifications will the true meaning of "working conditions" be explicated.

EXPLAINING DIFFERENCES

What can account for these extraordinary differences across NAFTA, the EU, and Mercosur in the targets and content of regional law? Many of the disparities can be traced to the legal traditions and power arrangements in which officials have operated. Let us consider each topic in turn.

---

[12] EU Regulation 574/72 lays down the procedures of implementing Regulation 1408/71.

[13] A worker can also leave his or her country of residence in search of employment in a different member state and receive benefits from his original country for a period of three months. Note as well that the regulation did not cover self-employed persons. Regulation 1390/81 was thus introduced to cover those workers as well.

[14] See, for example, Commission for Labor Cooperation (2001, 2003), where the rights of migrant workers (especially as they apply to the agricultural sector) are discussed.

Women in the Workplace

A number of EU member states experienced a surge in women's activism in the late 1960s and early 1970s. "By 1969," an observer noted, "women's groups were forming all over Western Europe" (Warner 1984: 147) "The late 1960s and early 1970s," a second observer wrote, "were characterized by the growth of women's movements throughout Western Europe" (Mazey 1995: 597). Quickly, these groups mobilized to pressure national governments to introduce, in their respective countries, progressive legislation on work and other matters. "Employers and national governments began," from then on, "to face new demands from women for equal pay" and other rights (Mazey 1995: 597). The major political parties could not ignore them. They took action that advanced the position of women in society and the workplace. The resulting legal victories set important precedents for EU officials. As integration progressed, and under much pressure from women's groups, those officials moved quickly to replicate at the EU level some of the most important legal principles already in place in the member states.

Consider the advances made in key member states during the 1960s and early 1970s. Nondiscrimination and equal pay laws were passed in France, West Germany, and Great Britain. In France, in response to the feminization of the workforce of the 1960s and a strong women's movement, "which put a strong emphasis on equality issues in the labour market" (Fagnani 2002: 110), the government produced a significant quantity of laws on women and work. Some could still be viewed as protectionist and hence designed to preserve the country's traditional family structure (Stetson 1987: 138).[15] Yet others signaled a progressive turn intended to grant women the status of equal workers (Fagnani 2002: 108; Jenson 1988). One of the most important laws was the Law of December 22, 1972. Building from the 1946 Constitution and a general statute on equality of pay in the public sector, the law asserted three principles. It imposed the principle of equal pay for equal work or work of equal value (Title 2), a wide definition of pay (Title 2), and the nullification of all prior discriminatory collective agreements and laws (Title 3). Pushing for the measure was the Comité d'Études et de Liaison des Problèmes du Travail Féminin (Committee on Women's Employment), an agency created by the government in 1965, comprised of representatives from labor, employers, and women's organizations, and situated within the Ministère

[15] For instance, the Law of July 11, 1975 was passed to protect maternity and pregnancy rights at work; in 1977, a family-income supplement was adopted in support of one-wage earner families; a series of proposals for maternity leaves and creative use of part-time work were also put forth (Duina 1999).

du Travail (Ministry of Work) with the explicit mission of pressing for equality and women's right to work. The same committee pushed successfully for a minimum wage increase—helpful mainly to women—in 1968.[16] Other initiatives included the reduction of the single-salary allowance that encouraged mothers to stay at home and the establishment of community-funded day-care centers to enable women to work (Fagnani 2002: 110).

In West Germany, a combination of legal measures was created to promote women's positions in the labor market. The 1949 Constitution, drafted at a time when German women had acquired a strong voice, held prestigious political positions, and were poised to flood the labor market (Moeller 1989: 417–18; Schlaeger 1978: 62), listed certain basic and directly enforceable rights. These were binding on the legislature, the executive, and the judiciary (Articles 19[2] and 1 III). The prohibition of discrimination on the basis of sex was one such right. Article 3 thus stated: "Men and women shall have equal rights" and "no person shall be favored or disfavored because of sex." In that spirit, a number of laws were passed to encourage women to function as regular workers. One such law (known as Mutterschutzgesetz) was adopted in 1952 to prohibit employers from firing pregnant workers. The same law also instituted health insurance payments to help with maternity leaves (Moeller 1989: 412).[17] Several years later, the Betriebsverfassungsgesetz of 1972 (Works Constitution Act) required that employers in the private sector ensure that every employee is treated in accordance with the principle of equity and in particular that there is no discrimination based on a person's sex.[18] The women's movement then became relatively conservative in the 1960s and 1970s (Schlaeger 1978), and, as a result, legal advances stalled for some time. Advances in progressive federal-level laws would begin again in the 1980s, mostly in reaction to EU law (Schiek 1998: 148).[19]

[16] The act suffered from severe implementation problems. To rectify this, the government passed the Law of July 13, 1983 or Loi Roudy (Roudy Law), a measure that gave birth to the Conseil Supérieur de l'Égalité Professionnelle (Council for Professional Equality), located within the recently created Ministère des Droits de la Femme (Ministry of Women's Rights), and a number of other initiatives.

[17] The law also imposed mandatory six-week resting periods before and after birth. This and other characteristics of the law prompted Moeller (1989) to observe that the law was, in fact, in part protectionist, since it reinforced views of women as different from men and in need of special attention.

[18] The act empowered plant-level work councils (which existed in every enterprise with more than five employees) to represent the interests of workers and impose certain conditions, such as no discrimination on the grounds of gender.

[19] For instance, in 1980, Article 611a of the Bürgerliches Gesetzbuch (German Civil Code) was created to prohibit discrimination in employment access and promotion in both the private and public sectors. The Act on Equality between Men and Women was also adopted in 1980. Equal Opportunity Offices were then also set up in all the states.

In Great Britain, as early as 1950s, the Women's Conference of the
Trade Union Congress was pressuring the government, with little success
at first, for equal rights in the workplace (Soldon 1978: 145–51). Subject
to one of Europe's largest wage differential and least progressive environments, British women faced opposition from both government and the
male-dominated trade unions.[20] With the help of visionary Labor Minister Barbara Castle and others, they began circulating drafts for an Equal
Pay Act in the late 1960s. The act would prove less impressive than those
found in France or West Germany: it had a narrow definition of pay and
only called for equal pay for equal work (and not for work of equal
value).[21] Submitted to the government in 1970, the act was eventually
passed in 1972. In 1975, the government then introduced the Sex Discrimination Act, a comprehensive measure intended to protect women
from discrimination in a number of social spheres. One of the most important sections (Part II) concerned employment, where powerful language outlawed discrimination in hiring, promotion, training, dismissal,
and other areas. It also created the Equal Opportunity Commission, a
body currently still active, whose mission is "to work towards the elimination of discrimination" and "promote equality of opportunity between
men and women generally" by, among other things, conducting investigations and writing reports (Part VI).

Among the large member states, Italy alone did not have significant progressive laws on women and work. Importantly, however, the country had
very advanced, and effective, collective agreements between national
trade unions and employers. Eager to recruit new members, unions had
declared an interest in women's issues since the days of their formation in
the late 1800s (Beccalli 1985: 410–25). Real progress, however, took
place right after World War II. The Confederazione Generale Italiana Lavoratori (CGIL, General Association of Italian Workers), the largest union
including both Socialists and Christian Democrats, won equality of pay
for some industrial sectors and cuts of 50% in wage disparities between
the genders in other sectors (Duina 1997: 168). The CGIL then pressed
forward with full force. Two years after a massive demonstration for
equality in 1954, it won the right to equal pay for work of equal value in
most industry sectors; by 1957, such agreements covered the entire private sector. In 1960, the other two main unions—the independent Unione
Italiana Lavoro (Italian Labor Union) and the Christian Confederazione

---

[20] The government feared the inflationary consequences of any increase in women's
wages and benefits; the trade unions, traditionally all-male organizations, sensed that progress for women might require significant sacrifices on their end (Duina 1997: 165–67).

[21] The act specified that comparisons between different jobs were possible only if the employer voluntarily had chosen to undertake such an exercise.

Italiana Sindacati Lavoratori (Italian Workers' Unions Association)—obtained the elimination of all discriminatory classifications based on gender in all manual occupations and, along with the CGIL, introduced objective evaluation codes. Finally, in 1962, an agreement on equal pay for nonmanual workers was signed and, a year later, a similar agreement was struck for all nonindustrial sectors (Beccalli 1985: 433–34; Beccalli 1984: 197). Wage differentials plummeted thereafter, decreasing by 15% in the following five years, making Italy the country with the lowest differential among the big economies of Europe by 1970 (Commission of the European Communities 1979: table 19).

Significant advances were made in some of the smaller states as well. In Denmark especially progress was made in the areas of nondiscrimination and equal pay but also beyond.[22] By the end of the nineteenth century, the newly founded General Union of Women Workers was already representing unskilled workers and demanding better conditions and pay. The first major victory came in 1919 with the adoption of the Tjenestemandslov (Public Employees Act): it required equal pay for equal work for all civil servants. In 1921 a law granted women equal treatment when seeking a public sector job (Walter 2001: 63). Perhaps the most impressive advances, however, centered on asserting the rights of women as workers, regardless of marital or maternal status. As early as 1857, a law gave unmarried women the right to represent themselves before the law: this meant that they could sign business and other contracts and control their economic affairs (59). That same year, women won the right to open their own businesses. Married women won parallel rights in the 1890s. In 1922 and 1925, in turn, women and men were made equally responsible for supporting their families. After a relative lull in advances during the 1930s and 1940s, impressive laws were adopted in the 1960s. These focused, above all, on ensuring that married women could work. Government child-care services were greatly expanded and paid parental leaves with a guarantee to an equal employment status were instituted. These measures proved highly effective, greatly increasing women's participation in the workforce.

The question facing EU officials in the 1970s, thus, was not *whether* they should produce laws regarding women and work, but *how* to best proceed with the articulation of powerful yet realistic principles that would translate, at the regional level, advances made at the national level. Developments at the national level, similar overall but certainly with some

---

[22] Belgium passed its equal pay law with the Pay Protection Act of 1965 and later in a collective agreement (No. 25 of 1975). In the Netherlands, an Equal Pay Act was passed in 1976, followed by the Equal Treatment for Men and Women Act in 1980. In Luxembourg, a grand ducal regulation in 1974 established equal pay for men and women. In 1981, a law was passed to establish equal treatment for men and women in the workplace (employment, training, promotion, etc.).

differences among them, set important precedents that required both replication and a degree of harmonization.[23] At the same time, "the political pressure of feminism and other social movements" for action at the regional level had become "intense", making the "1970s . . . the best period to advance the EC's social policies" (Rossilli 1999: 173). In some cases, Commission officials engaged in close and sustained "interactions with leading feminists and women's movements" (Liebert 1999: 198). In other cases, women mobilized in the streets to force the officials' hands. When, for instance, the social affairs ministers met in 1975 to discuss the fate of an antidiscrimination proposal, activists stood nearby, pressuring officials to adopt the text. "Approval" of Directive 76/207, a journalist noted, "came quickly, perhaps accelerated by a women's rights demonstration to greet the ministers' arrival" (Economist 1975a). Women were ready to play a "catalytic role in the development of EC equal opportunities legislation" (Mazey 1995: 592; Warner 1984). In such an environment, EU officials moved swiftly, producing impressive directives that would lay the ground for further legislation for decades to come (Mazey 1995: 593).

There were additional—but also closely related—factors that fueled the activism of EU officials in the 1970s. Two in particular should be mentioned. In 1976, in *Defrenne vs. Sabena* (Case 43/75 of 1976, ECR 455), a hostess of the Belgian national airline asked the European Court of Justice to determine the legal status of the principle of equal pay for equal work as articulated in Article 119 of the 1957 TEEC. The article had been ignored by all the member states as a "general declaration of good intent" intended to stimulate national legislators to produce equal pay law (Economist 1976; Heide 1999: 384; Warner 1984: 146).[24] The Court, however, found that the article had "direct effect": the article listed rights that national courts had to protect even in the absence of national laws on equality of pay. This extraordinary ruling provided a powerful precedent and stimulus for further action (Warner 1984; Mazey 1995). Secondly, a general interest in a EU-level "social" dimension developed in the 1970s (Rossilli 1999: 173). The adoption of the 1974 Social Action Program in particular seemed to have helped the cause of women (Warner 1984).

In Mercosur, by contrast, domestic legal traditions and political ar-

---

[23] There were differences in both the texts and the implementation of laws. In France and Great Britain, for instance, much evidence exists to suggest that equal pay legislation was very unevenly applied (Duina 1997; Hoskyns 1986: 310; Lorée 1980: 105 n. 11; Stetson 1987: 146).

[24] The article was introduced above all at the insistence of the French, who had one of the smallest wage differentials in the EU at the time and had ratified the International Labor Organization's Equal Renumeration Convention of 1951 (No. 100), which called for equal renumeration for work of equal value (Heide 1990: 384; Warner 1984: 143).

rangements simply precluded any possibility that officials would move to articulate at the regional level modern notions on women and work. In the 1990s, all four member states were young democracies emerging from long dictatorships, and were taking only the first steps to move away from "eminently paternalistic" legal regimes restricting most aspects of women's lives (Sardegna 2001: 79). Any regional initiative on work (or other matters) would have imposed enormous challenges to the normal functioning of those societies. There was, in addition, no single group at the national or regional level that could pressure officials into taking such a leap: women's groups were at the early stages of national mobilization. "Mercosur officials," thus noted Beatriz Etchecurry Mazza, a senior official in Uruguay's Instituto Nacional de la Familia y de la Mujer,[25] in an interview with the author, "could not have possibly made any progress on this front: the subject of women could not be touched—we need much more progress in the domestic realm before anything can be done at the regional level."[26]

Let us examine first the legal regimes in place in the four countries.[27] In Argentina, to this day, women's labor (and labor in general) is regulated mostly by Law 20744: the Ley de Contrato de Trabajo (LTC, Labor Contract Law). Crafted in 1974 under a conservative dictatorship and modified only slightly ever since, the LTC is above all conservative. It asserts that women are prohibited from working in physically demanding, dangerous, or unhealthy jobs (Article 176). It also asks that, if women are to engage in an uninterrupted day of work, there must be a two-hour pause at noon (Article 174). There must also be a pause of twelve hours from day to day (Sardegna 2001: 80). The same law prohibits employers from assigning women work to be executed at home (Article 175) and imposes wide-reaching maternity protections (Articles 177–79). The primary passage upon which Mercosur legislators could have built is Article 172, which forbids workplace discrimination and asserts the principle of equal pay for work of equal value.[28] It is, however, a brief and generic passage that has broadly been ignored in workplaces.[29] With the end of the dictatorship in 1983 important changes were introduced. These, however, entailed above all the derogation of very conservative principles,

[25] Assessor in the Instituto Nacional de la Familia y de la Mujer, Ministerio de Educación y Cultura.

[26] Interview with the author, Montevideo, Uruguay, August 2003.

[27] The following Internet site, made available by the Argentine government, offers a summary of laws on women in the four member states: http://www.mujer.gov.ar/.

[28] That same principle is stated by Law 20392 of May 1973.

[29] Law 24576 of November 1995 adds to the LTC a passage (Chapter 8, between Articles 89 and 90) that asserts the principle of equal opportunity in the area professional development. This, however, is a minor and rather vague passage.

mostly regulating family and social matters (Navarro 2001: 12).[30] Regarding work, only Article 173 of the LTC was repealed in December 1991 (with Law 24013): it forbade women to work at night.[31]

In Brazil, until very recently, no text asserted that men and women were equal before the law. The position of women in society was regulated by a 1916 statute "which formally enshrined the hierarchical, patriarchical view of family and sexual relations" and permeated all aspects of a woman's life.[32] A law in 2001 finally changed the situation: "After 26 years of debate, amendments, delays and parliamentary maneuvering, the Brazilian Congress . . . approved a legal code that for the first time in the country's history makes women equal to men in the eyes of the law" (Rohter 2001).[33] In such a legal environment, women in the workplace throughout the 1990s expectedly enjoyed very few modern rights. As in Argentina, most laws were designed to protect the role of women as mothers and domestic caretakers. Thus, well into the 1980s, women's labor (and labor in general) was regulated by the 1943 Decree-Law No. 5452 of May 1943, known as the Consolidação das Leis do Trabalho (Consolidation of Labor Laws). The decree had one, largely ignored, principle of importance for women: equal pay for work of equal value (Articles 5 and 461). This principle was matched in spirit by Law 5473 of July 1968 prohibiting discrimination in employment for jobs requiring selection. The decree had, on the other hand, a number of paternalistic laws. Article 379 prohibited night work (until 1989, when it was repealed by Law 7855 of 1989). Article 383 set out special rest times for women. Article 376 restricted overtime work for women. And a number of articles protected maternity (Articles 392 and 396).

The situation for working women improved significantly in the late 1980s, at least on paper. An impressive new constitution in 1988 put forth

---

[30] Examples of steps taken include the sale of birth control devices, marrying after a divorce, and illegitimate children were made legal; men were no longer granted exclusive rights to children (*patria potestad*); and women could enter the military. See Laws 23264 of September 1985, 23515 of June 1987, and 24429 of December 1994.

[31] An important law unrelated to working women but worthy of mention because of its progressive character is the 1991 Ley de Cupo (No. 24/012) (Quotas Law), requiring political parties to have at least 30% of their election candidates for the Chamber of Deputies to be women. The law has had a major impact on female presence in the chamber (Gray 2003).

[32] Husbands, for instance, had the right to keep their wives from working outside the home and restrict their travel (Epstein 1994: 6).

[33] The new code, which did not enter into force until 2003, repealed regulations that allowed men to divorce their wives on the grounds that their wives were not virgins and granted fathers exclusive legal rights to children. It recognized as well that single women are heads of their household and should be allowed to remarry even if found to have committed adultery in their first marriage.

a number of provisions related to social and work matters. Article 7 promised women protection within the labor market by means of incentives for the hiring and retention of female workers. The same article affirmed the principle of equal pay and dismantled protectionist regulations, allowing women access to night work and to work in unhealthy conditions. Additional measures included increases in the social benefits and rights of domestic servants, and new provisions for child care. These were important advances; yet the constitution required enabling statutes and laws for its application (Women's International Network 1995). Many of these were put into place only in the late 1990s or later, or are still missing (Htun 2002: 739–40). Judges have hesitated to enforce these principles in practice until recently (Pitanguy 1998: 104; Verucci 1991).

The legal and practical realities in Paraguay also precluded much progress at the regional level. Democracy in Paraguay came only in 1989 after forty years of repression and a new democratic constitution was adopted in 1992. The constitution put forth, for the first time in the country's history, important principles of equality, including a few workplace rights. Article 88 prohibits discrimination on the basis of sex and states that a woman may not be removed from her work during pregnancy or during her maternity leave. That same year, Congress rescinded legislation giving husbands the right to keep their wives from working outside the home (Epstein 1994). A new labor code was then instituted in 1993 (Código del Trabajo, Law 231/93 of October 1993). The code grants women and men identical rights and obligations at the workplace (Article 128) and equal pay for work of equal value (Article 229), in addition to abolishing contracts awarding women lower wages on the basis of sex (Article 47). These were important steps in a historically very conservative environment.[34] They were also theoretical measures whose application in practice is still largely unrealized.

Perhaps Uruguay alone offered Mercosur officials a legal base upon which to build progressive regional laws on women. On the whole the country lacked a tradition of repressive and discriminatory laws on women, and in fact had a few old but rather progressive laws.[35] Then, in the late 1980s, the government produced a series of impressive laws on women and equality. Among the most important was Law 16045 of June 1989: it prohibited discrimination in opportunity and treatment on the basis of gender, wage discrimination, and the evaluation of productivity

---

[34] The labor code contains as well regulations that still qualify as conservative. Women are prohibited, when pregnant or soon after birth of the child, from working at night, working extra hours, or engaging in unhealthy or dangerous work (Articles 129–31).

[35] For example, Law 10783 of September 1946 recognized the right of women to enter into employment agreements, own the fruits of their labor, and end any such agreement.

based on discriminatory criteria. It also introduced the possibility of positive actions for women and a special judicial procedure for enforcement. Two laws, in turn, eliminated the possibility of many types of discriminatory practices. Law 15996 of November 1988 and Decree 242 of 1987 established, respectively, an equal "regime" for men and women in the area of overtime and daily rest. These initiatives were then matched by the establishment of the Instituto Nacional de la Familia y de la Mujer in 1987, located inside the Ministerio de Educación y Cultura, whose mission was concretely to advance equality by charging existing administrative organs with new mandates.[36]

Yet, we should note, in Uruguay legal progress did not mean practical progress. As Assessor Beatriz Etchecurry Mazza put it in the interview with the author, Uruguayan women have suffered enormous discrimination: "We operate," she explained, "in a man's society where laws make little difference."[37] Many others share her view: women, noted a prominent women's organization, "enjoy equality under the law but experience a number of forms of discrimination stemming from traditional attitudes and practices" (Women's International Network 1993). Statistics from the labor market seem to confirm such claims. Despite having the highest participation in the labor force in all of Latin America, women with jobs identical to those of men in the 1990s averaged 50% of men's wages (Ronzoni 1995).

If the belated evolution of labor law on women made it unlikely for Mercosur officials to pursue regional-level laws on the topic, the absence of pressure from women to do so guaranteed that nothing would, in fact, be done. All major domestic groups were only beginning to form in the 1980s and 1990s. Understandably, they were preoccupied above all with domestic legislation. In Argentina, the Subsecretaria de la Mujer (Subsecretariat for Women) was established in 1987 within the Ministerio de Salud y Acción Social (Ministry of Health and Social Action) and in 1991 the Consejo Nacional de la Mujer (National Women's Council) was created to coordinate policies and report directly to the Presidency. Much of their attention, however, was directed to domestic improvements, especially the condition of women in the family and Argentine society in general (Navarro 2001). Brazil's most important organization—the Conselho Nacional dos Direitos da Mulher—was born in 1985. The council's objective was clear: to lobby domestic legislators to ensure that the new 1988 constitution would state that men and women were equal citizens

---

[36] For instance, the Ministerio de Trabajo y Seguridad Social was charged with conducting workplace inspections.

[37] Interview with the author, Montevideo, Uruguay, August 2003. See note 25 for Etchecurry Mazza's full job title.

(Pitanguy 1998: 104). Hence they organized seminars and public forums throughout Brazil, where lawyers, feminists, legislators, and the general public analyzed women's legal situation and formulated proposals for the constitution. They succeeded, but were then effectively silenced until 1995 by the conservative and powerful Ministério da Justiça do Brasil (Ministry of Justice) (Pitanguy 1998: 108). The 1990s witnessed the development of a feminist movement. The Centro Feminista de Estudos e Assessoria set itself up in Brasilia to provide advice to women in Congress; track the progress of all women's rights legislation; and conduct research projects, meetings, and exchanges involving women's groups from all over the country (Htun 2002: 735–40). Yet, as in Argentina, the focus of these new groups was also almost exclusively domestic (Stephen 1997).

Paraguay's women's movement was practically nonexistent for much of the twentieth century: the country's repressive regimes allowed for very little radical mobilization. Again, only in Uruguay could one see some encouraging trends. Uruguayan women in the 1990s could point to nearly a century of activism and organizing. Important groups, such as the Uruguayan Consejo Nacional de Mujeres (National Women's Council), the Alianza de Mujeres para los Derechos Femeninos (Women's Alliance for Women's Rights), and the Uruguayan chapter of the Federación Abolicionista Internacional (International Abolitionist Federation) were established and very active in the 1910s and 1920s (Ehrick 1998: 408). Yet, as Assessor Beatriz Etchecurry Mazza explained to the author, Uruguayan women shared similar objectives as those of their counterparts in the other three member states: to improve their conditions on the domestic front, which in this case meant ensuring the application of laws.

The absence of laws in NAFTA is, at first sight, somewhat more perplexing than in Mercosur. Though perhaps not as much as in the EU, the three member states shared a legal base upon which to build a regional set of modern laws on women and work, even if important differences certainly set them apart.[38] This alone, however, could not prove sufficient to motivate NAFTA officials—naturally inclined to minimalism, as we have seen—to take action on women's behalf. Pressure had to come from

---

[38] In the United States, women have made major progress in social and personal issues (abortion, divorce, etc.) but more limited progress in workplace issues (Stetson 1997). An Equal Rights Amendment to the Constitution with significant workplace clauses, passed by Congress in 1972, could not get ratified by thirty-eight or more states and thus failed. Canadian women have probably obtained the most advanced legislative principles on economic rights, with the passing in the late 1970s of an impressive federal plan (Gabriel and Macdonald 1994: 540; Women's International Network 1996). Mexico's constitution and labor law provide for "equal pay for equal work in equal jobs," a limited principle which was eventually broadened in 2003 with the passage of a more comprehensive law on women's rights (Women's International Network 2003).

women's groups as well. As it turned out, these groups proved surprisingly uninterested in mobilizing. As one critic noted:

> During the NAFTA debate, women's groups failed to make the gendered dimension of regionalization visible in public debate and have had virtually no impact on either the NAFTA text or on broader public policy related to integration. This failure to influence the policy outcome can be contrasted with the greater success of other social movements, like labour and the environmental movements. . . . [O]nly the Canadian women's movement organized widely at the national level in response to NAFTA. (MacDonald 2002: 152)

The absence of pressure from women's groups in the United States was especially conspicuous. "US-based women's organizations were virtually absent from transnational organizing around the passage of the North American Free Trade Agreement" (Liebowitz 2002: 145). Two key organizations—the National Organization for Women and the Fund for the Feminist Majority (now the Feminist Majority Foundation)—"showed little interest" in influencing the course that NAFTA would take (177). There were only smaller groups participating from the United States. These had stronger interests in issues related to trade, economics, immigration, and other topics directly related to NAFTA. They included Alternative Women in Development, the Women's Alternative Economic Network, and the Coalition of Labor Union Women (177). They did not participate, however, in the main alliance that formed around NAFTA (the Citizens' Trade Campaign) though they were active in the Alliance for Responsible Trade, managing to "inject a gender component into the coalition's analysis" (Macdonald 2002: 163). Yet, their objectives were not to influence NAFTA's texts as such, but rather to address how the texts, once approved, would affect women in certain economic sectors (Liebowitz 2002: 178). As a result, their efforts had little impact on the choices of NAFTA officials.[39]

Much of the behavior of the major groups was the result of a longstanding disinterest in international events and, especially, international trade. Even when considering topics like "pay equity . . . large multi-issue US women's organizations rarely consider[ed] the relationship between the domestic economy and international economic change." These groups simply "did not have a history of defining their interests as encompassing international economic issues. . . . [They did] not see their agenda as relevant to the trade debate" (Liebowitz 2002: 180). The same groups shared as well a preference for struggle through the private, rather than

---

[39] Importantly, major nonwomen groups from the United States involved in the crafting of NAFTA and the NAALC also did not advance gender or women's rights in any meaningful way (Liebowitz 2002: 178). These included groups such as labor unions, think tanks, and development organizations.

the public, sphere of society (Macdonald 2002: 160). The fact, moreover, that NAFTA would have most likely affected women of color and poor women working in the manufacturing sectors of the industry played a role: "these women were not key constituents of the large organizations in the United States" (Liebowitz 2002: 182; Macdonald 2002: 162).

Mexican women failed to mobilize as well. Those groups that were critical of NAFTA were "relatively small, often located away from the capital (particularly in the border region or in the South) and marginal both in political and even ethnic terms . . . to the mainstream middle-class women's movement" (Macdonald 2002: 167). Only one group, Mujer a Mujer (MM), emerged to represent women in any meaningful fashion. MM coordinated activities at the transnational level with its Canadian counterparts (Liebowitz 2002: 177). One of its most important initiatives was the organization of the First Tri-national Working Women's Conference on Economic Integration and Free Trade. The conference was organized with a second group—Mujeres en Acción Sindical (Women in Trade Union Action)—and took place in the state of Toluca, Mexico, during February 1992. Participants included representatives from "unions, women's and community groups, church and justice organizations, research and policy institutes, as well as national coalitions and networks" (Canadian Dimension 1992: 20). They were active in a variety of sectors, such as education, health, clothing and textiles, telecommunications, banks and service, and border maquiladora industries. The conference ended with unanimous agreement on several items for action. Two such items are reproduced here:

> Because economic integration is based explicitly on women's participation in the paid labour force, we—women of Mexico, Canada and the United States—demand that our respective governments guarantee basic rights to adequate education, health care, food, nutrition, housing, stability of employment, living salaries and training, voluntary maternity, and peace (that is the ability to live free from violence) within any trilateral agreement.

> Women are prepared to participate actively and to be subjects and protagonists in the dramatic process of change currently taking place throughout the continent, and globally. Thus we demand also that women's interests and organizations be represented in discussions and negotiations of any trilateral trade agreement between our countries. (Canadian Dimension 1992)

The agreement and later activities by the MM, however, proved to be isolated cases of activism. The one alliance with real access to leading officials in Mexico was the Red Mexicana Ante el Libre Comercio (RMALC). The RMALC granted only minimum attention to the MM or to women's issues (Macdonald 2002: 164).

Structural and ideological factors, rather than programmatic priorities, above all precluded mobilization in Mexico. The women's movement in Mexico lacked a national dimension: it was comprised of several, "disorganized and fragmented" groups (Lamas 1998: 113). These groups historically lacked resources and access to policymakers and were thus not accustomed to mobilization (Macdonald 2002: 164).[40] An antagonistic stance toward the state did not help their cause, for it prevented the establishment of a permanent lobbying presence in the corridors of power. Thus, by the 1990s, the women's movement could "not be considered a key participant in the [Mexican] policy-making process relating to women" (Lamas 1998: 113, 121).[41] At the same time, a number of other women's groups were actually supportive of NAFTA—even without progressive clauses for women—and had little desire to challenge it. To many, NAFTA represented an important step towards modernity. They hoped that NAFTA would "provide a beneficial influence on women's position in Mexico by increasing women's incorporation in the labour force and expose the Mexican government to pressures from northern countries with more advanced labour codes and social practices around women's rights (Macdonald 2002: 166).

Canadian women alone mobilized aggressively to shape NAFTA's texts. Macdonald notes: "Only the Canadian women's movement responded to the challenge of continental integration with some degree of unity," avoiding those "fractures along lines of ideology, strategy and identity" that had plagued movements in the United States and Mexico (2002: 155). The National Action Committee on the Status of Women (NAC) played a special role, including that of attempting to mobilize its counterparts in the United States (Liebowitz 2002: 181). An umbrella organization of five hundred women's groups, NAC voted in June 1992 to oppose the NAFTA agreement then under negotiation, calling as well for the termination of CUSFTA (Lalonde 1992). Thereafter, in collaboration with Action Canada Network—a broad coalition of social forces (including labor, antipoverty activists, and others) whose previous major goals included challenging CUSFTA—it became a powerful voice in the movement against adoption of the NAFTA texts (Sornberger 1992). NAC's call to action in 1993 as vocalized in a speech by its president, Judy Rebick, is representative of the group's determination and goals: "We must use every means at our

[40] Civil society in general has had limited access to political processes in Mexico (Lamas 1998: 113). This alone, however, cannot explain why a number of constituents (environmentalists, labor, and even animal rights activists) other than women were able shape the direction of policymaking in NAFTA.

[41] Lamas observes that the antistate attitude of the women's movement gradually changed in the 1990s, making it more likely that they may enjoy more access to the corridors of power (1998: 123).

disposal, including direct action, including disruptions of Parliament. . . . Whatever we can do to stop this deal from going through" (Pelletier 1993). In her view, "NAFTA and the related changes to our economic and social policies are the biggest threat to women's equality right now" (Pelletier 1993).

The aggressive mobilization of NAC stemmed from a history of lobbying state and public officials, a focus on trade and work issues, and strong alliances with labor organizations. Like other women's groups in Canada, NAC was committed to the "ordinary political process, and a belief in the welfare state and the importance of state action to remedy injustice, in contrast to the more liberal and individualistic character of US movements" (Macdonald 2002: 156). During the 1970s, NAC worked hard to lobby the federal government for progress in a number of areas, including equal pay (157). Partly in response to those pressures, the Canadian government produced a number of impressive laws advancing the cause of working women.[42] In the 1980s, NAC "helped initiate a coalition for farmers, unions, the poor and unemployed, seniors, religious groups, aboriginal peoples, immigrants, and artists" against CUSFTA (Cohen 1996). NAC's visibility and position during the NAFTA negotiations simply followed decades of similar activism.

Dairy Products

How are we to explain the expressed desire of EU officials not to standardize the world of dairy products, and especially that of cheese? Standardizing procedures and outputs would have challenged longstanding traditions in key member states of granting farmers and companies the exclusive right to manufacture specific types of cheeses, butters, and creams. These traditions reflected strong partnerships—grounded in a commitment to safeguarding cultural heritages and, in the eyes of many, the quality of food—between dairy producers and state actors. National representatives in Brussels thus fought hard to ensure that the interests of dairy producers would be protected by competition and other forces.

Dairy producers gained special recognition in three countries especially. Beginning in the early 1900s, Italian, French, and Spanish farmers had fought for, and obtained, protected denominations for a large variety of products. In 1954, the Italian government passed Law 125/1954 authorizing such denominations. In 1955, it recognized four cheeses as protected (De Roest and Menghi 2000: 440–41).[43] By the late 1990s, nearly

---

[42] For an overview of Canadian laws on women, see Loney (1998).

[43] The cheeses were Fontina, Grana Padano, Pecorino Siciliano, and Parmigiano Reggiano.

80% of all cheeses in the country had come under protection (Food and Agriculture Organization of the United Nations 1997: chap. 9). In France, the early battles centered on wine. Later, they concerned dairy products. Powerfully represented at the national level by the Fédération Nationale des Syndacats Exploitants Agricoles (National Federation of Farmers' Unions) and other organizations,[44] farmers won denomination protections under the system of Appellation d'Origine Controllée (AOC, Controlled Origin Denomination) in the late 1970s, 1980s, and 1990s for a large number of cheeses, butters, and creams.[45] The AOC system specified the geographical location for collection of milk, specific ways of preparing cheese, butter, or cream, and strict production controls. By the 1990s, there were well over forty protected cheeses, with all of the major dairy companies in the country producing at least one of those cheeses (Deeprose 1997). In Spain too the first efforts concentrated on wine (with Law 26 of May 1933) but were then expanded to dairy and other farm products in 1970 (with Law 25/1970 of December 2). Denominations for cheeses today amount to almost thirty, and the country has a Consorcio de Quesos de España con Denominación de Origen (Origin Denomination Consortium for Spanish Cheeses) for representative purposes at the national and EU levels (Spanish Newswire Services 2001a, 2003b).

These legal advances led to the creation of powerful administrative units designed to aid producers and ensure compliance. In Italy, the Comitato Nazionale per la Tutela della Denominazione di Origine e Tipiche dei Formaggi (National Committee for the Protection of Cheese Origin Denonimations) was set up in the 1950s within the Ministero delle Risorse Agricole, Alimentari e Forestali (Ministry of Agricultural, Nutritional, and Forest Resources). In 1947, the French government founded by legal decree the Institut National des Appellations d'Origine (National Institute for Origin Denominations). Within that institute, the government established the Comité National des Produits Laitiers (National Committee of Milk Products) exclusively for the protection of dairy products (Echikson 1998). The Spanish government followed in 1970 with the establishment of the Instituto Nacional de Denominaciones de Origen (National Institute for Origin Denominations). These and other governmental and nongovernmental bodies helped dairy producers retain their exclusive

---

[44] Analysts agree that the Fédération Nationale des Syndacats Exploitants Agricoles enjoyed a corporatist relationship with the French state (Montpetit 2000: 580).

[45] See Decree 93-1239 of November 15, 1993 for a list of cheeses and butters covered through time. In the case of butters, for instance, we find (for the year 1979) Beurre Charentes-Poitou, Beurre des Charentes, and Beurre des Deux-Sèvres. For cheeses, we find (for the year 1986) Bleu d'Auvergne, Bleu des Causses, Bleu du haut Jura, Bleu de Gex or Bleu de Septmoncel, Brie de Meaux, Camembert de Normandie, Cantal or Fourme de Cantal, Chaource, Comté, and Crottin de Chavignol or Chavignol.

rights to an array of products. They also invariably helped farmers cement their ties with the political establishment in their respective countries.

The same dairy producers and farmers that enjoyed such protection at home acquired remarkable power in EU affairs from the very early days of European integration.[46] At first, mostly due to the demands of France, EU officials adopted the CAP, a program primarily concerned with giving dairy producers and farmers in general a great deal of financial support. In a speech in 1962, President of the Commission Walter Hallstein would succinctly capture what the spirit of the CAP would be for decades to come. In his words, "the agricultural market is not such that it could be left to itself and to that free competition which renders us good services everywhere else. . . . [T]he first aim of all agricultural policy is to ensure an adequate income for the farming population" (Hallstein 1963: 7, 9). The program quickly "entrenched," noted an observer, in the minds of EU officials "ideas of the farmer as a special producer, requiring extraordinary attention both qualitatively and quantitatively" (Roederer-Rynning 2002: 111). To that end, insulated and specialized bodies eager to protect the interests of all the farming world were set up.[47] They would set very favorable prices and quotas, to the great benefit of dairy and other producers (Marsh 1977: 609). The program was so powerful as to consume as much as 90% of the EU's budget in the 1970s and 50% by the end of the century.

During the 1960s, 1970s, and 1980s, dairy product standardization remained a relatively minor issue. A few definitions were certainly crafted, but only to support the CAP as needed. All else was left untouched. As European integration proceeded, however, matters began to change. On the one hand, consumers throughout Europe were becoming more familiar with foreign dairy products. As the market for a given product gained in size, imitators began to produce their versions of cheeses and other products. On the other hand, new scientific evidence on hygienic requirements in food processing pressured EU officials to regulate production processes (Blythman 1992). The largest dairy companies supported this: small producers would be put out of business by higher costs, while shared guidelines for hitherto protected products would open whole new markets.

It was then that small French, Italian, and other farmers began to fight back. Their desire to take action was further intensified by a reduction in the CAP program—itself under severe criticism. Farmers, with their

---

[46] See Feld (1979: 348–49) and Roederer-Rynning (2002: 112–13) for an excellent overview of the influence of farmers in the EU.

[47] See, for instance, the Special Committee on Agriculture or the European Parliament Committee on Agriculture, Fisheries, and Food (Roederer-Rynning 2002: 111).

strong representation in Brussels and years of experience in protesting any EU proposal that seemed against their interests, would not easily relinquish their privileges.[48] Depending on the specific topic at hand, different national and transnational coalition of farmers and national representatives mobilized to oppose EU efforts towards standardization. The governments of dairy producers, for decades happy to grant their support on the domestic front, made their views clear in Brussels. They too, as Mauro Poinelli—a representative from Italy's largest lobby organization in Brussels (Coldiretti)—noted, mobilized in recognition of "the financial, as well as cultural, importance of these products."[49]

Commission efforts to standardize whole milk, for instance, caused an uproar in Italy, Ireland, the United Kingdom, and other countries (Agri Service International Newsletter 1993). In reaction to EU efforts to outlaw the use of unpasteurized milk, French dairy producers vehemently protested the measure (Economist 1991). So did Italian mozzarella makers (Roell 1993). Throughout, the European Farmers' Coordination, the European Council of Young Farmers, and the Committee of Agricultural Organisations in the European Union and General Committee for Agricultural Co-operation mobilized in Brussels in defense of national traditions.[50] Their position, reflecting the view of a spectrum of farmers and farming cooperatives, was simple. A letter to several European newspapers by French agriculture minister Hervé Gaymard, along with six other agriculture ministers, summarized it: "For us, agricultural products are more than marketable goods; they are the fruit of a love of an occupation and of the land, which has been developed over many generations. . . . For us, farmers must not become the 'variable adjustment' of a dehumanised and standardised world" (Economist 2002b: 18). Henriette Christensen—Secretary General of the European Council of Young Farmers—paraphrased this sentiment in an interview with the author. "The French," she noted, "continue to believe in their product and thus challenge the market. . . . They are not interested in trade as such, but in the concept of 'food sovereignty': self-sufficiency helped by trade when needed."[51]

In this acrimonious atmosphere, EU officials naturally developed a

[48] Throughout the 1980s, dairy producers and farmers (especially from France) staged massive protests against proposed changes to the price or quota systems. See, for example, Betts (1984) and United Press International (1990). Those protests continued during the 1990s, as more reforms to the CAP were introduced. In one instance, "barbed wire was placed around a building in Brussels . . . to protect agriculture ministers from a demonstration by farmers protesting at planned reforms" (Lognonne 1998).

[49] Interview with the author, Brussels, Belgium, April 2004.

[50] Examples abound. In the case of cheeses, for instance, see *European Report* (2002) on Grana Padano and *European Report* (1997) on Roquefort.

[51] Interview with the author, Brussels, Belgium, April 2004.

timid approach to dairy standardization. On the one hand, they crafted Regulation 2081/92, a measure that recognized and protected denominations, and one that farmers would work hard to ensure that the Commission enforced. On the other hand, officials proceeded to advance a relatively slim legislative apparatus designed to cover some of the most essential health and hygienic considerations. Mauro Poinelli, the representative from Coldiretti, summarized events in the EU as follows:

> In the early days of the CAP, the concern with EU policymakers was with direct financial support. The standardization of most dairy products was not relevant for those objectives and was, therefore, not pursued. Later, explicit measures were taken against standardization. As with the CAP, this was done to protect the dairy sector, and especially small and medium companies. And, again, these steps were taken for the preservation of local culture and traditions, but also to promote the quality of the product itself.[52]

Matters developed quite differently in Mercosur, with officials moving quickly to standardize much of the dairy world. What can explain such an aggressive approach? We must again consider the domestic policy contexts in place in the early 1990s and the preferences of dairy producers in the region.

On the policy front, standardization was made easy by the fact that none of the member states had a history of protected denominations in the dairy sector. Production of specific types of cheese, butter, dessert, and other products could take place—and in fact had taken place—across the entire region for decades prior to Mercosur's formation. In the case of cheese in particular, precisely those denominations that were protected in the EU (such as mozzarella or parmesan) were the most widely produced, a fact largely explained by the European descent of most consumers in the region. The region also lacked rooted traditions of location-specific products and processes. Accordingly, officials could move swiftly through most product lines, and produced laws whose adoption into national legal systems and practical application posed "no major problems" (Nofal and Wilkinson 1999a: 255). It was a question of technical, rather than cultural, harmonization (Spanish Newswire Services 1999a, 1999b, 2000b). Products and procedures could be easily standardized and the industry quickly opened to competition—steps which made the protectionism of the EU a subject of criticism by Mercosur officials (Spanish Newswire Services 2000b).

More importantly perhaps, there was also a policy shift on the part of the governments of the member states during the 1980s and 1990s away from decades of discrimination against agricultural producers and to-

---

[52] Interview with the author, Brussels, Belgium, April 2004.

wards a more market-friendly approach. Since the 1950s, these governments had imposed on producers indirect and direct taxation, punitive price controls, and other burdens. Their objective was to discourage investment in agriculture and to encourage the growth of more "modern" industries (through direct subsidies, tax credits, and other tools made possible by discrimination against farming) (Helfand 2000: 462).[53] Hence, in the case of Brazil for instance, the "historical record shows that from the mid-1960s through 1982 . . . an implicit record of taxation on the order of 25%" was placed on farmers (Helfand 2000: 463, 1999: 7). Similar measures were taken in Argentina, Uruguay, and Paraguay, all with the result of stifling growth.[54] Agriculture and its dairy sector were depressed, and trade suffered as a result.

The policy shift—itself a function of a number of factors[55]—involved helping dairy companies invest, grow, and engage in cross-national exchanges (Nofal and Wilkinson 1999b: 151; United States Department of Agriculture 1997: 25). In Argentina, "the more free-market approach" meant that "export taxes on most agricultural products [were] eliminated" and that import duties on inputs (fertilizers, pesticides, machinery, etc.) were lowered (26). In the case of Brazil, it entailed the elimination of export taxes on primary and semiprocessed agricultural exports and incentives to rationalize production (United States Department of Agriculture 1997: 26; Nofal and Wilkinson 1999b: 150). Direct incentives for investments and export activities were also introduced (Nofal and Wilkinson 1999a: 256). In Uruguay as well measures were taken to free the dairy sector from harmful intervention (255). In all countries, moreover, tariff and nontariff barriers were reduced (Nofal and Wilkinson 1999b: 161).

In such an environment, as Maximiliano Moreno—a participant in Mercosur's legislative activities on dairy[56]—explained to the author, "differences in production norms and sanitary requirements naturally came to be seen as hindering the development of the dairy industry."[57] This was

---

[53] Discrimination was not unique to the Mercosur countries. On the contrary, it was widespread across developing countries.

[54] We should note that these policies hurt most dairy producers, but not all. The largest agricultural enterprises received credit subsidies (loans at below-market rates) (Helfand 1999: 3–28).

[55] These include the economic crises of the 1980s, democratization, and a more neoliberal international policy environment. See Helfand (1999) for an excellent overview of events in Brazil.

[56] Legal Advisor in Argentina's Ministerio de Economía y Producción and, specifically, a lawyer in the Coordinación de Legislación Internacional, Dirección Nacional de Mercados Agroalimentarios, Secretaría de Agricultura, Ganadería, Pesca y Alimentos (International Law Coordination, National Directorate for Agricultural Food Markets, as found in the Secretariat for Agirculture, Hunting, Fish and Food).

[57] Interview with the author, Buenos Aires, Argentina, August 2003.

especially so because tariff barriers between Argentina and Brazil had been set to zero. Regulatory differences posed unnecessary barriers to the expansion and growth of dairy companies, in contrast to the new market-oriented policies of governments. They had to be eliminated—a matter that could be taken care of with the right resources and expertise (Gazeta Mercantil 1997a).

Yet very little could be achieved without the support of dairy companies. As it turned out, these eagerly supported any effort to eliminate trade barriers across the member states. They welcomed enthusiastically the reduction in tariffs,[58] but their attention also turned to standardization. As Maximilano Moreno would note, large players "pushed officials to do away with conflict in national regulation that blocked trade."[59] They were especially interested, as María Juana Rivera—another direct participant in the negotiations—described to the author, in doing away with "differences in quality and health standards, especially differences between Brazil, which had overall lower standards, and Argentina, which had higher standards."[60]

Such interest in full-scale liberalization was easy to understand. In the 1980s and early 1990s, due partly to national liberalization programs, companies in Brazil (and to a lesser extent Paraguay) were already importing significant quantities of processed and semiprocessed cheese from Argentina and Uruguay. Dairy companies from Argentina and Uruguay, in turn, relied heavily on Brazil as their major export destination (Nofal and Wilkinson 1999b: 161). The further removal of trade barriers promised to make transactions across these countries cheaper, faster, and easier. Everyone—especially the larger players—stood to benefit. The early years of integration proved these suppositions right and thus intensified the interest of dairy companies in market liberalization. Trade boomed and companies' revenues multiplied. All evidence suggests that cross-national trade exploded: "Intra-bloc dairy exports," noted two industry experts from the region, "rose by 800% between 1986–1988 and 1994–1996" (Nofal and Wilkinson 1999b: 154).[61] This contrasted with an increase in extra-bloc sales of only 54% during the same period. Pablo Costagma, Secretary for Economic Planning for Rafaela, a core city in the

---

[58] In one case at least, support was such that a company preceded Mercosur officials in striking tariff reduction agreements with recipient countries. In 1991, Conaprole (Uruguay's biggest dairy company) signed a series of contracts to sell fresh milk tariff-free to Argentina and Brazil (Xinhua General Overseas News Service 1991).

[59] Interview with the author, Buenos Aires, Argentina, August 2003.

[60] Interview with the author, Buenos Aires, Argentina, August 2003. See chap. 3, n. 25 for Rivera's full job title.

[61] In 1995 and 1996 alone, for instance, Brazil's imports of butter from the other member states (as a percentage of all butter imported) jumped from 46% to 65%, those for cheese from 16% to 65% (see Nofal and Wilkinson 1999b: 150).

dairy region of Argentina, would observe: "The Argentine Midwest, around the province of Santa Fe, is an island of prosperity. The principal dairy region of Latin America, it has benefited from the creation of Mercosur, which has served to awaken the dairy industry to the prospects of larger markets" (Gazeta Mercantil 1997b).[62]

Dairy companies had a second reason to support Mercosur. The general stabilization of currencies and incomes in all four countries in the early 1990s led to a steep increase in demand for dairy products (Nofal and Wilkinson 1999b: 149). Mercosur would offer companies easier access to expanding markets. Parallel GATT negotiations indicated that the heavily subsidized producers from North America and Europe would no longer be able to dump their products in Latin America.[63] The appeal of regional integration grew even stronger.

At first glance, the decision by NAFTA's officials not to standardize the world of dairy products could be seen as representative of a "hopeful" openness to trade: a desire to allow exchanges to occur and, if needed, to solve conflicts as they arise. We have seen that minimalism in NAFTA is generally intended to be conducive to trade. The presence of Article 713, which asks member states to comply with standards from international organizations as they engage in agricultural activities, would lend support to such an interpretation. Yet a closer inspection of the NAFTA text itself, the strong bargaining by officials from Canada over the question of dairy products, and the historical legislative and political dynamics responsible for such bargaining suggest otherwise. NAFTA officials would have had little reason to standardize, at the regional level, the world of dairy products. Eager to defend decades of domestic protectionism, Canadian officials in fact pressed hard for and took measures to ensure that dairy products would *not* be subject to trade liberalization, that they would be exempted from the NAFTA treaty (Scollay 2001: 1141). Without a single market for dairy products in the making, officials logically did not engage in any standardization of those products.

In the NAFTA text, Canadian dairy trade with the United States and with Mexico is simply *exempted* from trade liberalization. Chapter 7 in fact permits Canada to continue to protect its dairy producers. In the case of trade with the United States, Article 702 incorporates into the NAFTA

[62] We should note that the trade of dairy products was not without its conflict. In 1997, Brazilian officials began accusing Argentine and Uruguayan producers of dumping their products in Brazil (especially powdered milk and long-storage milk). The Brazilians retaliated by imposing bureaucratic controls on imports (such as import licenses and sanitary requirement checks). The conflict came to an end in 2001 with the introduction of minimum prices (Spanish Newswire Services 1999b, 2001b). The conflict certainly hurt exports from Argentina to Brazil (INTAL 2001: 47), though their precise impact is difficult to measure.

[63] We know now that those expectations were not fulfilled, as governments from those countries (and especially the EU) refused to comply.

text a series of articles found in the 1989 free trade agreement between the United States and Canada (CUSTFA).[64] One of these articles states:

> Unless otherwise specifically provided in this Chapter, the Parties retain their rights and obligations with respect to agricultural, food, beverage and certain related goods under the General Agreement on Tariffs and Trade (GATT) and agreements negotiated under the GATT, including their rights and obligations under GATT Article XI. (CUSFTA Article 710)

Article XI of the GATT states that countries have the right to use selected trade restrictions on dairy products. These include tariff-rate quotas: the imposition of high tariffs over goods once certain import quotas are met.

Chapter 7 then has similar provisions for trade between Canada and Mexico:

> The rights and obligations of the Parties under Article XI:2(c)(i) of the GATT . . . shall apply with respect to trade in agricultural goods only to the dairy, poultry and egg goods . . . and with respect to such dairy, poultry and egg goods that are qualifying goods, either Party may adopt or maintain a prohibition or restriction or a customs duty on the importation of such goods consistent with its rights and obligations under the GATT. (NAFTA, Section B of Annex 703)

Measures were taken to liberalize only trade between the United States and Mexico. Section A of Annex 703.2 asked for the elimination of all tariff and nontariff barriers by the year 2003 (a date that was in fact largely met on time).[65]

As it turned out, while the United States took unilateral steps to open somewhat gradually its borders to Canadian products, the Canadian government proceeded to impose tariffs on dairy products that reached 350%.[66] In 1996, for instance, Canadian tariff-rate quotas were 343% for butter, 275% for cheese, and 270% for milk and cream. The government indicated that those quotas would be lowered, but only to 299%, 246%, and 241% respectively, by the year 2001 (United States Department of Agriculture 1997: 19–20).[67] These measures proved utterly frustrating to the United States. That same year, officials from the United

[64] These are CUSFTA articles 701, 702, 704, 705, 706, 707, 710, and 711.

[65] Mexico, for instance, eliminated any barrier to imports of fresh milk, fresh cheese, processed cheese, hard cheese, yogurt, whey, casein, lactose, condensed milk, evaporated milk, and dairy blends. For milk powder, the United States was allowed 52,191 tons duty-free, with out-of-quota imports taxed at 58.71%.

[66] In prior years, Canada used strict quotas to limit imports, also allowed by Article XI. But, after 1994, the GATT legislation allowed for tariff-rate quotas but not traditional quotas. The Canadians asked GATT officials in Geneva to allow them to continue using quotas, but to no avail (Financial Post 1996a)

[67] These reductions were necessary to keep in line with agreements made at the Uruguay Round of negotiations regarding GATT's Article XI.

States filed a complaint against Canadian tariffs on imported dairy products, arguing that they went against the provisions found in NAFTA.[68] The panel mechanism for dispute resolution was used for the first time for this occasion. After some deliberation, the five judges (two of whom were from the United States) unanimously concluded that the tariffs were perfectly legal and in line with both the GATT and the NAFTA texts.

The complaint by the United States was clearly disingenuous. Much evidence exists to suggest that officials knew all too well what they had agreed to during the NAFTA negotiations. In their argument, those officials made no mention of Chapter 7, and instead referred to the more generic trade liberalization principles found in Chapter 3 of the NAFTA text. Clearly, such an omission only served to confirm that these officials knew the meaning of Chapter 7. Throughout the negotiations over the NAFTA text, moreover, the subject of dairy protectionism was openly debated on numerous occasions and in no unclear terms (Bailey 2002: 9). Ira Shapiro, Ambassador from the United States Trade Representative's Office, would unambiguously state in a testimony before the House Committee on Agriculture (Subcommittee on Dairy, Livestock, and Poultry) that "there were no agricultural market access negotiations between the United States and Canada during the NAFTA negotiations" (Federal News Service 1996). In fact, at the time officials from the United States were actually themselves interested in protecting their own domestic industry. Their change in viewpoint was quick and unexpected, driven by a change in the preferences of the dairy industry and a related policy shift at home. The turnaround, of course, did not go unnoticed. Claude Rivard, President of Dairy Farmers of Canada, would bluntly state at the time: "The United States is trying to secure through the NAFTA dispute settlement process something that was never agreed to through eight years of bilateral, trilateral and multilateral trade negotiations." These were agreements made, he added, "openly and in good faith" (Canada NewsWire 1996). A frustrated Richard Doyle, executive director of the same organization, would for instance note: "The story is always the same with the Americans. They sign an agreement, and then when they find it doesn't suit them exactly, they turn around and try to get out" (Gazette 1996).

Why, then, were the Canadians so adamantly opposed to trade liberalization in the case of dairy products? The Canadian position was simply a continuation of a deeply rooted—stretching from the 1920s but truly put into place in the 1970s—tradition of domestic protectionism of dairy farmers. The policy had a number of components: production restrictions,

[68] The complaint (which also covered eggs and poultry) actually had two parts. First, the argument was made that the NAFTA member states had agreed to work towards the elimination of tariffs. Second, the argument was made that the NAFTA text states that no country can impose tariffs higher than those in place before NAFTA came into being (United States Department of Agriculture 1997: 19).

administered prices, import control, and direct payments. At the federal level, it was managed by the Canadian Dairy Commission, which acted on behalf of the government and in collaboration with other entities, such as the Canadian Milk Supply Management Committee.[69] Provinces too, however, exercised some control, especially through milk marketing boards (United States Department of Agriculture 1997: 20–21). The primary objective of all these measures was simple: "to ensure price, and hence income stability, at the producer level" (Financial Post 1996b). Of course, this came at a cost: higher prices for consumers and, as well, direct transfers from taxpayers to farmers.

The coming of NAFTA, and before that CUSFTA, posed a potential problem for Canada. Imports would certainly be much cheaper than domestic goods: they would flood the market, and wipe out a large number of Canadian farmers. One popular study conducted in 1996 by Informetrica, Ltd., an Ottawa research firm, predicted that opening the gates to dairy products (and also poultry and eggs) would cost Canadians "a C$3 billion drop in economic output during the first year, and $16 billion over five years" (Gazette 1996). Indeed, the government itself would lose C$2.7 billion in forgone taxes in the first year alone. Other studies estimated twenty-seven thousand lost jobs in farming and food processing (Gazette 1996). The Canadian government could not permit that, and mobilized early and decisively to avoid it. The decision by the NAFTA panel to allow Canada to continue in its path evoked quite positive reactions in Canada. Peter Clark, a representative of the Canadian dairy processing industry, reacted with relief: "This is a very important victory for Canada. . . . There could have been very serious political problems, including a rapid adjustment program that would have been difficult to manage" (Financial Post 1996c). An ebullient observer then noted:

> Canada's long history of ensuring price stability for farm commodities rests intact. So does the philosophical underpinning of the tight and complex Canadian legislative scheme aimed at maintaining the security of rural life and the family farm, values and virtues with which most Canadians probably agree. (Financial Post 1996b)

Why, we might also be tempted to ask, would the United States and Mexico agree to leave dairy products off the NAFTA project? Farmers from both those countries had enjoyed decades of protectionism, and their support for NAFTA was ambivalent at best. The United States had itself a long tradition of major quantitative restrictions on many dairy product imports, price setting, and subsidies for exports, especially when domestic production exceeded demand (Bailey 2002; Doyon and Novakovic

[69] For a concise overview of the Canadian system of government management of the dairy sector, see Bailey (2002: 5–7) and Doyon and Novakovic (1996: 1–3).

1996: 3–4).[70] In 1993, it seemed that the nation's biggest farm organizations, including the National Milk Producers Federation, were backing the agreement, "but cracks in the united front aren't helping their efforts to round votes for the pact in Congress" (Brasher 1993). Representative Tim Johnson from South Dakota described one dimension of the split: "Commodity organization leaders tend to favor it, but the level of support drops off drastically as you go to the coffee shops and grain elevators to talk to individual producers" (Brasher 1993). Yet even among commodity organizations there was much ambivalence. The Minnesota Milk Producers Association and the Florida Farm Bureau voted to oppose the agreement. The president of the Farmers Union Milk Marketing Cooperative (with ten thousand members in eight Midwestern states) voiced his view that NAFTA was a "huge gamble with the livelihoods" of dairy farmers, while the American Farm Bureau Federation was deeply ambivalent (Brasher 1993).

In Mexico, in turn, the government had supported the dairy industry with import licenses and quotas for many years. Indeed, well into the late 1980s, much of agricultural production was directly subsidized and the beneficiary of guaranteed producer prices and high import barriers. By the early 1990s, steps were taken to eliminate quotas, price setting, and subsidies (partly in response to GATT regulations but also as an effort to improve the efficiency of the sector). At the same time, Mexico retained import licenses and tariffs (Burfisher, Robinson, and Thierfelder 1998: 68). In the midst of such a transition period, Mexican officials found it acceptable to proceed with liberalization with the United States and not Canada, with which they retained the right to permanently use import protection measures against dairy products (as well as poultry and eggs).

The absence of standardizing laws on dairy products at the regional level is then to be understood first and foremost in light of the fact that NAFTA itself was designed to allow one of the three member states to continue protecting its markets. As long as such protectionism continues, we are indeed unlikely to see any move towards standardization any time in the near future.

Labor Rights

Officials from the EU, Mercosur, and NAFTA have endowed workers with certain rights. In this regard, all three regions share some form of interventionism. As we have seen, however, the specific rights granted to

[70] Restrictions on dairy products put in place in the 1950s, for instance, allowed imports not to exceed 2% of domestic consumption. Export subsidies were in place throughout the 1990s with the Dairy Export Incentive Program (started in 1985) (Bailey 2002).

workers vary from RTA to RTA. How are we to understand such variance? The content of regional law, much as what regional law targets, is most easily understood in light of preexisting legal and power arrangements in the member states.

Consider first EU legislation in the area of social security. Recall that Regulation 1408/71, requiring member states to extend to migrant workers the same benefits that they made available to domestic workers, includes (unlike in Mercosur or NAFTA) an explicit clause guaranteeing access to unemployment benefits. The approach does not entail the development of a single set of provisions to be applied homogeneously to migrant workers everywhere in the EU. Instead, it says that migrant workers should be given the same unemployment benefits as those enjoyed by local workers. What can explain the presence and specific "reciprocal" qualities of this approach to the protection of migrant workers in unemployment?

The most obvious answer is that Regulation 1408/71 actually builds from two of the earliest legal measures taken in the EU—Regulation 3 and Regulation 4 of 1957, adopted the same year that the TEEC was signed. These regulations aimed at putting into practice Article 51 of the TEEC, which stated in very general terms that the Council shall take steps to "secure for migrant workers . . . payment of benefits." The regulations themselves built directly on a number of recommendations, conventions, and other documents developed by the International Labor Organization (Wedel 1970: 459, 465–66). These previous documents already put forth the principle of reciprocity, including in the area of unemployment. The existence of Regulation 1408/71 may thus be explained as a form of incorporation of earlier EU and International Labor Organization documents. Yet, EU officials in the early 1970s could have easily pushed for a different approach: a more aggressive one centered on harmonization or, perhaps less likely, a reversal entailing the elimination of any benefits. We thus still need to explain why officials opted in the 1970s to continue with a system based on reciprocity.

As it turned out, in the early 1970s all the member states were in the midst of building impressive but also increasingly quite different social-security schemes (Crijns and Laurent 1978: 577; Gallie and Paugam 2000). Differences existed in relation to entitlements, financing, administration, and operations.[71] Retirement benefits, for instance, differed across all six member states in terms of levels and sources. In Belgium, the state would give retirees 60% of their career-covered earnings, adjusted for cost of living. Private employers then provided 60% to 65% of final

---

[71] See De Montigny and Schmahl for a concise review of pensions and benefits related to disability, medical conditions, and death (1970: 41–44).

average pay in excess of the social security ceiling for a full career. In France, a complex multi-employer institutional scheme and state pension system gave workers up to 65% of final average pay for all employees (including hourly ones). In Italy, the figure could reach 100% of final pay, but most if not all of it was state sponsored. In Luxembourg too the state was the primary source of pay, but only for a total of 60% to 70% of final coverage (De Montigny and Schmahl 1970: 41–44).

Unemployment benefits in particular were central to this expanding range of social-security programs, and were indeed poised to register the biggest increase of any program during the period 1970–75 (Crijns and Laurent 1978: 571). As with all other programs, each member state had different policies in place, all of which reflected local economic problems and industrial relations. Variation related to levels, lengths, conditions, and the funding sources of benefits. This would mean that by the mid-1970s in France benefits were 90% of the previous year's gross earnings, free of tax but minus other social security payments, such as family allowances. Benefits dropped after one year to 40% of previous earnings, plus a flat-rate sum. In Germany, benefits varied between 80% and 68% of previous pay, net of tax. Yet there was also a weekly maximum for a single person and the length of benefit was scaled to how long in the last three years the worker held a job. In Italy, benefits were set to be 80% of gross and 93% of net wages, to be paid for an initial three months and possibly extended for another six months (Economist 1975b, 1975c, 1975d).

In the early 1970s, EU officials thus faced a variety of national systems that had been systematically applied—as required by Regulations 3 and 4—to migrant workers from other member states. The Acting Secretary-General of the Administrative Commission on Social Security for Migrant Workers (ACSSMW) of the EU described the social-security programs for migrant workers found in the member states soon after the time of the passage of the 1971 regulation as offering "every possible variant" of benefits: "The European Community is . . . marked by the heterogeneousness of social security systems of its member States both in terms of the actual concept of social security and as regards the level of benefits, structures, methods of financing and administration" (Coëffard 1982). At such a juncture, a regional law that would have established a precise set of benefits that all member states should have extended to all migrant workers would have been unthinkable. Granting migrant workers the right to existing national benefits would instead prove more acceptable.

Thus, in the words of the Acting Secretary-General, the "harmonisation of national legislation" was "rejected as soon as it was mooted" (Coëffard 1982: 255). The preferred choice was one of "coordination" of the different national schemes, a terminology that continues to be used by

EU officials. As the Secretary put it when, again, discussing migrant workers:

> It is easy to imagine the difficulties involved in introducing uniform regulations for systems as different as the Danish one which, in almost all branches, offers all residents a personal entitlement to benefits without contribution or employment conditions and is financed almost exclusively out of public funds, and the Italian system which is organised primarily for the benefit of workers and where entitlements to benefits and the amount of these depend on the length of the period of insurance. (244–45)

EU officials had but one choice: to design a flexible system and avoid introducing a uniform set of benefits. Villars, a Swiss expert on international social security, thus described the benefits of Regulation 1408/71 as follows:

> The formula adopted by the Council of Europe has made it possible to take account of the diversity of national security schemes and to give the [regulation] the flexibility without which it would never have proved acceptable to all the member States. As regards sickness, maternity, unemployment and family benefits, the [regulation] proposes solutions which . . . allows [sic] the Contracting Parties the possibility of adopting procedures more appropriate to the problems facing them, bearing in mind the nature of their sickness, maternity, unemployment and family benefits schemes. (Villars 1981: 296)

Such flexibility would remain a characteristic of the formula for decades to come, as unemployment and other social-security programs continued to differ across the EU, especially as new member states joined the common market and as "the specific provisions for unemployment insurance and assistance [continued to] differ widely from country to country" (Snower 1995: 633).[72]

---

[72] Snower offers some powerful examples:

In many European countries (e.g. Denmark, Germany, Luxembourg, Portugal and Spain) unemployment insurance benefits are granted as a percentage of gross wages, up to specific ceilings. In other countries (e.g. France, United Kingdom and Ireland) these benefits have substantial flat-rate components. There is wide variation across countries as to the duration of benefits, the conditions under which people can qualify for unemployment insurance and the degree to which the benefits are financed by employers, employees and the state. . . . There is also a large inter-country variation in benefits pertaining to unemployment assistance. In some countries, such as Germany and Greece, they depend positively on earnings . . . whereas they are largely flat rates in France, Ireland, the Netherlands, Portugal, Spain and the United Kingdom. By contrast, Belgium, Denmark, Italy and Luxembourg have no unemployment assistance at all, relying instead on welfare provisions that are not related to people's unemployment status. (1995: 633)

In the case of the rights to strike and to associate, any regional law based on reciprocity, let alone harmonization, was out of the question. The primary difficulty encountered by the Commission from the 1970s on was a conflict of worldviews among its member states. The French were above all responsible for promoting both the early Community Charter of Fundamental Social Rights for Workers of 1989 and the European Charter of Fundamental Rights in the 1990s. For French President François Mitterand, the 1989 charter constituted a priority (Economist 1989). For the government of Prime Minister Lionel Jospin at the time of the Treaty of Nice, the charter was also a priority and something that French officials reasoned should be made compulsory (Times 2000). Indeed, Employment Minister Martine Aubry warned that France would push for other compulsory goals related to employment (Times 2000). Driving the French position was a rich collection of domestic legislation granting to workers many of the same rights as found in the charters, importantly including the rights to strike and form associations.

Yet working assiduously against the French and any legal recognition of both charters was the United Kingdom, backed intermittently by Ireland, Denmark, the Netherlands, and other countries. In the United Kingdom, the right to strike and association were not enshrined in any legal document (Roberts 2003). They were recognized in practice through common law, but workers could not point to any legal document where those and other rights were listed. A succession of British governments, backed by the Confederation of British Industry, feared that a formal EU declaration of those rights would seriously jeopardize the functioning of the national economy. Thus, British Prime Minister Margaret Thatcher steadfastly opposed the 1989 charter: "At the Madrid summit last month," reported a journalist in July 1989, "Mrs. Thatcher single-handedly blocked the approval of a draft of the charter" (Economist 1989; Dowdy 1990). Referring to it as a "socialist charter," (Meade 1989) Thatcher firmly asserted that she would not tolerate "attempts by Brussels to impose worker participation and other sensitive issues on Britain" (Xinhua General News Service 1989). Her views were then further voiced by Employment Secretary Norman Fowler, who launched "a fierce attack on the European Social Charter" (Press Association 1989). As Fowler put it, the charter "would pave the way for a virtually unqualified right to strike," something that, along with the other principles in the charter, "would have one inescapable effect: to add to the labour costs of industry and of every company in this country, and put jobs at risk" (Press Association 1989).

Having succeeded in blocking the adoption of the 1989 charter as a legal text, the United Kingdom then turned its attention to the subsequent European Charter of Fundamental Rights. Consistent with their past position, the British opposed its formal adoption in the Nice Treaty. In 2000, "Blair and other more sceptical EU prime ministers insisted that the charter of fundamental rights should not be legally binding." Other British government officials pointed out that they would work assiduously to ensure "that the finished product will not create new rights or be in conflict with the law in any member state" (Castle 2000), and that it would ultimately be "subject to national law and practice." As a government spokesman put it in reassuring fashion, the final document "will be a political declaration and not a legal text. . . . [I]t will not create law or be a springboard to new laws. It will not extend the power of the EU institutions but will help ensure that Europe's citizens are aware of the rights they already enjoy" (Mead 2000).

A few years later, the same government fought hard to dilute the charter's scope and reach in the proposed European constitution. Thus, it was "largely at Britain's insistence [that] the charter's remit is supposedly confined to Union law and institutions, implying that what is a fundamental right for an employee of the Union is no right of any kind for somebody not in that fortunate position" (Economist 2003b). Again, the most salient issue was the introduction of hitherto noncodified normative principles and their consequences. "Downing Street fears," a reporter wrote, that the charter "could open the way for police, doctors and the armed forces to demand the right to take industrial action" (Roberts 2003). As another journalist noted:

> The British . . . worry that the list of rights includes a lot of vaguely worded social rights, including the right to work, bargain collectively and strike. . . . They fear that such rights could be used to roll back Thatcherite labour laws which have let Britain avoid some of the rigidities of continental labour markets. . . . The British believe that they can safeguard their position if they can get an explanatory commentary, limiting the charter's impact on national legislation, attached to the constitution. (Economist 2003c)

In Mercosur, the situation was remarkably different from that in the EU. The 1980s were turbulent years in all of the four member states, as those countries were transitioning from dictatorships to democracies. The dictatorships of the 1970s and 1980s had outlawed in brutal fashion many progressive labor rights that unions and supportive government leaders, such as Juan Domingo Perón in Argentina, had secured for workers over the decades (Bronstein 1995). These included the right to strike and form associations, which had been in place in the four member states for quite some time. The generals in power also jailed or killed hundreds of union leaders (Cieza 1998). As the military regimes came to an end, trade unions mobilized with force to regain their lost rights. The new government leaders, though not sympathetic to union interests, worked with labor representatives towards a series of compromises.[73]

Hence, during these important years "labor organizations obtained many prolabor reforms and secured the restoration of rights in labor law" (Cook 2002: 2). High on their agenda were the rights to strike and associate. In all four countries, key advances where made in both constitutions and law. In Argentina, the Confederación General de Trabajadores (General Workers Association) struggled bitterly with the Alfonsín government in the 1980s for a broad sanctioning of the rights to strike and form unions (6). In 1988 they won such sanctioning in the form of a revised labor code. In Brazil, the Central Unica dos Trabalhadores (Central Workers' Union) fought successfully to ensure that those same rights be recognized in the new 1988 Constitution (9), with later regulations (such as Act 7783 of June 28, 1989) facilitating their practice (Bronstein 1995: 172 n. 30). In Uruguay, those rights were quickly reinstituted after the election of Julio María Sanguinetti and the Partido Colorado (Colorado Party) in 1985, as also happened in Paraguay in 1992 with the adoption of a new constitution.[74]

The 1990s followed, bringing neoliberal economic policies and thus new challenges to labor, but the final result was the establishment of trade unions as major—and politically independent—players in national politics (Bronstein 1995: 166). In Argentina, Carlos Menem embarked on a series of reforms, some of which (such as the 1991 Ley Nacional de Empleo, or National Employment Act) centered on increasing the flexibility of the labor force. Many of these reforms were at first tolerated but then vehemently opposed by unions after the economic crisis of 1994–96, which followed a sharp devaluation of the peso. Bitter struggles ensued between Menem (acting under severe pressure from the IMF), trade unions, and opposition parties. The end result was the adoption of a labor reform bill in 1998 that embodied significant victories for labor (Cook 2002: 17). A similar course of events took place in Brazil, albeit with a few years' delay, due to the impeachment of Fernando Collor in 1992 and the arrival of reformist Fernando Henrique Cardoso in 1994. Like Menem, Cardoso pushed for labor reforms that challenged the strength and resources of labor. Some of these reforms passed, but several stalled. Throughout, unions managed to assert themselves as powerful political actors that could not be ignored by the country's leadership (17–23). In

[73] In both Argentina and Brazil, trade unions were associated most directly with the parties that lost the elections (Cook 2002: 2). They had nonetheless acquired legitimacy because of their instrumental roles in the fight against the dictatorships.

[74] I do not intend to offer here a complete overview of all the relevant constitutional and legal measures in the four member states, but of only the critical advances made in the 1980s.

Uruguay and Paraguay too, trade unions established themselves as powerful fixtures of the political landscape (Buchanan and Nicholls 2001; Bronstein 1995: 168–69).[75]

The legislative victories of the 1980s and the increasing relevance of trade unions in the 1990s formed the context in which Mercosur officials generated the Declaración Sociolaboral of 1998. Officials directly involved in the crafting of the declaration described it as a logical extension of principles that were already recognized in all the member states. Gerardo Corres,[76] one of the crafters of the declaration, described it to the author as "something fundamental, something that we had to do if we wished to retain the rights that workers already enjoyed in their respective countries and also to ensure the backing of unions."[77] Ruben Cortina,[78] a senior official from Argentina deeply involved in Mercosur's labor legislation, articulated a similar point of view during the same meeting with the author: "The right to strike was very much in the regulatory history of the member states, a history that is shaped by intensive collective bargaining." Indeed, he added, this was a history in which the state had learned to work with, and even represent, the interests of labor. Hence, Cortina added, the "Ministries of Labor from the four member states themselves were very active from the very beginning of Mercosur in representing labor's interests."[79] They wanted to have a voice, he continued, and they managed to have one.

At the same time, trade unions pressured those officials to introduce labor-friendly principles into regional law. In October 1996, union leaders from the four member states gave life to the Coordinadora de Centrales Sindicales del Cono Sur: a "unified movement of power" fighting against the "neoliberal" mission of Mercosur (Calloni 1996). In one of the first shows of strength in December 1996, thousands of union members from all four member states clashed with Brazilian police in a major demonstration protesting Mercosur and asking that their respective leaders take labor issues into consideration. Those protests were paralleled by transportation workers from the four member states in a town on the

[75] In the case of Paraguay, trade unions "developed as never before in that country's history" (Bronstein 1995: 168–69).

[76] Argentina's Representative to the Comisión Sociolaboral del Mercosur (an entity created to oversee the implementation of the declaration throughout Mercosur) and also a member of Argentina's Ministerio de Trabajo, Empleo y Seguridad Social.

[77] Interview with the author, Buenos Aires, Argentina, August 2003.

[78] Coordinator of International Affairs at Argentina's Ministerio de Trabajo, Empleo y Seguridad Social and member of Mercosur's Subgrupo No. 10 (Work, Employment and Social Security) and of the Comisión Nacional (National Commission) for the implementation of Mercosur's Declaración Sociolaboral in Argentina.

[79] Interview with the author, Buenos Aires, Argentina, August 2003.

Brazil-Argentina border, by a paralyzing four-hour strike for workers' rights in Uruguay, and by other protesters in Paraguay demonstrating in front of the embassies of the member states (La Jornada 1996a). These activities followed an earlier demonstration in September in Argentina against Mercosur and the IMF. There, three hundred thousand workers asked their leaders to consider labor and other issues as they pushed forward with integration and reforms (La Jornada 1996b).

These were protests focused mostly on basic labor and social rights, however, and far less on more advanced matters, such as the issues faced by migrant workers. The question of whether migrant workers should be entitled to unemployment benefits was hardly entertained by labor organizers. It was totally ignored by Mercosur officials. This is easily understood when one considers the traditionally underdeveloped unemployment systems of the two largest member states. Contrary to reality in the EU, neither Argentina nor Brazil had well-developed (even if perhaps different) unemployment benefits programs for domestic workers in place at the time of integration. In Argentina's case, the state had successfully pursued full-employment policy approaches for decades prior to the 1990s (Cieza 1998). As a result, it had little experience, capability, and interest in dealing with supporting the unemployed in financial terms. Indeed, except for construction workers, there was no national unemployment benefit system in Argentina until 1991, with the exception of a brief period between October and December 1985 (Campbell 1991).[80] The program introduced in 1991 departed so much from the norm that only 4.5% of the country's unemployed claimed their benefits, and the Ministerio de Trabajo, Empleo y Seguridad Social planned for a publicity and outreach campaign (Campbell 1993). The state's traditional effort had instead focused on creating jobs and placing workers in the labor market. In the case of Brazil, the government had faced enormous levels of official unemployment and a related large number of workers (by some estimates, over 60% of the workforce) active in the informal economy. These conditions, coupled with limited funds and poor management of resources, made it very difficult for the state to build a well-funded and functioning national unemployment benefit program (Chiarelli 1976; De Oliveira and Beltraõ 2001: 101–2). Until the 1990s, the existing benefit programs helped only a fraction of salaried workers. In 1990, following the introduction of a new unemployment insurance scheme, a higher percentage of salaried workers was covered (De Oliveira and Beltraõ 2001: 102), though informal economy workers were again left excluded.

---

[80] This changed in 1991 with the introduction of a new labor law covering all workers except those in construction (who still retain their traditional set of benefits), domestic workers, and civil servants who lost their job because of an administrative reorganization (Campbell 1991).

All this made it very unlikely that Mercosur officials would grant workers unemployment benefits as they migrated from one member state to the next.[81] "Unemployment and benefits," noted senior administrator Ruben Cortina from Argentina's Ministerio de Trabajo, Empleo y Seguridad in his conversation with the author, "have not preoccupied the minds of regional planners." The recent financial crisis in Argentina, he continued, "has made all of us realize that the state has no institutions for supporting with financial help the unemployed." This may change over the next ten years or so, he added, but for the moment "there are no foundations upon which we can build a regional system."[82]

Events followed yet a different course in NAFTA. Recall that with the NAALC officials produced, as in Mercosur, an explicit recognition of the rights to strike and to form associations. Yet they adopted far more ambiguous language in the case of unemployment benefits for migrant workers, stating only in general terms that migrant workers should enjoy the same protection with regard to their working conditions as domestic workers. Here they proved more aggressive than Mercosur officials but more timid than their EU counterparts. What can explain this particular approach to labor rights?

Consider first the recognition of the rights to strike and associate. As was the case with Mercosur, all three NAFTA member states already granted workers those two rights in their national legal systems. In this sense, officials introduced nothing new in the NAALC other than asking member states to commit to enforcing existing national legislation.[83] In Canada, the rights to strike and form unions had been in place since the Public Service Staff Relations Act of 1967 and the Canada Labor Code of 1971 (Taylor 1997). A number of provincial-level legal texts also had parallel or more specific legislation. In Mexico, Article 123 of the Constitution of 1917 recognized the right to strike and form labor unions. In 1931, a federal labor law (Ley Federal de Trabajo) codified that right (Patroni 1998). In the United States, after a period of intense labor unrest, in 1935 the National Labor Relations Act (known as the Wagner Act because of its sponsor, Senator Robert Wagner of New York) recognized the rights to strike and form labor unions. Of course, important differences in scope

---

[81] Indeed, past efforts at some form of collaboration in this area have already failed. One example comes from the Asociación Latinóamericana de Libre Comerció in the 1960s. The founding Treaty of Montevideo provided for some form of coordination of social provisions for migrant workers. Yet, little was achieved, mostly as a result of the tremendous differences that existed among the major players in the region (Moles 1982: 165).

[82] Interview with the author, Buenos Aires, Argentina, August 2003. See note 78 for Cortina's full job title.

[83] The NAALC also allows organizations and other entities outside a given member state to monitor the implementation of national legislation (Phelps 2001: 24). Yet in this sense too, the NAALC works closely with existing national legislative regimes.

and application set those legal measures apart from each other.[84] But again, NAFTA officials did not seek a harmonization of differences but only a commitment to respect existing law.

Equally importantly, however, trade unions from the United States and Canada put enormous pressure on the NAFTA crafters to add a labor dimension to their texts, especially one that would prevent Mexican employers from enjoying cost advantages derived from illegal abuses of their workers. The words of United Auto Workers president Owen Bieber at a typical union meeting in Canada in the months preceding the approval of NAFTA are representative of the unions' position. As Bieber put it, "if NAFTA really was a free trade agreement, it would have a structure for correcting disparities in wages and working conditions" among the three member states (Fowlie 1993). Similar complaints came from the AFL-CIO and other unions in the United States (Hall 1993). High on the list of demands was that the Mexican government would take action to protect the legal rights of workers to strike and form unions. If workers in Mexico were denied those rights, the unions reasoned, they would be in a poor position to extract wage and other concessions from employers.[85] The NAALC was developed as a direct response to these pressures, and was indeed immediately used in a series of high-profile cases related to the right to strike and organize in Mexico.[86]

President Clinton in particular seems to have pushed for the NAALC as a way to address the concerns of the unions (Morton 1993). "It is widely agreed," wrote one observer at the time, "that the labor side agreement was included in NAFTA to provide then–U.S. President Bill Clinton with 'political cover' to support the deal and mollify his labor union constituency" (MacDonald 2003: 181). Clinton, wrote a second observer, "hopes to steer a middle ground. He supports the basic concept of NAFTA, but at the same time promises to negotiate side agreements that will mollify the critics" (Hall 1993). The NAALC, noted yet another observer, was "created to diminish NAFTA opposition and prevent the kind of labor atrocities that would give opponents of free trade broader recog-

---

[84] For a comparative analysis of the right to strike in the United States and Canada, especially as it applies to public sector employees, see McGuire (1987). On some of the limitations concerning Mexico, see Diebel (1993).

[85] Indeed, trade unions and leading politicians in the United States were eager to see that Mexico do more than ensure implementation of existing law and take steps to repeal a key restriction on strikes: that they be organized by a government-recognized union. On this very point Senator Richard Gephardt withdrew his support of NAFTA in 1993 (Deibel 1993).

[86] Examples abound. For a list of cases filed under the NAALC, see the Internet site of Human Rights Watch: http://www.hrw.org/reports/2001/nafta/nafta0401-05.htm#P772 _114554.

nition and support" (Phelps 2001: 24). Whether, in fact, the NAALC could win the support of skeptical unions became clear over time, as a number of organizations voiced their disappointment with Clinton and the president himself began criticizing the unions for their inflexibility (Bradsher 1993; Walker 1993).

It is in the context of union interests and politics that we can also understand the absence in NAALC of a direct affirmation of unemployment rights for migrant workers. As we already learned, NAALC was crafted above all to address concerns about wages and all matters associated with the workplace that influence costs of production (and thus the competitiveness of different enterprises and, ultimately, job security). Unions from the United States worried above all about regulatory practices in Mexico: poor working environments there translated into lower costs of production. Unions had far fewer concerns about the rights of workers who were not employed, especially migrant workers who might come into the United States to take jobs.

At the same time, unions did worry about the rights of migrant workers who were already employed in the United States. It is this worry that can explain the presence in Annex 1 of NAALC of a protection for migrant workers at the workplace—a clause that has indirect and only potential implications for unemployment rights.[87] Workers in the United States fretted about cheap and unregulated labor performed by illegal or legal Mexicans within the United States: this form of labor too represented a source of unwelcome competition. Eager to prevent employers from taking advantage of those workers, union leaders made sure that the governments of the United States (as well as Canada) and of the various states (and provinces of Canada) would apply their existing legislation to legal and, whenever appropriate, illegal workers. The resulting clause in NAALC was designed with those objectives in mind. Its implications for workers and their entitlement to unemployment benefits were largely unintended and in any case unclear. Thus, as one would expect, this aspect of the law remains seldom a topic of conversation or legal confrontation.[88]

---

[87] See, for instance, the analysis of the Commission for Labor Cooperation (2003) of the all-important agricultural sector.

[88] No case has so far concerned unemployment benefits, though there have been important cases on migrant workers and their rights. Of those, the most prominent is probably the Washington State Apples Case (Mexican NAO Case No. 9802). The petitioners alleged that the United States government failed to enforce the rights of migrant workers to organize and bargain collectively, and enjoy minimum labor standards, nondiscrimination in employment, job safety and health, workers' compensation, and migrant worker protections. To the uninformed but observant reader of the NAALC, the presence of any principle related to migrant workers must surely seem very surprising. NAFTA was designed to liberalize trade for goods, capital, and selected services, and not the movement of labor. When

Conclusion

There exist important differences in the specific character of regional law across RTAs. In the EU, officials have taken impressive steps to help women assert themselves at the workplace. The same has yet to take place in Mercosur or NAFTA. In those two RTAs, the world of working women remains defined and regulated at the national level. In the case of Mercosur, however, we see extensive intervention in the world of dairy products. Officials there have taken significant steps to standardize products and processes. Their counterparts in the EU and NAFTA have not taken a similar approach. In the case of the EU in particular, steps have been taken not to standardize many dairy products. Finally, in the case of workers' rights, we have learned that officials in all three RTAs have given workers an array of rights. Yet we saw important differences in what those rights actually entail. In NAFTA and Mercosur, the rights to strike and form unions are recognized at the regional level. In the EU, they are not. On the other hand, migrant workers in the EU enjoy more extensive rights than those in NAFTA and Mercosur, especially in the case of unemployment benefits.

We can account for these important differences among the three RTAs when we consider the national legal and power contexts upon which regional law is built. Women had made impressive gains in most EU member states in the 1960s and 1970s. EU officials, working under pressure from powerful women's groups, translated at the regional level principles already present in most of the member states. Women in the Mercosur region had not enjoyed much progress in their respective countries and, expectedly, lacked regional representation. Women in the NAFTA region certainly enjoyed more favorable legal histories. Yet groups in the United States and Mexico, in line with their historical position toward international trade issues, proved largely uninterested in shaping NAFTA.

In the case of dairy products, liberalization of the agricultural sector in the Mercosur member states during the 1980s and 1990s prepared companies for participation in the international economy. There was no history of protected denominations. With the arrival of Mercosur, officials and businesses alike were ready to create a single marketplace for dairy. EU and NAFTA officials could not do the same. In the EU, powerful dairy producers—after having made sure that many of their products would be protected from competition at the national level—mobilized with the help of government officials to ensure that Brussels would grant them regional-

---

the NAALC is properly understood as an instrument intended to assuage labor from the United States, however, the confusion should dissipate.

level protection. In NAFTA, while the policy environment in the United States and Mexico had been moving towards open trade, that of Canada had not. Canadian officials accordingly removed dairy products from the NAFTA negotiations.

Labor rights legislation in the three RTAs also reflects the legal and political realities in the member states. In the EU, the rights to strike and form unions were vehemently opposed by the British, who lacked national legislation on the matter. Those rights were quickly recognized in NAFTA and Mercosur: there, under pressure from unions, officials simply translated at the regional levels principles already in place in all of the member states. The same officials could not, by contrast, grant migrant workers unemployment benefits. In Mercosur, such an initiative would have departed from legal and administrative practices in Argentina and, to a lesser extent, Brazil. In NAFTA, where labor movement is largely restricted for fear of massive migration from Mexico into the United States, the topic was hardly relevant. It became an important issue in the EU, however, where all the member states had well-established but also quite different systems for dealing with unemployment and migrants. The EU response was, cleverly, not to harmonize those differences but simply to recognize, at the regional level, that migrant workers have rights to benefits and then to ensure the coordination of national programs.

We conclude, then, that regional law varies across RTAs in ways that ensure continuity with existing realities on the ground. If accurate, this observation raises some important questions. We wonder about change in each RTA: do RTAs always provide some degree of continuity and is this continuity tantamount to the absence of change? Questions arise as well about other potential explanatory variables, such as the level of economic and social development in the three RTAs. We will consider these and other questions in chapter 6. We continue now with our comparative examination of the EU, Mercosur, and NAFTA by moving away from the realm of law and investigating how societal organizations have responded to integration.

Chapter 5

SOCIETAL ADJUSTMENTS TO INTEGRATION

WE HAVE SEEN that regional law varies significantly across the EU, Mercosur, and NAFTA in ways that reflect local legal and power contexts. Yet law represents only one dimension of difference across RTAs. As market building progresses, additional transformations shape the physiognomy of each region in unique fashion. This chapter explores a second dimension of difference among RTAs: how organizations—specifically interest groups, businesses, and state administrations—have responded to regional integration. Chapter 4 analyzed laws in the areas of women's rights, dairy products, and labor rights. This chapter focuses on the evolution of three sets of organizations active in those areas: women's interest groups, dairy companies, and state administrative units dedicated to the promotion of labor rights.

We will observe important differences across the three RTAs. In the EU, impressive regional-level lobbying groups dedicated to working women flourished during the 1980s and 1990s. In Mercosur and NAFTA no equivalent regional groups have developed. In Mercosur alone, in turn, major dairy companies have acquired a regional profile. In all three RTAs, national administrative units have developed regional structures and programs dedicated to labor rights. Yet the specific nature of those structures and programs varies across RTAs. These differences in the evolution of organizations require an explanation. Our attention turns again to institutional and political variables. As with regional law, national legal and power contexts have shaped organizational developments, preparing some organizations for expansion but not others. At the same time, the very presence of regional law itself regulating certain realms of social life has stimulated the rise of regional organizations, while its absence has deprived organizations of a powerful stimulus. We note a certain amount of coherence, therefore, in the legal and organizational development of any given RTA.

THE EVOLUTION OF WOMEN'S GROUPS

During the 1980s and 1990s, women in the EU established a number of impressive regional groups: organizations with membership bases from across the member states whose primary mission is to influence the course of EU activities and integration. In Mercosur and NAFTA, by contrast, women's groups have remained fundamentally national in character. In this section, I examine and account for these divergent developments. I relied on a variety of sources to collect the necessary data: official Internet sites, interviews with group officials, analysis of groups' programs and reports, and various secondary reports and other types of texts.

Most, if not all, organizations representing women's interests across Europe in the 1960s and 1970s were national in character. They had purely national membership bases and their objectives focused almost exclusively on the advancement of women's positions in their national contexts. These, as seen in chapter 4, were strong groups, capable of scoring impressive legal victories in their respective member states and lobbying for EU law. By the 1980s and 1990s, the organizational landscape had changed. A number of transnational groups emerged. These recruited their members from several EU member states, including both individuals and national groups. They also shared, as their main objective, the advancement of women at the European, rather than national, level.

Table 5.1 lists some of the most important European women's interest groups established in this important period, identifying their year of birth, membership bases, and agendas. As we examine these groups, one fact becomes clear: the mission—indeed raison d'être—of many of these groups has been to influence the development of EU law on women as well as ensure the implementation of favorable legislation. EU law thus lies at the very core of these groups' existence and, without such law, it is difficult to imagine how these groups might have developed. As an expert put it, EU law on women and the "transnational European women's lobby" live in a close symbiotic relationship, each influencing the other in fundamental ways (Mazey 1998: 142, 1995: 592, 2000).

The most prominent European group is the European Women's Lobby (EWL). Established in 1990, the EWL has over three thousand national and EU-wide member organizations, and close links with national women's groups that are not formal members (European Women's Lobby 2000: 14; Sperling and Bretherton 1996; Mazey 1998). Within a few years of its founding, it represented over one hundred million individuals. Board members come from every EU member state, and the presidency itself rotates as women from different nationalities assume leadership.

The EWL centers most of its efforts on shaping EU law. In the words of Cécile Greboval, policy coordinator for the group, the organization "lives in a close symbiotic relationship with EU law . . . since the legislative and policy agenda of the EU shape directly what we do."[1] Above all, the EWL's objective is to pressure EU officials to produce laws that can help European women improve their positions and power in society: to

---

[1] Interview with the author, Brussels, Belgium, April 2004.

TABLE 5.1
Major European-Level Women's Interest Groups

Group & Year of Birth	Membership Base	Program
European Women's Lobby (EWL), 1990	3,000 national and EU-wide groups	Lobby and work with the EU to promote equality, rights
	Individuals who are members of national groups	Coordinate activities of national and European women's groups
	Dutch President, French and Portuguese Vice Presidents	Ensure implementation of EU gender laws
	Board members from every member state	
European Women Lawyers Association (EWLA), 2000	National women lawyers' associations	Improve public understanding of EU laws on women
	Individual lawyers from member states	Defend women's interests in the EU
	25 board members: one from each member state	Strengthen links and understanding among female lawyers in the EU
European Institute of Women's Health (EIWH), 1996	Individuals from member states	Promote health and wellbeing of women as a priority for the European Commission
	Health care professionals from member states	Research on women's health issues on a European level

	Women's interest groups	Promote equality in health care treatment and options for women in the EU
	Patient organizations	Present recommendation to European Parliament
European Federation of Women Working in the Home (FEFAF), 1983	Organizations from EU member states and Switzerland	Lobby EU Parliament and Commission to recognize worth of domestic work
		Ease transition from domestic work to workplace for European women
Business and Professional Women–Europe (BPWE), 1985	Individuals and groups from the EU but also Switzerland, Iceland and other countries	Equal opportunity and status for women in economic, civil, and political life
	Officers from all EU countries	Promote the number of women in decision-making positions

Note: Internet addresses of these groups are as follows: EWL: www.womenlobby.org; EWLA: www.ewla.org; EIWH: www.eurohealth.ie; FEFAF: www.fefaf.org; BPWE: www.bpw-europe.org.

"promote equality between women and men and to ensure that gender equality and women's rights are taken into consideration" in all of the EU's policies (European Women's Lobby 2000: 2). In practical terms, the EWL conducts a variety of activities. Based in Brussels, it interacts regularly with the European Commission, which supports much of its budget, sends legislative proposals to the group for expert commentary and opinion, and relies on the EWL for data and figures (Mazey 1995: 605; European Report 2004). The EWL also watches quite closely, and then publicly supports or criticizes, most EU activities related to women, such as fund allocation, educational initiatives, enforcement programs, and so on. In 1995, for instance, it criticized in the strongest possible terms the decision taken by the EU's Social Affairs Council to allocate only ECU 30 million to the program for equal opportunities between men and women for the period 1996–2000 (European Report 1995).

The EWL has also direct access to the European Parliament, enjoying meetings with legislators and their staff, and regular exchanges through electronic mail and other means (European Report 1998). "Just this morning," explained Cécile Greboval to the author, "I was working on a reply to a parliamentarian interested in our opinion about a policy idea; this happens all the time. . . . They know we have much technical knowledge and experience." A primary objective of the group has been to increase the number of women working in the parliament. To that end, it has created and made available to its members and anyone else interested memos, facts, figures, and lobbying material to pressure leaders of various European parties to recruit more women. It has also directly lobbied citizens to vote for women's candidates by sponsoring advertisements, going on road trips, and holding public meetings across Europe. Cécile Greboval emphasized to the author the educational mission of the EWL: "We play a role in explaining to the public what's happening at the EU level. . . . No one else does that."

In 1994, for instance, "a white and purple double decker bus, complete with [a] woman bus driver, left London for a three week tour of England, Scotland and Wales stopping off in market places and supermarkets to persuade women to use their votes" (McEvoy 1994). Most recently, with the arrival of ten new member states, the EWL has mobilized its base to pressure the new member states to appoint women to work in the European Commission. Other initiatives have included drafting proposals for revising the Maastricht Treaty, lobbying officials working on the new European constitution, the release of official declarations and recommendations evaluating existing legislative proposals and demanding new policies, and much more (Liebert 1999: 226–27).[2]

___

[2] See Strid (2003: 16–19) for a recent overview of the EWL's activities.

The European Women Lawyers Association (EWLA) is a second major group. Born in 2000, it links thousands of female lawyers across member states. Its constitution spells out its membership requirements: "Any person who is a qualified woman lawyer according to customs and practice of the member state where the relevant woman has her principal residence, or has studied law, or is a student of law, in one of the EU member states is eligible for membership." Organizations active in the legal field can also become members: "Any association of women with legal capacity in legal professions with its principal seat in one of the EU member states is eligible for membership" (Article 4.1).[3] The organization boasts several thousand members spread out across the EU. Its administrative leadership is composed of four women from as many member states: Germany, Greece, Spain, and Belgium. It also includes twenty-five members, each responsible for (and coming from) one of the member states.

More exclusively focused on law than the EWL, the EWLA has two related goals. The first is "to improve the understanding of European legislation in relation to equal opportunities, with particular reference to women" (European Women Lawyers Association 2002: 1). Armed with such an understanding, the EWLA then develops viewpoints and recommendations on law that are delivered to EU institutions and other public forums. The second objective is to foster a network of female EU lawyers across the member states (2). To attain those two objectives, the association sponsors conferences, working groups, publications, and numerous other events. Like the EWL, the EWLA has established a strong presence in EU policymaking bodies. Its representatives have participated in meetings of committees of the European Parliament and the European Commission. In February 2003, for instance, the EWLA participated in a hearing of the European Parliament on new EU legislation on equal treatment. Throughout 2002 and 2003, the association participated in Commission-sponsored events related to gender, EU law, and the crafting of the EU constitution.[4]

A number of additional groups established themselves in the EU space in the 1990s and 1980s. Table 5.1 identifies three rather different ones: the European Institute of Women's Health (EIWH), the European Federation of Women Working in the Home (FEFAF), and Business and Professional Women–Europe (BPWE). All three groups share a desire, on the

---

[3] Individuals and associations not in the EU but in Europe can apply for associate membership only and must be approved by the board (Article 4.2)

[4] See, for instance, the participation of Sophia Spiliotopoulos, EWLA Vice-President, at the Commission's Conference on Gender Equality and the Future of Europe, held on March 4, 2003, in Brussels (Rapid 2003).

part of European women, to push the EU to legislate and take initiatives in areas beyond the strict confines of the workplace. The EIWH, born in 1996, identifies its mission as "working to make the health and well being of women a priority for the European Commission and Member States of the European Union" (http://www.eurohealth.ie/). Based in Dublin, it is supported by individuals from the member states as well as patient and other types of organizations. It promotes research on women's health issues and lobbies the EU decision-making bodies. The FEFAF, established in 1983, wants the EU institutions to recognize domestic work as regular employment and grant associated benefits and rights. Its membership is again composed of European Union members, though Swiss individuals and groups participate. The BPWE, born in 1985 as the regional branch of the International Federation of Professional and Business Women, aims for the empowerment of women and their participation in decision-making forums related to areas ranging from the environment to health and agriculture. To obtain those ends, the BPWE has established permanent links with the EWL and regularly lobbies the European Commission.

Table 5.1 is by no means comprehensive: numerous other groups flourished in the European space. By some counts, a total of twenty-one new groups were founded in the late 1980s and 1990s (Strid 2003: 15). We should mention here a set of three closely related organizations. In reaction to legislative activism in the EU, the Women's European Action Group spent considerable energy in the 1980s studying "how the European institutions work and what they did (or didn't do) for women" (15). The group would later become the Center for Research on European Women, a nonprofit research organization that worked regularly with the Commission to develop legislative proposals (Strid 2003: 15; Cichowski 2003). The center would in turn give birth to the European Network of Women, with funding from the Commission itself. The network has sought to synthesize a coherent vision and policy agenda from various feminist organizations spread throughout Europe, though scarcity of financial resources and access points to the EU limited its effectiveness (Strid 2003: 16).

Women have responded to EU integration by establishing organizations both in civil society and *inside* the walls of the EU itself. Once again, a dominant stimulant and focus of attention has been EU law. The Equal Opportunity Unit was set up inside the Commission in 1976, more specifically as a part of Directorate General V (Employment, Industrial Relations, and Social Affairs). The unit created nine European Networks of Experts, each comprising between twelve and twenty-four people from the member states and charged with monitoring the impact of legislation and/or collecting data to drive further legislation and administrative programs. One such network is the Expert Network on the Application of the Equality Directives, made up of lawyers, and a second is the Network on the Position of Women in the Labor Market, made up of economists (Mazey 1995: 604). In 1981, the Advisory Committee on Equal Opportunity was created, a body similarly reliant on a rich network of women across Europe. In the European Parliament we find instead the Standing Committee for Women's Rights, established in 1984. It has lobbied for women's causes, held public hearings on women's issues, and initiated parliamentary debates on a variety of issues such as sexual harassment, contraception, prostitution, and so on (Mazey 1995: 605).

This impressive regional mobilization on the part of European women has had no parallels in NAFTA. To this date, in North America there simply does not exist a truly transnational organization dedicated exclusively to the representation of women at the NAFTA level. This is so regardless of whether we consider organizations in the civil society space or inside NAFTA structures. There was one exception: MM, the group responsible for organizing the 1992 Tri-national Working Women's Conference on Free Trade and Continental Integration discussed in chapter 4. The group ceased to operate in the mid-1990s, however, because of lack of funding. At first a Mexican organization founded in the 1980s, it became over the years a regional organization with women members from Mexico, the United States, and Canada, a focus on NAFTA, and offices in Mexico City, San Antonio (Texas), and Toronto.

In NAFTA, all other activism has taken place within the confines of national-level groups.[5] These are organizations with purely national membership bases and leadership that have responded to economic integration with a partial broadening of their agendas and, in some cases, some collaboration with like-minded groups across frontiers. Perhaps the most relevant group is the Coalition for Women's Economic Development and Global Equality (EDGE), which operates in the United States—the country where women's groups were the most indifferent to the question of NAFTA. The organization was born in 1998 and boasts a leadership that comes only from the United States. The group's objectives are to influence the trade and investment policies of the United States government and to educate the citizens of that country about gender and trade. As one observer put it, EDGE was born "precisely to fill a number of critical gaps in US activism around gender and international economic issues that were evident during the debate over NAFTA" (Liebowitz 2002: 187). In that spirit, in November 2003 the group announced the completion of a

---

[5] The exceptions are international organizations with members from countries across the globe dedicated to the advancement of women in a wide variety of settings, including NAFTA. The Women's Environment and Development Organization, once a large organization focused mostly on activities related to politics and the United Nations, is an example (Liebowitz 2002: 186). See http://www.wedo.org/about/about.htm.

"groundbreaking case study" on the impact of NAFTA on Mexican women farmers.[6]

In that study, EDGE was bitterly critical of NAFTA, linking the agreement to a variety of adverse developments for women. "With this study," the authors wrote, "for the first time there is a quantifiable, accurate picture" of the differential impact that NAFTA has had "on men versus women" (White, Salas, and Gammage 2003: iii). For example, they noted that poverty increased by 50% in female-headed households since the implementation of NAFTA; the trade agreement, they continued, eliminated reliable and safe jobs, and instead created jobs in the informal sector or, if in the formal sector, in poorly paid enterprises, such as the maquiladoras. EDGE called for the Mexican government to resurrect its protection programs for small farmers and develop training programs for displaced workers.[7]

NAC is a second important organization. As discussed in chapter 4 in the analysis of the position of women's groups in relation to NAFTA's passage, the group is by far the most influential representative of women's interests in Canada, though it has recently run into serious financial difficulties (Macdonald 2002: 159; Carlyle 2002). With around seven hundred member groups to date, the group experienced a major transition from the 1970s, when it was mostly focused on domestic issues. After joining the struggle against CUSFTA in the 1980s and NAFTA's passage in the early 1990s, NAC became the most important women's group in Canada to monitor progress at the NAFTA level, educate citizens, sponsor reports, and lobby (Cohen et al. 2002).[8] Its 2001–2002 Priority Campaign, for instance, was dedicated to understanding how women were affected by transnational trade, both in NAFTA and beyond. From the early 1990s on, the group has also led working groups, conferences, and meetings with NAFTA and international trade at the center of its attention (Gabriel and Macdonald 1994: 549–54).

Additional, but less noteworthy, examples come from Mexico, where women have relied on existing labor and other organizations to express their concerns about economic integration. Women have continued their participation in RMALC, a major coalition against NAFTA composed of unions, peasant organizations, indigenous groups, environmentalists, and a number of women's organizations (MacDonald 2003: 185). The

[6] For details on the study, see: http://www.womensedge.org/pages/aboutus/detailpage.jsp?id=177.
[7] Another but less relevant group from the United States is the Coalition of Labor Union Women, operating within the AFL-CIO. With twenty thousand members from sixty unions, it has included NAFTA as a major point of study and protest.
[8] Thus, in recognition of their position against NAFTA and free trade, the Solidarity Network, the new name of Action Canada Network (Canada's most relevant antitrade group), gave financial support to the NAC (Banks 2000).

RMALC has given some voice to women's issues. Women have also been fairly successful in joining the the Ejército Zapatista de Liberación Nacional (Zapatista National Liberation Army). According to observers, "Indian women in dozens of communities have produced a code of women's rights, which was adopted unanimously by the EZLN leadership." Their demands have included the right to work and receive a just salary, and have represented "perhaps the most visible and successful of the challenges to the NAFTA" in the country (Macdonald 2002: 557).

These and other national groups have engaged in important forms of transnational but also ad hoc cooperation. Scholars have described with excitement (and perhaps a bit of optimism) these changes. Gabriel and Macdonald, for instance, state:

> [NAFTA] has engendered new forms of cooperation among women. Across the continent, women, drawing on their particular experiences, have challenged the terms of the agreement. Their mobilisation is premised on the fact that in all three countries women will pay a disproportionate share of greater economic insecurity. (1994: 535)

In a similar vein, Domínguez describes the arrival of "transnational advocacy networks," "cooperation," and "cross-border connections" in response to NAFTA, which has "provoked" reactions no one could have expected (2002: 217, 218). Liebowitz also points to increasing "cross-border collaboration" and "transnational organising around gender and NAFTA" (2002: 175, 176). She notes "a shift in women's organizing in the USA between the period of the NAFTA debate (1990–1993) and the period after NAFTA's inception in 1994" (175). The shift is one towards engagement at the international level.

Except for the now defunct MM, however, transnational activism has so far taken the form of international meetings, joint statements, coordinated actions, and exchanges of information and plans, rather than the establishment of stable and permanent regional organizations. Both NAC and EDGE, for instance, have actively sought international links with women from across North America and beyond. The most interesting examples, though, involve different organizations. One case is the long-term cooperation between the Canadian Auto Workers and the Red de Mujeres Sindicalistas de México (Network of Female Trade Unionists of Mexico) (Domínguez 2002: 230). "Armed with weapons furnished by the cooperation with CAW, the RMSM is undertaking a new transnational advocacy campaign on sexual harassment and discrimination in the workplace, which is being 'framed' as 'an issue' in relation to regional integration" (232). A second example can be seen at the border between Mexico and the United States, where we find the Comité Fronterizo de Obreras (Border Committee of Women Workers), an organization dedicated to women working in the maquiladoras. The committee was from the start a product of the American Friends Service Committee, and now has contacts with Canadian unions and in the United States with three powerful unions: the United Steelworkers of America, the United Auto Workers, and the United Electrical Workers (227).

Yet a third example involves unprecedented networking among businesswomen at the helm of small and medium enterprises in the United States and Canada. Eager to take advantage of the opportunities created by free trade, three hundred of these women met at the first-ever Canada-U.S.A. Businesswomen's Trade Summit in Toronto in May 1999 (Hanson 1999). Sponsored by the governments of the two countries and large firms from the private sector, the event had as its primary objective "to develop and grow existing cross-border business so as to capture a larger percentage of [the] lucrative export market" (Canada Newswire 1999). Seminars from representatives of the legal, financial, and government sectors offered attendees crucial information on cross-border trade. Present were high-level government officials, such as Canada's Minister of International Trade and the Secretary of Commerce of the United States. The meeting culminated with the signing of a Joint Cooperative Declaration aimed at promoting cross-border trade by women-led businesses.

As in NAFTA, women in Mercosur have not established truly regional representative associations. We note only two regional-level organizations. Established as an independent organization in Buenos Aires in 1995, the Foro de Mujeres del Mercosur (FMM) quickly opened official chapters in all four of the member states. The primary objective of the FMM has been, as Laura Velázquez—president of the forum in 1999—put it, to "make space" for 51% of the population of the region (Spanish Newswire Services 1999c). The mission of the group, then, is to strengthen and deepen the leadership of women in the region (INTAL 1998: 32).[9] In pursuit of these objectives, the FMM has held a number of meetings and programs in the four member states throughout the years on a wide array of topics, such as democratic participation, work, women's rights, law, and social issues, as well as women in entrepreneurial positions and business. Its ninth meeting, for instance, was held in August 2003 in Montevideo and had representatives from the four member states, nongovernmental organizations active in gender issues, and professional women's organizations, as well as diplomats. Interestingly, the group has also sought to establish links with other extraregional entities, as happened in 1999 when it participated in the meeting of the Free Trade Areas of the Americas in Toronto or in 2003 when it invited representatives from the EU to participate in its meeting.

---

[9] For information on the FMM, its mission, composition, and activities through the years, see the organization's website: http://www.forodemujeres.org.ar/.

The FMM interacts with a second regional organization: the Reunión Especializada de la Mujer (REM, Specialized Women's Group). The REM is a body created in 1998 by Mercosur officials (Resolution 20/98) partly in response to pressure from the FMM itself and other organizations, such as the United Nations Development Fund for Women (Espino 2000). It is composed of representative of all the member states. It is supported by, and works closely with, national governmental bodies in each country. These include the Subsecretaría de la Mujer in the Ministerio de Relaciones Exteriores (Subsecretariat for Women, External Relations Ministry) in Argentina, the Conselho Nacional dos Direitos da Mulher in Brazil, the Secretaria de la Mujer (Women's Secretariat) in Paraguay, and the Instituto Nacional de la Familia y de la Mujer in Uruguay. The REM is also in regular contact with national trade unions and workers' organizations (Ulshoefer 1998).

The REM's mission has been to "analyze the situation of women, in light of national legislative regimes in the member states on equality and opportunities, with the objective of contributing to the social, economic and cultural developments of the communities of Mercosur's member states" (Article 1 of Resolution 20/98). In its position, the REM has offered the Grupo Mercado Común and the Consejo del Mercado Común a gender prospective as it produces laws that affect women directly.[10] It has also encouraged the analysis of women's problems, the advancement of equality, and the promotion of women in decision-making organs. Yet we should note that the REM has had limited success. Assessor Beatriz Etchechury Mazza from Uruguay's Instituto Nacional de la Familia y de la Mujer and an active participant in REM described the organization in an interview as "having one major problem: it has no strategy or capacity to influence Mercosur's key decision makers."[11]

Though interesting, then, the FMM and the REM are the only two truly regional women's organizations in the Mercosur space.[12] National groups, we should add, have largely ignored the question of regional integration, preferring instead to solidify their position in society by either focusing on purely domestic issues (such as domestic violence or representation in local political processes) or women's rights on the global level. In Brazil, for instance, the Centro Feminista de Estudos e Assessoria—one of the

[10] The REM is housed inside the Foro de Consulta y Concertación Política (Consultation and Political Coordination Forum), a body within the Consejo del Mercado Común.

[11] Interview with the author, Montevideo, Uruguay, August 2003. See chap. 4, n. 25 for Etchecurry Mazza's full job title.

[12] The Articulación Feminista Mercosur (Mercosur Feminist Articulation) appears to be a third regional group for women within Mercosur. Its purported mission is to infuse Mercosur's decision-making processes with a feminist perspective, and to do so in part by interacting with the REM. Very little data exists, however, about the group or its activities.

most important feminist organizations in the country—retains a remarkably national agenda.[13] Similarly, the Movimento de Mulheres Trabal-
hadoras Rurais (Rural Working Women Movement), born in 1989—a
major rural women's movement—has focused its efforts with much success on domestic issues related to work and other areas (Stephen 1997:
210–19). Conversely, the Atriculacão das Mulheres Brasileiras (Brazilian
Women's Voice) was created in the early 1990s to coordinate the work of
feminist organizations all over the country in preparation for the 1995
Beijing Women's Conference (Htun 2002: 736), while the Comisión Nacional de Mujeres de Seguimiento de los Compromisos de Pekin (National
Women's Commission for Monitoring the Promises of the Beijing Conference) was instead set up in Uruguay to monitor progress since that conference (Spanish Newswire Services 1999d).[14]

We can thus easily concur with UNESCO observers in their analysis of
organizational change and women in Mercosur. "It needs to be asked
whether the Mercosur process is encouraging the creation of a women's
movement that is regional in nature" (Jelin et al. 1998: 9). The answer is
clearly "no": by and large, the process of integration in the area has not
generated a concomitant transnational organization of women. As in
NAFTA, women have retained mostly national organizations for interest
representation. Active in domestic groups, they have sought some collaboration with their counterparts across national borders. These efforts,
however, have not generated regional organizations dedicated to representing women at the NAFTA or Mercosur levels.

What can explain the absence of regional women's groups in either
NAFTA or Mercosur? In both regions, the position and interests of national women's groups across the member states played a crucial role in
shaping their responses to integration. We learned in chapter 4 how
starkly different ideologies and perspectives on regional integration set
women apart in the NAFTA region. Women from Canada have had both
the ability and interest to react to NAFTA, partly in response to their experience of CUSFTA (Gabriel and Macdonald 1994: 548). Women from
the United States have had the resources to react but have thus far shown
little interest in "engaging seriously with issues related to international
political economy" (Macdonald 2002: 152). Mexican women, on the
other hand, have remained weak players in their political system and in

---

[13] See http://www.cfemea.org.br/ for an overview of the group's mandate.

[14] We should mention that government representatives have also begun working together
on women's issues in Mercosur, but their work is in its exploratory phases. For instance, see
the 2002 statement of the Secretary of State for the Conselho Nacional dos Direitos da Mulher of Brazil at a meeting with her colleagues from the other member states: "We want to
discuss the participation of women in the political, financial, and professional arenas in the
Mercosur member states" (Spanish Newswire Services 2002).

any event have viewed NAFTA with rather ambivalent eyes. These contrasts have made it quite unlikely that women across NAFTA would seek permanent forms of transnational organizing. As Gabriel and Macdonald put it:

> There can be no axiomatic unity between groups of women. . . . The politics of location and the contradiction between privilege and non-privilege finds expression in the varying nature of women's employment in Canada and Mexico, and women's experiences of economic crisis. These differing experiences have significant implications for feminist mobilisation and cross cultural alliances. (1994: 539–40)

In a different passage, Macdonald reasoned that "the nature of the women's movements in the three countries *foreclosed* the possibilities of greater contestation of the form of economic liberalization at . . . the transnational levels (2002: 152, italics added). Hoping for increased "transborder cooperation among women," she then warned, is simply "unwise" (152). An alignment of needs and priorities of women across the region is needed. At the moment, most indications are that such an alignment is far from taking place.

Women in the Mercosur member states have certainly shared more similar experiences. What they have missed is power. In chapter 4, we explored their limited access to domestic and regional legislative and policy processes. By the time of Mercosur's arrival, the same women were still very much in the process of establishing themselves as national players, with the result that most of their attention focused on domestic considerations rather than Mercosur. The establishment of strong national groups remained throughout the 1990s a distant objective. Beatriz Etchechury Mazza—from Uruguay's Ministerio de Educación y Cultura—dismissed the possibility of any major change in the near future. "Women in the Mercosur countries," she said, "are decades behind their European counterparts. . . . It will take time and a lot of work for us to become strong players in our societies. Perhaps then we will be able to make a difference in the Mercosur arena."[15]

Women remain also separated by the different challenges shaping their agendas at home. In Uruguay, women have enjoyed a fair amount of equality in education levels, employment, and the family, but not in politics or law. In Brazil, the feminist movement has had strong rural and work components, though women there too have little voice in the state power structures. Women from Argentina and Paraguay have focused more on access to government and on law. In Paraguay, moreover, do-

---

[15] Interview with the author, Montevideo, Uruguay, August 2003. See chap. 4, n. 25 for Etchecurry Mazza's full job title.

mestic labor and the position of women in the family have been a top priority. These differences, explains Beatriz Etchechury Mazza, have limited how much representatives of women's interests could mobilize. Thus, Maricela Viera—active in the Mercosur unit of the Ministerio de Trabajo y Seguridad Social[16]—explained that "the dialogue continues, but we face different problems in our countries, and this colors how we view Mercosur . . . in terms of priorities and objectives."[17]

A rich system of regional law could have possibly provided the stimulus for regional organization in both NAFTA and Mercosur. As with the EU, it might have offered a tangible, realistic target that could have fueled, granted legitimacy, and given meaning to collective mobilization. It is difficult to imagine what the actual impact might have been, in part because the very institutional conditions that produced regional law in Europe (rich national legislative precedents, and strong and interested networks of women) are not present in South America. Yet we can consider how regional law has prompted other types of organizations in the two RTAs to become regional players. In North America, the NAALC and NAAEC have given labor and environmental groups ground for regional mobilization. As Domínguez writes:

> International labour and environmental activism existed long before NAFTA, particularly in the US-Mexico border area, where maquiladora production was the focus of this activism. But NAFTA "framed" this activism, giving different organizations more basis for organizing across borders. Moreover, NAFTA provided these organizations with an institutional framework in which to direct their demands. The NAFTA side agreements on labor and the environment, at least in theory, give grassroots actors (individuals and organizations) a mechanism for articulating their complaints under the terms of the treaty. (2002: 225)

Nascent labor and environmental organizations in NAFTA have formed. The filing of labor violation claims, for instance, noted an observer in the 1990s, "has helped Mexican unions forge stronger ties with their North American counterparts" (Donnelly 1998); these "alliances," noted a Mexican labor activist, are "something new, something interesting" (quoted in Donnelly 1998). Indeed, 1998 was the first year that a labor leader from the United States (AFL-CIO President John Sweeney) met and worked with representatives from a Mexican union that was independent from the government (the Union Nacional de Trabajadores, or the National Workers' Union) (Donnelly 1998). In the case of the environment, an ex-

---

[16] Coordinator for the Secretaría del Area Mercosur (Secretariat for Mercosur) in Uruguay's Ministerio de Trabajo y Seguridad Social.

[17] Interview with the author, Montevideo, Uruguay, July 2003.

ample is the Green Parties of North America—an effort to increase co-operation among the green parties of the three member states.[18] Similarly, recall in South America the establishment in October 1996 of the Coordinadora de Centrales Sindicales del Cono Sur. This was described as an organization "without precedents in the history of the region," which has brought together in a formal setting union leaders from all four of Mercosur's member states to demand the recognition of additional labor issues in the direction of Mercosur policies (Calloni 1996; Agence Presse 2003c).[19] In contrast to events in the areas of the environment or labor, women in both NAFTA and Mercosur have had no tangible declarations, laws, or texts that would provide them with a common language and targets.

THE EVOLUTION OF DAIRY COMPANIES

The 1990s brought spectacular changes to the dairy industry in the Mercosur member states. The major dairy companies underwent an unprecedented international expansion in their productive infrastructures beyond national boundaries. The expansion has had no parallel in Europe or North America, where many dairy companies have kept their national character. In this section, we consider the divergent evolution of the five largest dairy companies in each of the major dairy-producing countries in the three RTAs:[20] Argentina and Brazil for Mercosur; Germany, Great Britain, and France for the EU; and Canada, the United States, and Mexico for NAFTA. I collected data on plant location by analyzing company annual reports, industry reports, and media articles, and by corresponding with or talking to a large number of company officials.[21] I offer again a political-institutional explanation for the course of events. The neoliberal agricultural policies of the Mercosur member states in the 1980s and 1990s, and the rich standardizing body of Mercosur laws stimulated the expansion of dairy companies in the region. Prolonged protectionism and minimalism in the EU and NAFTA, on the other hand, had the opposite effect.

---

[18] The effort is part of a global initiative to bring parties in certain regions together. It is coordinated by Global Greens.

[19] In the context of that organization, we should note, women have been able to have some voice (Espino 2000: 21).

[20] The size of a company is calculated in terms of revenues. For companies involved in more than dairy products, only revenues coming from dairy products were taken into consideration.

[21] Note that plants located beyond national boundaries were not considered part of a company's transnational network if 95% or more of their products are imported for domestic consumption.

Let us consider events in Mercosur first. Until the early 1990s, the major dairy companies in Mercosur had only national production infrastructures. By 2001, *eight of the ten* most important companies in the region had established plants beyond domestic borders. Consider Argentina first. By 2003, all of Argentina's five largest producers possessed plants in Brazil, their major export market. In 1990, only one (Nestlé) did. Expansion was rapid. In 2001, Sancor—Argentina's largest dairy company—signed an agreement with Mococa of Brazil to have branded products produced directly in Brazil. In 1998, Mastellano (Argentina's second largest firm) bought Leitesol of Brazil, a powdered milk facility to be used for the breakdown of large powdered milk shipments, packaging, and labeling of Mastellone products.[22] And in 1998 Milkaut (Argentina's fourth largest dairy company) bought Ivoti in Rio Grande del Sul (Brazil) to produce milk products there. Danone (today the country's third largest dairy producer) established its production capacity in Argentina in 1997, after being in Brazil since 1970. This rapid, impressive transformation of the Argentine dairy companies did not go unnoticed. "In addition to new [domestic] investment geared to the sub-regional [Mercosur] market," wrote two observers, "the leading companies are also committed to *direct* investment and the creation of alliances in order to secure greater presence in the Brazilian market for end products" (Nofal and Wilkinson 1999b: 152, emphasis added).

Very similar changes have taken place in Brazil. By 2003, three of Brazil's five largest dairy companies had manufacturing operations in Argentina. Two of the three expanded their operations into Argentina in the 1990s. Parmalat, in Brazil since 1977, entered Argentina in 1992 with the purchase of La Vascongada.[23] It then established plants in Uruguay in 1992 and Paraguay in 1994. Danone, as already noted, expanded into Argentina in 1997 after being in Brazil since 1970. Table 5.2 captures the transnational character of the largest dairy companies in Argentina and Brazil as of 2002.

We should add that the biggest company in Uruguay has hinted at expanding in Brazil. Conaprole accounts for 80% of milk processing in the country, 85% of the country's dairy exports, and is one of the most important dairy companies in South America (Nofal and Wilkinson 1999b: 152). In the late 1990s, the company acquired 85% ownership of Leben, a major distributor in Rio Grande do Sul. Leben owns pastures. This positions Conaprole for a direct presence in the country. In 1999, there were

---

[22] Data according to a Mastellone official, telephone interview with the author, July 2002.

[23] Thus making Parmalat the sixth largest company in Argentina by 2000, with revenues of US$200 million.

TABLE 5.2
Major Dairy Companies in Mercosur

	Revenues in US$ (millions)	Plants in Home Country (2002)	Plants in Other Mercosur Countries (2002)
ARGENTINA			
Sancor	870 (2000)	18[b]	1[d] (Brazil)
Mastellone/La Serenísima	700 (2000)	6	1[d] (Brazil)
Danone–Argentina	288 (2000)[c]	1[e]	2[e] (Brazil)
Milkaut	240 (1999)	17[d]	1[d] (Brazil)
Nestlé–Argentina	n.a.	5[b,e]	10[b,e] (Brazil)
BRAZIL			
Nestlé–Brazil	n.a.	10[b,e]	5[b,e] (Argentina)
Parmalat–Brazil	963 (2000)[d]	17[b]	20[b] (8 Argentina, 12 Paraguay and Uruguay)
Itambé	550 (1996)[a]	14[e]	0[b,e]
Danone–Brazil	179 (2000)[c]	2[e]	1[b,e] (Argentina)
Grupo Vigor	n.a.	3[d]	0[d]

Sources: [a] = Taccone and Garay (1999: 259); [b] = Company Website; [c] = Company Annual Report; [d] = Telephone Interview with Company Officials (July 2002); [e] = E-mail Exchange with Company Officials (July 2002). A general source of information for the Brazilian case was the Ministério da Fazenda (Parecer N.172/COPGA/SEAE/MF, 22 May 2002, Brasilia, Brazil). If no source is given, figures are from media releases and articles.

Notes: An alternative method for identifying the most important companies is to consider daily kilos of milk processed. Nestlé–Argentina matches Milkaut, with 1.6 and 1.5 million each during 1999, and can thus be considered the country's fourth or fifth largest dairy company. Media sources and figures for daily kilos of milk processed unquestionably point to Nestlé–Brazil as the biggest dairy company, and Grupo Vigor as either the fourth or fifth largest company in Brazil. See, for instance, the statistics section of the Internet Homepage of the Associação Brasileira dos Produtores de Leite (http://www.leitebrasil.org.br/).

then tentative plans to establish a plant in Brazil: "Conaprole's next investment in Brazil is likely to be construction of a plant in the port of Santos" (Rebella 1999: 6). Those plans have yet to materialize, however.

Such a remarkable reshaping of the dairy industry has not happened in the EU, where economic integration has been under way for over four decades. Germany is the EU's biggest producer of dairy products. Nonetheless, its two largest companies (Nordmilch and Humana) only produce in Germany. The third company, Campina, is Dutch and has plants in the Netherlands and beyond. Hochwald and BMI (both tied for fifth place) are, however, also purely national. Great Britain's companies exhibit an even stronger national character. The two largest dairy companies have all of their production plants in Great Britain.[24] Only the third company has transnational capacity. It is a Danish company with an extensive network of plants. In several interviews with company officials, respondents seemed genuinely surprised when asked to elaborate on their operations abroad. For them, dairy production has been, and will continue to be, a purely national endeavor. Only in France do the major dairy companies have transnational production capacity. The five largest companies all have international capacity. This is a noteworthy fact, but it is also rather unique in the region.[25] Table 5.3 reports the data for the three countries.

The situation in NAFTA is quite similar to that in the EU. In the case of the United States, where the biggest dairy companies in North America are located, the picture could not be any clearer. The three largest dairies in the United States have no plants in either Canada or Mexico. The fifth largest also has no such plants. Only Schreiber Foods—the fourth largest company—has a single plant in Mexico. Mexican companies have also not expanded in the NAFTA regions. The two largest companies—Alpura and the Lala Group—have no plants in the United States or Canada. Nor does GILSA, the fifth largest company. The only two companies that do have plants are multinationals from Europe: Danone and Nestlé. In the case of Nestlé, moreover, expansion in the three member states preceded the arrival of NAFTA.[26]

Canadian companies alone in North America have expanded their operations across borders. The largest companies in Canada all have a presence in the United States and some in Mexico as well. Important phases

[24] Dairy Crest has a cheese manufacturing plant on the coast of Ireland. However, 98% of its products are intended for the British market (telephone interview with company officials, July 2002). As discussed in note 21, such a plant is not categorized as part of a transnational production infrastructure.

[25] For this project, data was also collected for companies in the Netherlands and Denmark, given the presence of Dutch and Danish companies in Germany and Great Britain. The three largest companies in the Netherlands (Friesland, Campina, and Nestlé) have an international presence in other member states, making the Netherlands somewhat similar to France; only one company in Denmark (Arla), however, has international productive capacity. Irish, Spanish, and Italian companies are known to have little production capability in other EU member states.

[26] E-mail exchange with company officials, April 2004. Data on the timing of Danone's expansion is not available.

TABLE 5.3
Major Dairy Companies in the European Union

	Revenues in US$ (millions)	Plants in Home Country (2002)	Plants in Other EU Countries (2002)
GERMANY			
Nordmilch	2000 (2000)[a]	15[a]	0[d]
Humana Milchunion	1608 (2000)	11[a]	0[d]
Campina - Germany	1266 (2000)[a]	6[a, d]	22[e] (18 Netherlands, 3 Belgium, 1 France)
Molkerei A. Müller	1335 (2000)[a]	2[d]	1[d] (Great Britain)
Hochwald	572 (2000)[a]	5[a]	0[e]
BMI	486 (2000)[a]	7[d]	0[d]
GREAT BRITAIN			
Dairy Crest	2077 (2001)[c]	15[d]	0[a,d]
Express Dairies	1282 (2001)	10[d]	0[d]
Arla	712 (2000)[b]	6[b,d]	62[b,d] (36 Denmark; 25 Sweden; 1 Greece)
Robert Wiseman Dairies	434 (1999)[c]	5[c,d]	0[c,d]
The Milk Group	187 (2001)[b]	2[b]	0[b]
ACC-Manufacturing	n.a.	8[b,d]	0[b,d]
Danone	6597 (2001)[b]	7[e]	13[e] (6 Spain; 3 Germany; 1 Belgium; 1 Greece; 1 Italy; 1 Portugal)
Groupe Lactalis	5000 (2000)	65[e]	7 to 9[e] (Belgium, England, Germany, Italy, Luxembourg, Portugal, Spain)
Bongrain S. A.	3500 (2000)[c]	over 12[b,g]	4[b,f] (Spain)

continued

TABLE 5.3
Continued

	Revenues in US$ (millions)	Plants in Home Country (2002)	Plants in Other EU Countries (2002)
Sodiaal	2563 (2000)[a]	28[a]	4[d,e] (1 Great Britain; 1 Ireland; 2 Finland)
Fromageries Bel	1557 (2000)[a]	8[b]	9[b] (1 Belgium; 1 Germany; 2 Italy; 2 Portugal; 3 Spain)

Sources: [a] = European Dairy Magazine (Special Report: The Leading Dairy Companies in Germany and Mainland Europe 2001); [b] = Company Website; [c] = Company Annual Report; [d] = Telephone Interview with Company Officials (July 2002); [e] = E-mail Exchange with Company Officials (July 2002); [f] = Bongrain Financial Report 2001. If no source is given, figures are from media releases and articles.

Note: In terms of daily kilos of milk processed, BMI ranks fifth in Germany, with 2.8 million kilos (vs. 2.3 for Hochwald). Given their similar revenues, both BMI and Hochwald are included in the table.

of the expansion happened in the 1990s, with Saputo—the country's largest dairy company—aggressively moving into the United States in the second half of the decade. "It started in 1997 with our acquisition of Stella [Foods Inc]," observed a company official in an interview with the author; "from then on, we have been expanding and looking to expand even more"[27] (Hamilton Spectator 1997). Table 5.4 reports the findings for the United States, Mexico, and Canada.

In the EU and NAFTA, then, many of the most important dairy companies have retained a national character. In Mercosur, by contrast, eight of the ten most important companies have expanded their activities across borders—with seven of those eight doing so in the 1990s. What can explain these differences between Mercosur on the one hand and the EU and NAFTA on the other? We would do well to consider again legal and power contexts in the member states and the nature of regional law.

In the Mercosur area, the liberalization of the dairy and—more generally—agricultural sectors in the 1980s and 1990s prepared dairy companies for international trade. We examined this policy shift in chapter 4, and described it as a transition away from discriminatory policies against dairy producers and towards true market economies. As we saw, large dairy players welcomed this liberalization, for it would help them both

[27] Telephone interview with the author, March 2004.

TABLE 5.4
Major Dairy Companies in NAFTA

	Revenues in US$ (millions)	Plants in Home Country (2004)	Plants in other NAFTA countries (2004)
UNITED STATES			
Dean Dairy Group	8120 (2002)[a]	95[a,b,c]	0[a,b,c]
Kraft	4100 (2002)[a]	18[a]	0[a]
Land O'Lakes	2899 (2002)[a]	12[a,c]	0[a,c]
Schreiber Foods	2300 (2002)[a]	16[a]	1 [a,b,d] (Mexico)
National Dairy Holdings	2148 (2002)[a]	32[a,c]	0[a,c]
MEXICO			
Ganaderos Productores de Leche Pura (Alpura)	1328 (2001)[f]	2[c]	0[c]
Lala Group (including Evaproadora Mexicana)	1152 (2001)[f]	14[b]	0[b]
Nestlé - Mexico	462 (2001)[f]	6[f c,d]	13[f,b] (11 United States, 2 Canada)
Danone	251 (2001)[f]	14[d]	25[d] (20 United States, 5 Canada)
Grupo Industrial de la Leche S.A (GILSA)	234 (2001)[f]	1[e]	0[e]
Saputo	2503 (2002)[a]	35[a]	15[a] (United States)
Parmalat - Canada	1800 (2002)[a]	20[a]	6[c] (5 United States, 1 Mexico)
Agropur Coop	1327 (2002)[a]	20[a, c]	1[a,c] (United States)
Kraft - Canada	n.a.	2[d]	19[a, d] (18 United States, 1 Mexico)
Nestlé - Canada	n.a.	2[d]	17[d] (11 United States, 6 Mexico)

Sources: [a] = *Dairy Foods Magazine* (Annual Report on Top 100 Dairy Companies in North America, 2003); [b] = Company Website; [c] = Telephone Interview with Company Officials (February - March 2004); [d] = E-mail Exchange with Company Officials (Feburary - April 2004); [e] = Telephone Interview with Alpura official; [f] = Figures estimated from data assembled from Datamonitor Industry Market Research reports from January 2002 ("Mexico: Liquid Milk"; "Mexico: Powdered Milk"; "Mexico: Concentrated Milk"; "Mexico: Yogurt"; "Mexico: Processed Cheese").

domestically and regionally. Intraregional exports boomed (Spanish News-wire Services 2001c). In the 1990s, Mercosur officials solidified this export-oriented environment by adopting laws that not only reduced tariff barriers to zero but also removed technical barriers to trade. The result, as one might expect, was a boom in intraregional dairy trade and a decrease in costs associated with expansion.

Thus, today Brazil represents the primary export market, and a major source of revenue, for dairy companies from Argentina and Uruguay (San-guinetti 2004; El Pais 2003). Estimates put Argentina's current dairy exports to Brazil as a percentage of all dairy exports at around 70% or higher. In the case of Uruguay, the figure is around 50%. Truly astonishing data is available for the period 1986–88 to 1994–96. Argentina's dairy exports to Mercosur countries increased by a factor of 25 during that period, those of Brazil by 160, those of Uruguay by 4, and those of Paraguay by over 22. Total Mercosur intratrade increased by over 900%. By comparison, total dairy exports to the rest of the world increased by only 50% in the same period (Nofal and Wilkinson 1999b: 168).

It was this combination of national and regional export-friendly policies, and the resulting widening of company's markets, that made direct infrastructure investments across national borders attractive. Maximi-lano Moreno of Argentina's Ministerio de Economía and Producción discussed with the author the importance of the Mercosur initiatives. He noted: "It was that environment above all which prompted regional expansion. . . . The removal of technical barriers made it a single-level playing-field, stimulating companies to expand."[28] His views are widely shared by other policymakers and business experts alike. Two such experts described, for instance, how "the impact of Mercosur on alliances, joint-ventures, mergers and acquisitions has been very significant" (Nofal and Wilkinson 1999b: 156). They continued, "Mercosur's impact can be seen at different levels: it has had an effect on market competition for finished products (long life milk, butter), on shaping investment decisions in the powdered milk and cheese sectors, and on prompting a greater level of organization of the actors in the chain" (156). Because of Mercosur, foreign companies invested heavily in the region, penetrating "the sector through mergers and associations with companies already established in the domestic markets of the member countries" (Nofal and Wilkinson 1999b: 156; Presidents and Prime Ministers 1997).[29]

---

[28] Interview with the author, Buenos Aires, Argentina, August 2003. See chap. 4, n. 56 for Moreno's full job title.

[29] There were of course other factors that shaped the decision of dairy companies to expand: most nonetheless become relevant only in the context of integration. For instance, the sharp devaluation of the real (Brazil's currency) in the late 1990s has been said to have driven Argentina companies to expand in Brazil (their products would have otherwise been unaffordable for most Brazilian customers) (Spanish Newswire Services 1999e). Yet devaluations

In the EU, matters developed quite differently. The market liberalization that transformed the dairy industry in Mercosur never took place in the EU. Dairy producers have operated in policy and political environments that have long prevented the formation of a genuinely single European market. We discussed some aspects of those environments in chapter 4. These include protected denominations, which encourage local production and reliance on local supplies for raw materials. But they also include the exclusive and longstanding agreements between local dairy producers and local milk suppliers. Those agreements are strongest in France, but they are present in most of the major dairy countries, especially in Great Britain where marketing boards controlled milk supply well into the 1990s. They grant, in effect, a monopoly over the supply of milk to local producers. The EU, moreover, has helped cement those ties. When production quotas were introduced in 1984 through the CAP, for instance, the EU allocated given volumes of local milk to dairy producers.

These variables have posed a significant barrier to entry for foreign competitors. As Pierluigi Londero, of the Directorate General on Agriculture of the European Commission, explained to the author:

> In theory, a German company can therefore set up shop in, say, France. In practice, this is actually quite difficult. There is a tremendous variety of products across countries: the required knowledge and familiarity is simply not there for foreigners. I have a hard time imagining a German company setting up shop in France to sell a certain type of Brie to the French. . . . Then, there is the supply side of things. There exist negotiated deals between suppliers and buyers of milk. This makes it very difficult for anyone to arrive in a given market and have access to the local raw material. The only choice would be to acquire a local company, but that is rather difficult to do and, besides, the incentives are not there: the CAP's inflated price structure for dairy goods has made lots of companies complacent. . . . They are happy to stay where they are.[30]

There is, Londero continued, an "artificial stability" to the market, one that has prevented financial problems from occurring and has thus deprived the marketplace of a certain dynamism. Such stability is reflected in the modest growth rates of intraregional trade. European Commission data shows a mere 50% increase in the period 1989–2002.[31]

---

happened in the past too, without prompting companies to expand. The choice to expand was ultimately driven by the increasing importance of the Brazilian market—itself the result of the new open-market policies in the region.

[30] Part of the difficulty stems from the ownership structure of companies, many of which are cooperatives not structured for expansion. Interview with the author, Brussels, April 2004.

[31] The figure comes from Londero's database. Note that it refers to the twelve member states that the EU had in 1990 (i.e., not Finland, Sweden, and Austria—countries with lit-

Interviews with officials of large dairy companies in Germany and Great Britain revealed a frame of mind that is highly focused on the national dimension. A representative from Britain's Dairy Crest thus explained his company's domestic focus as follows: "We have a healthy market here in the U.K., and really see no need to set up shop elsewhere."[32] A second representative from Germany's BMI stressed her company's attachment to domestic standards and traditions. "How," she asked, "could we set up a plant in, say, France? We would need to bring our German milk all the way there. . . . That would be impractical."[33]

In the NAFTA region, matters followed a fairly similar course. We recall from chapter 4 that Canada successfully resisted the liberalization of dairy trade with both the United States and Mexico. Clinging to a policy tradition of strong protectionism and heavy market regulation, Canada has opted out of any NAFTA agreement on dairy. At least partly as a result of this, NAFTA today does not have laws that standardize processes and products. The result is a fragmented marketplace: regulatory regimes are different in each country, and intraregional trade remains low. Consider, for example, that in the decade 1991–2001, only 6% of all dairy imports into Canada came from NAFTA countries (Brunke 2002: 3). For the United States, in turn, Canada has represented a minor trading partner at best, taking in only 11% of its dairy exports and accounting for only 2.5% of its dairy imports.[34]

All this has obviously not prevented Canadian companies from expanding into the United States, for whom—despite the barriers—the United States represents an important destination. It has prevented, however, companies from the United States from considering expansion into Canada or Mexico. A representative from Land O'Lakes aptly summarized the implications of Canada's position for the behavior of companies from the United States: "Canada is a very difficult country to enter: the regulatory environment is tough, the country is closed. . . . With all those difficulties, I cannot imagine a company that would be willing to enter the country."[35] David Phillips, Chief of *Dairy Foods Magazine* (a publication based in the United States) and an industry expert, reflected on this possibility in an interview with the author:

---

tle weight in this sector). Figures for the EU fifteen for 1996–2002 point to an increase in intraregional trade of about 20%.

[32] Telephone interview with the author, July 2002.

[33] Telephone interview with the author, July 2002. In this context, the expansionist tendencies of French dairy companies require explanation. One key factor seems to have been the extraordinary support that those companies (much as French companies in other sectors) have received from the government for exporting their goods.

[34] Calculated from figures in Brunke (2002: 3).

[35] Telephone interview with the author, February 2004.

Certainly, had Canada and Mexico been willing to adopt, say, to agree that all dairy companies use USDA [United States Department of Agriculture] standards, that would have really stimulated the industry in unprecedented ways. It would have made it a lot easier for U.S. companies to think of Canada as part of their market and playing field.[36]

There is, of course, hope that the bilateral agreements between the United States and Mexico might one day generate more favorable policy environments. "It is not beyond the realm of possibility," wrote a group of experts at the time of the agreements, "that some US dairy farmers may decide to move or expand their operations to Mexico" (Outlaw et al. 1994: 14). By 2004, that possibility remained just that.

STATES AND THE PROMOTION OF LABOR RIGHTS

As we have seen, the rise of women's interest groups and dairy companies active on a regional level has been a rather selective affair. Only in the EU have women set up organizations with regional membership bases and regional programs. Only in Mercosur have most major dairy companies expanded their productive infrastructure across national borders. In contrast to these trends, the transformation of labor and employment departments has been ubiquitous. In all of the member states of the EU, Mercosur, and NAFTA, these departments have become active in permanent transnational bodies. They have also developed units that specialize in the administration of regional-level policies and regulations. Yet here too we notice important differences across RTAs: the specific structure and programs of those transnational and new domestic units vary significantly across RTAs.

In this section, we consider developments in two specific thematic areas: the unemployment rights of migrant workers, and the rights of workers to strike and form trade unions. We observe that labor departments in the EU participate in transnational coordinating bodies dedicated to migrant workers and unemployment; they have also established domestic units active in that area. The labor departments of Mercosur and NAFTA's member states have not experienced the same changes. They instead participate in transnational bodies and have created domestic units dedicated to the protection of the rights of workers to strike and form unions. In all three RTAs, the link between regional law and changes in labor departments is direct and obvious: regional law either *mandated* those changes or created formidable pressures in the same direction. The empirical data

[36] Telephone interview with the author, February 2004.

comes from EU, Mercosur, and NAFTA official publications, governmental publications, interviews with state officials, government Internet sites, and secondary sources.

Let us first consider change in the EU. The labor and employment departments of EU member states are involved in one major transnational administrative body concerned with the unemployment (and other social security) rights of migrant workers. Composed exclusively of representatives of national departments,[37] and attached organizationally to the European Commission, the ACSSMW is charged with overseeing all administrative, technical, and financial questions associated with the implementation of the principles of Regulation 1408/71, including its unemployment requisites. With a budget of €1.6 million for 2002, it meets several times a year.[38] Its meetings and activities regularly concern unemployment benefits. Thus in 1996 for instance, the ACSSMW, recognizing the need to inform migrant workers of their rights, published a practical guide with a special section on unemployment benefits (1996: section 5.8). In that same year, it also produced one important binding decision (Decision 96/172/EC), in which it streamlined the unemployment benefit procedures for workers in professions, such as international transport or diplomacy, where the country of residence varies often over short periods of time or is unclear. And again in that year, with Recommendation No. 21 of November 28, 1996, the ACSSMW outlined for the competent institutions of the member states an efficient process for handling unemployment requests of persons accompanying their spouses abroad.

Aiding the ACSSMW is a second transnational administrative body: the Advisory Committee on Social Security for Migrant Workers.[39] Also attached to the European Commission, it serves as a forum for representatives from national labor and employment departments to meet with representatives of trade unions and employer organizations from every member state of the EU. The main function of the committee is to supply the ACSSMW with opinions on all aspects of social security rights for migrant workers, including unemployment rights.[40]

---

[37] Participants are of course not exclusively from labor and employment departments. In the case of Great Britain, for instance, two officials from the Department for Work and Pensions and one each from the Departments of Health and Inland Revenue participate.

[38] Based on a report discussed in the British Parliament (House of Commons, Hansard, written Answers for May 24, 2002: col. 654W).

[39] The European Commission adopted a measure to merge and streamline the work of various committees that work on social policy. See Communication Concerning the Development of the Social Dialogue Process at Community Level (COM[96] 448). But the ACSSMW remains in place to date.

[40] For the composition of the committee in 2000, see Council Decision of February 28, 2000 (2000/C 69/02). Two members of the Department of Work and Pensions, for instance, made up the British contingent.

Domestically, European labor and employment departments have developed institutional capacity to process and oversee unemployment claims by migrant workers. At a general level, Regulation 1408/71 and its implementing measure Regulation 574/72 specify functions that national administrations are expected to fulfill (Villars 1981: 298–99). They are expected to exchange information on legislative changes, provide mutual administrative assistance free of charge, communicate directly with each other as needed, and accept documents and claims in foreign languages. Yet it is the practical application of the principles set out in the legal texts that has caused the most significant transformations.

The management (i.e., information dissemination, processing, reimbursement requests, etc.) of Form E-303 offers an example. Form E-303 allows citizens of one country to receive unemployment payments for three months as they search for work in a second country. The host country is to process the request, but workers are required to complete the form before leaving their home country (the home country must then reimburse the host country for its payments). In Sweden, offices of the Arbetsmarknadsverket (Labor Market Administration) manage Form E-303.[41] In Belgium, a more decentralized country, regions have a branch of the Ministère Fédéral de l'Emploi et du Travail (Department of Employment and Labor) charged with the task: VDAB for Flanders, FOREM for Wallonia, and BGDA/ORBEM for Brussels. In Denmark, the Arbejdsformidlingen (Public Employment Service), located in the Danish Ministry of Employment, handles those forms. We can examine the Danish case to assess the type of impact of Form E-303 on the national administration.[42]

According to representatives of the Arbejdsformidlingen, a total of 1,553 E-303 forms were issued in 2003 to Danish citizens ready to seek work outside of Denmark, for a total of almost US$10 million in benefits. To fulfill these functions, the service relied on 60–65% of the time of nine full-time civil servants. Officials did much more than simply issue the forms, however. They handled a fair amount of complaints from individuals regarding erroneous accounting, addresses, deposit issues, and much else. In addition, the Arbejdsformidlingen relied heavily on the help of the AK-Samvirke.[43] This association is a private national organization closely affiliated with unions and the state. The association has one assigned per-

---

[41] In Stockholm, a major office is Arbetsformedlingen City.

[42] At the time of writing, the EU has just welcomed a number of Central and Eastern European countries as full members. The administrative functions of these countries have already undergone important transformations to comply with the EU's requirements on the rights of migrant workers. See Wiktorow (2001) for the case of Poland.

[43] All data for the Danish case comes from a group interview with the author in Copenhagen, Denmark, April 2004. Jørgen Kappel and Jes Flatanand spoke for Arbejdsformidlingen. Ingmar Jørgensen spoke for AK-Samvirke.

son for each of its thirty-three offices charged with processing the initial request of Danish citizens wishing to emigrate and look for work. The Arbejdsformidlingen and the AK-Samvirke have thus entered into very close collaboration to handle Form E-303.[44]

As part of their work, officials from the Arbejdsformidlingen interact regularly with fellow colleagues from other member states, in particular Sweden and Germany, where most Danes go in search of work. Indeed, as representative Jes Flatan explained to the author:

> I have a long list of contacts from key countries in the EU. I know who they are and they know me. We also gather with our colleagues from Sweden and other key countries three to four times a year as part of an informal working group. . . . We do not mind: we can all learn from each other how to improve what we do.

Similarly, officials from the AK-Samvirke have also established important transnational networks and working groups with counterparts in other member states. Contacts are strongest with Sweden. As AK-Samvirke's Ingmar Jørgensen explained to the author, "we hold meetings with our Swedish colleagues four or five times a year: there will be something like eighty of us, and we talk about issues related to the flow of workers across our borders, including of course matters related to Form E-303."

The labor and employment departments of Mercosur member states do not exhibit analogous transnational linkages or domestic capabilities in the area of migrant workers and unemployment. Decision 19/97, with its limited vision of social security for migrant workers, envisions the creation of the Comisión Multilateral Permanente (Permanent Multilateral Commission) as a forum for transnational cooperation among national administrators, trade unions, and employer representatives. The commission, however, is to focus on sickness, old age, invalidity, and death benefits for migrant workers, and not on unemployment benefits. The commission remains in any case in the planning phases.[45] In the words of María Carmen Ferreira, a senior Uruguayan official directly involved with social security negotiations in Mercosur,[46] Decision 19/97 has thus far had "no impact. . . . There has been no coordination among [member states'] ministries" in any area of social security for migrant workers.[47]

---

[44] There now exist plans for the state to rely increasingly on the AK-Samvirke for managing most aspects of Form E-303. This would entail a more decentralized approach.

[45] The commission will come into existence after Paraguay ratifies Decision 19/97.

[46] Former National Director of Employment at Uruguay's Ministerio de Trabajo y Seguridad Social, and National Coordinator for Uruguay for Mercosur's Subgrupo No. 10 (Work, Employment, and Social Security).

[47] Electronic mail exchange with the author, September 2002.

Domestically, Mercosur member states have not developed specialized units to deal with the unemployment benefits of migrant workers.

The labor and employment departments of Mercosur member states have, however, established transnational and national structures in the area of workers' rights, including the right to strike and form unions. The Comisión Sociolaboral del Mercosur, created with Resolution 12/2000, was established to promote the rights of workers covered by the Declaración Sociolaboral of December 1998, which—as we saw in chapter 4—include the rights to strike and form unions. National departments have a permanent representative in the commission (national employer and labor unions also have one representative each). The commission inspects yearly reports on member states' formal and practical compliance with workers' rights (Article 9 of Resolution 12/2000), and formulates action programs and recommendations. It also holds meetings multiple times a year (for instance, four in 1999 and 2000 respectively, and at least two in 2002).[48] In an interview with the author, Gerardo Corres, an Argentine representative to the commission,[49] described the intensity of the work taking place at the regional level. "There is now a regional theme to which we must all pay attention," he noted; "there is a lot of mobilization, a lot of work that is done in the commission."[50] Ruben Cortina, a colleague of Corres, then proceeded to elaborate:

> We are [as a result of the commission] in permanent and regular contact with our counterparts in Brazil, Uruguay, and Paraguay. . . . We have no choice on that; our thinking about labor issues, including the right to strike—let alone form unions—has become more regional: we do not think of problems in Argentina but of problems in the Mercosur area. . . . By now, I know my counterparts very well. . . . We are friends, we go out to dinner, we speak often. . . . This was not so ten years ago, before Mercosur. . . . I must tell you that a person like myself and my colleagues do not per se belong fully to a regional bureaucracy, but our heads certainly operate more at the regional level than the national. We are subject to national pressures, but we have a regional vision.[51]

To aid the Comisión Sociolaboral del Mercosur, member states have in turn set up Comisiones Nacionales (National Commissions) (Resolution 85/2000). These commissions are situated within the departments of labor or employment in each country to gather information on all issue

[48] Interview with Maricela Viera, Montevideo, Uruguay, August 2003. See n. 16 for Viera's full job title.

[49] See chap. 4, n. 76 for Corres's full job title.

[50] Interview with the author, Buenos Aires, August 2003.

[51] Interview with the author, Buenos Aires, August 2003. See chap. 4, n. 78 for Cortina's full job title.

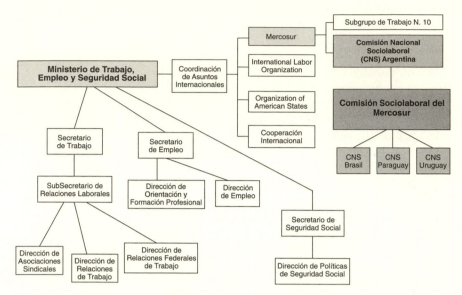

Figure 5.1. Argentina's Ministerio de Trabajo, Empleo y Seguridad Social: Adjusting to Mercosur's Declaración Sociolaboral. Sources: Ruben Cortina, Coordinator of International Affairs in the Ministerio de Trabajo, Empleo y Seguridad Social and member of Mercosur's Subgrupo 10 (Work, Employment and Social Security) and of Argentina's CNS; Internet Homepage of the Ministerio: http://www.trabajo.gov.ar/

areas covered by the declaration. Each year, these commissions are asked to place special focus on selected rights. To date, seven out of nineteen rights identified in the declaration have been thoroughly discussed. The 2002 Program of the Comisión Sociolaboral del Mercosur, for instance, put Article 8 (which affirms the right to form unions) on the agenda. The right to strike is certain to be on future programs, most likely in 2005 or 2006.

Figures 5.1 and 5.2 identify the location of the commissions of Argentina and Uruguay in their respective labor departments. They offer a clear indication of the structural transformation of these departments in response to the Declaración Sociolaboral, including its principle ensuring workers the rights to strike and form unions. In the words of Ana María Santestevan, a counterpart to Ruben Cortina in Uruguay,[52] "our institutional setup has certainly undergone a change in response to the arrival of Mercosur and its labor declarations. . . . We have all had to adjust."

[52] Technical Assessor, Asesoría en Relaciones Internacionales (International Relations Office), Ministerio de Trabajo y Seguridad Social.

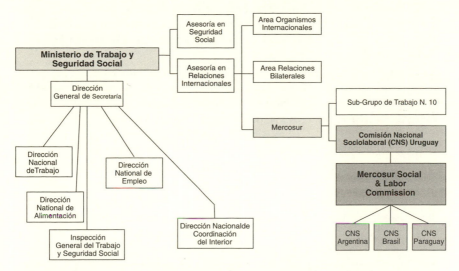

Figure 5.2. Uruguay's Ministerio de Trabajo y Seguridad Social: Adjusting to Mercosur's Declaración Sociolaboral. Sources: Maricela Viera, Mercosur section of the Asesoría en Relaciones Internacionales; Ana María Santestevan, Asesora Técnica in the Asesoría en Relaciones Internacionales; Internet Homepage of the Ministerio: http://www.mtss.gub.uy/

NAFTA too has witnessed the rise of institutions with regional characteristics. There are none, however, dedicated to helping migrant workers receive unemployment benefits. Instead, we note that national departments of labor and employment have undergone changes in order to protect the rights of workers as specified by the NAALC—including, therefore, the right to strike and form unions. At the transnational level, representatives from the labor and employment departments have a permanent structure for interaction: the Commission for Labor Cooperation, an organ created explicitly for overseeing the implementation of the NAALC.

At the heart of the commission is the Council of Ministers. This is a body composed of the Secretary of Labor from the United States, the Secretario del Trabajo y Previsión Social (Secretary of Work and Social Security) from Mexico, and the Minister of Labor from Canada. The modus operandi of the council is simple: to act as a single entity aiming to promote the principles of the NAALC. As such, the council carries out several functions. These include conducting research and proposing policies on topics of relevance to the NAALC text, participating in the process of dispute resolution for NAALC-related complaints, and keeping the public abreast of developments related to labor issues.

We should note that the commission also supports a second venue for transnational collaboration among labor officials from the member states. These take the form of several yearly collaborations and meetings on a variety of topics related to the NAALC. Thus, in February 2001, for instance, representatives from Canada and the United States held in Toronto a "one-and-a-half day cooperative activity under the NAALC to examine the general scope of protection of the right to organize" in the two countries (Commission for Labor Cooperation 2001: 11).

The internal structure of national labor departments has also changed, in ways that reflect directly the principles set out in the NAALC. The NAALC text states that each department must establish a National Administrative Office (NAO), an entity charged with developing and receiving complaints about alleged violations of the labor principles, publishing reports, exchanging information, and much more. There now exist NAOs in the labor departments of the three member states.

Per the NAALC text, the three NAOs are in a permanent relationship with the commission itself. Thus, there is a close connection between the transnational body in which the departments function and the domestic units that they have created to oversee the NAALC. Figure 5.3 offers a schematic overview of both the regional and domestic impact of NAFTA on labor departments. It takes the example of the United States to show the regional and domestic dimensions of change. The reader will note the presence of a "tri-national" Secretariat in the commission. This organ also draws its officers from the three member states, but these officers come from a variety of public and private sources rather than the labor departments. The Secretariat, however, does support the Council of Ministers directly and, moreover, conducts research and publishes on matters of direct relevance to the NAOs.[53] Similarly, there are two dispute resolution organs (the Evaluation Committee of Experts and the Arbitration Panel) aiding the council. Both are temporary bodies (i.e., reconstituted on an ongoing basis as cases reach the commission) and have had only limited impact on national departments.

As of January 1, 2001, nearly twenty-five complaints had been filed with the three NAOs (Compa 2001: 454), all of which were closely monitored by the council. Thirteen involved the right of workers to associate. One, however, also involved the right to strike. The AeroMéxico Case (U.S. NAO Case No. 9801) was filed in August 1998 by the Association of Flight Attendants of the United States. The association accused the Mexican government of violating NAALC standards related to the right to strike by forcing striking flight attendants at AeroMéxico to go back

---

[53] Two important publications are the North American Labor Markets Series and the Comparative Guides to Labor and Employment Law in North America.

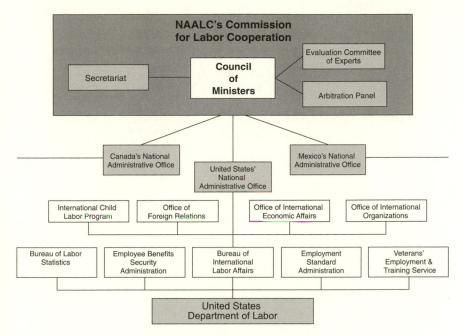

Figure 5.3. The United States Department of Labor: Adjusting to NAFTA's North American Agreement on Labor Cooperation (NAALC). Sources: United States General Accounting Office, *North American Free Trade Agreement: U.S. Experience with Environment, Labor and Investing Dispute Settlement Cases, 2001*; Internet Homepage of the United States Department of Labor: http://www.dol.gov/ilab/

to work. Justifying their actions on national security grounds, the Mexican government intervened by executive order to take over the airline and end the strike. The U.S. NAO considered the case but eventually declined to hear it, arguing that the takeover was carried out according to Mexican law. The submitters asked the U.S. NAO to reconsider its decision in a letter dated November 9, 1998. On December 21, 1998, the U.S. NAO informed the submitters that it would not reconsider its decision, but agreed to conduct a research project evaluating how the three NAALC countries can reconcile the issue of the right to strike in light of national interests of safety, security and general welfare.

CONCLUSION

Organizations respond to regional integration, expanding their structures and programs. As this chapter has shown us, however, such an expansion is selective: which organizations expand regionally varies from RTA to RTA. When similar organizations expand, their specific regional structures and programs differ. We thus saw the formation of regional women's groups in the EU, but not in NAFTA or Mercosur. Dairy companies exploded in Mercosur, but less so in the EU or NAFTA. Labor and employment departments in all three RTAs developed regional structures and programs. Yet the very nature of those structures and programs varies from one RTA to the next.

In accounting for such variation in organizational development, we paid attention to the national legal and power contexts in which organizations functioned prior to and during integration. We also noted that regional law itself (its presence or absence, and its specific content) has shaped the evolution of organizations. Women's groups in the EU have grown in response to EU law on women. Dairy companies in Mercosur have expanded their productive infrastructure in response to the creation of a single marketplace in the region. States have developed new administrative units charged with implementing regional laws on workers' rights.

Two major conclusions emerge from this empirical analysis. First RTAs affect not only abstract law but also practical reality. RTAs are giving rise to regional *societies*: real-life spaces where people conduct their everyday lives. Second, those regional societies are different from each other. What dimensions of social life are subject to regional expansion varies across RTAs. Women think and act regionally only in the EU. Dairy producers think and act regionally only in Mercosur. National administrators in all three RTAs think regionally in terms of labor rights; yet they have different understandings of those rights.

These observations raise a number of important questions about the nature of RTAs. How permanent are these differences in organizational fields? As with law, questions of change and causality come to mind. This book cannot account for all variables responsible for the evolution of organizations. We note as well that our observations in this chapter concern three very specific areas of organizational activity. It is reasonable to wonder how pervasive organizational differences are across RTAs. The next chapter addresses these and other questions raised by the three empirical chapters of this book.

PART III

Conclusion

Chapter 6

REFLECTIONS ON THE PRESENT AND FUTURE

MARKET OFFICIALS pursue trade liberalization in the midst of complex social realities. As they mobilize to erect structures to support a new regional
economic space, a number of variables limit their options, constrain their
behavior, and guide them toward certain solutions. The resulting regional-
level arrangements seldom represent abrupt or major departures from existing reality. They instead offer much continuity with that reality, translating at the transnational level conditions and dynamics present in most
or all of the member states before integration. At the same time, the resulting new regional spaces generate unprecedented opportunities and
pressures for societal players. How those players respond to these opportunities varies from region to region, in line with their capabilities and interests—as they developed in the given domestic contexts prior to integration—as well as the nature of the regional opportunities presented to
them. Thus, societal developments in a given RTA also provide much continuity with existing realities on the ground.

The preceding chapters considered two dimensions of regional market
building: law and organizations. With regard to law, I showed that RTA
officials have made rather distinct choices concerning the use of law to address the question of standardization for market participants. In NAFTA,
they have avoided creating complex cognitive guidebooks to reality, relying instead on international standard-setting organizations and reactive
conflict resolutions systems. EU and Mercosur officials have opted, by
contrast, to use law to standardize much of the world. I explained this difference in legal approaches in terms of national legal traditions and the
preferences of powerful actors in each region. NAFTA's minimalism is
highly consistent with the common-law approaches of the United States
and Canada; the rich legal systems of the EU and Mercosur resemble the
civil-law approaches of member states in those two regions. I then presented evidence that the specific targets and content of regional law differ
across the three regions, again in ways that generally prove consistent
with existing legal approaches and power configurations dominant in the
member states. Taking as examples the cases of working women, dairy
products, and labor rights, I showed that there exist major differences in
what has been made subject to standardization and the very content of
those standardizing laws.

With regard to organizations, I presented evidence to show that organizations have responded quite differently to integration across RTAs. Attention turned to three types of organizations: women's interest groups, dairy companies, and state departments of labor and employment. The analysis revealed a great deal of variation across RTAs. Only in the EU have women's groups developed truly regional programs and membership structures. Only in Mercosur have most of the largest dairy companies expanded their production infrastructures. In all three RTAs states have developed units dedicated to the promotion of regionally defined labor rights: at the same time, important differences exist in the specific structures and programs of those units. As with law, I offered a political-institutional explanation for the evolution of organizations in each RTA. Preexisting national legal traditions and power arrangements shaped which organizations would become regionally active. At the same time, the very nature of regional law shaped to varying degrees how organizations responded to regional integration.

Regional law and the evolution of organizations in a given RTA, then, share similar causes (national legal traditions and power contexts) and are themselves causally related (regional law shapes the evolution of organizations). This, I argued, accounts for the coherence between regional law and the evolution of organizations that is present in any one RTA: as figure 2.1 suggested, in given spheres of social life, law and organizations move in tandem. In the EU, for instance, we noted that the world of working women has acquired a regional dimension. In Mercosur, we observed the same for the world of dairy. In NAFTA, we saw the same for workers and their rights to form unions and strike. Additional empirical analysis would certainly produce many more examples. This coherence between law and organizations in a given RTA suggests that the differences among RTAs are *systematic, meaningful, and enduring*. Entire, but different, sections of social life undergo a regional expansion from one RTA to the next, ultimately in line with the history of a given area.

We are now in position to step back and reflect on the evidence presented in chapters 3, 4, and 5. Along the way, we noted that the evidence raised a number of important questions about RTAs. The next section discusses three which merit special attention: the desirability of legal minimalism and interventionism, the possible sources of conflict in future interregional trade, and the possibility of change in each RTA. The subsequent section revisits the three broader debates discussed in chapter 1: globalization, the process of building markets, and the spread of neoliberalism. Attention then turns to venues of future research. Even within the theoretical confines of this book, much empirical work remains to be done; variables other than institutions and politics may shed additional light on the process of regional integration. The fourth and final section offers some concluding remarks on RTAs and this book.

REFLECTIONS ON BEST PRACTICES, INTERREGIONAL TRADE, AND CHANGE

This book has paid considerable attention to NAFTA's legal minimalism and the more aggressive approach of the EU and Mercosur. These constitute fundamentally different approaches: the former is lighter, looser, more flexible, and less intrusive. The latter is much heavier, tighter, and it interferes with social life in countless ways. The parallel existence of the two systems raises some questions. Perhaps the most important concern the desirability of each approach. Is one model superior to the other? Is there a "best practice" in regional approaches to standardization? These questions cannot be easily answered in a few pages. Some of the most important advantages and disadvantages of each approach, however, can be readily identified.[1]

Minimalism offers a clear set of benefits. First, it requires fewer resources. The EU and Mercosur have spent (and continue to spend) enormous quantities of money, human assets, and time to produce their legal systems. Overseeing the implementation of those legal systems has also taken enormous quantities of resources. By itself, the need to translate EU legal texts into eleven languages during the 1990s has been a massive enterprise. To whatever costs the EU has incurred, we must add the extraordinary transformation that nation states have had to undergo to comply with EU law. A similar observation applies to Mercosur. The process is cumbersome and highly intrusive. In the case of NAFTA, costs of operations are minimal. The NAFTA Secretariat is a small office. The number of government officials from each country working on NAFTA matters is miniscule when compared to the numbers for the EU and, to some extent, Mercosur. There are no major legislative bodies requiring constant physical and clerical support. NAFTA is an efficient, slim operation.[2]

---

[1] There is currently much debate over the merits of common- versus civil-law in relation to economic performance at the *national* level. The debate informs our evaluation of the merits of minimalism versus interventionism in regional law. See Woo-Cumings (2003) for a review of that debate.

[2] The size of the EU's budget—around €100 billion—is actually quite small when one considers all the operations of the EU. Figures for NAFTA's budget are not easy to find. I estimate expenditures (for the Secretariat, the NAALC, and the NAEEC) to be around US$25 million.

Minimalism has a second advantage: it allows a particular RTA to interact with the outside world with more ease. The officials of a minimalist RTA can contemplate an expansion of their scheme to include additional member states. The reverse is true for the EU or Mercosur. As highly integrated economic entities, they must approach expansion as a major process. Potential member states must comply with eighty thousand pages of EU legislation or almost two thousand Mercosur laws. In the EU, accession is preceded by intensive, multi-year negotiations and adjustment processes matched by close monitoring of progress. ASEAN's AFTA—an RTA with significantly less legislation than either the EU or Mercosur—welcomed Vietnam and Cambodia in the 1990s without extensive legal preparation. An expansion of NAFTA would certainly prove similar.

Yet minimalism also seems quite risky, for it leaves much room for conflict, even in the case where member states have common-law traditions. NAFTA is experiencing serious internal tensions. As we saw in chapter 2, many see higher levels of industry standards and compliance rates in the United States and Canada (as opposed to Mexico) as weakening the competitiveness of companies from those two countries. Trade unions as well as some business leaders wish to put an end to NAFTA for this very reason. Had NAFTA officials developed a single harmonized regulatory framework, such discontent would have been far less. In their current format, the NAFTA texts were a contested issue in the United States presidential election of 2004. Minimalism also can create pressures for a "race to the bottom" in national regulatory frameworks. Faced with competition from Mexico, for instance, companies in the United States and Canada have had to reduce their costs. To do so, some have pressured government officials to loosen their regulatory frameworks in the areas of the environment, labor, safety, health, and so on.

A minimalist approach also imposes limitations on how much can actually be traded. In a harmonized system of regulation, consumers do not face an influx of foreign products that do not comply with domestic standards. Producers in turn have a wider array of compatible products from which they can select. In a minimalist system, moreover, companies are more likely not to respect the guidelines of international standard organizations—the preferred option found in the NAFTA text. In a harmonized system, by contrast, evasion is more difficult: national and regional watchdogs are generally in place, and in any case the relevant standards are more clearly delineated (and therefore both easier to follow and to investigate).

An interventionist approach has its own advantages and limitations. It certainly avoids some of the shortcomings of minimalism. A harmonized system of laws presumably makes economic integration smoother. It is likely to create a single playing field where forces of production (companies, labor, capital) can move without incurring penalties or difficulties. Such a move would translate into a better use of those forces and therefore more efficiency throughout the industry. This, in turn, generates further pressure for more efficiency. A harmonized system of law is also likely to reduce production and transaction costs. Companies must follow only one set of requirements as they produce their goods and services. Border inspections are gone and compliance checks are done with only one regulatory book in mind. Moreover, components and services are more likely to complement each other: it will be easier for a manufacturer of telephone equipment, for instance, to shop around for parts throughout the region. This will decrease costs and therefore prices. Overall, more goods and services will cross national borders, hence increasing the benefits of free trade.

Interventionism also increases pressure to respect the law. In a given RTA, the number of parties interested in a given company's compliance with, for instance, manufacturing laws is greatly increased: that number will include many, if not all, of the players competing in that industry throughout the region. Before integration, most players have limited knowledge of foreign regulatory regimes and have little interest in monitoring compliance. In parallel, the governments of the member states themselves face increased pressure for implementing law. Before integration, legal compliance is largely a matter in the hands of national authorities; if, in a given country, respect for the law is low, few outside actors have the inclination or the means to pressure the relevant governments to take action. With the arrival of regional law (which, as discussed in the appendix, supersedes national law) regional bodies (such as the EU's Commission, for instance) are involved in monitoring, overseeing, examining, and at times enforcing compliance. More informal mechanisms are also at work. Information on laggard member states is made publicly available through reports and the media. Governments thus feel a certain pressure to take steps to improve their image. This is more than a matter of national pride, of course, since businesses and external investments are likely to be attracted to countries with good reputations.

Interventionism is, in addition, likely to improve the stability and performance of the member states. Participation in the EU or Mercosur is conditional on compliance with regional law. Such compliance, though certainly costly, offers regional officials an opportunity to shape domestic policy regimes in fundamental ways. When these regimes are in the first instance weak or ineffective, regional law introduces an element of coherence and stability. In Mercosur, regional law has certainly improved regulatory regimes for product manufacturing in Paraguay and Brazil: they are more rational, predictable, and more difficult to evade. The enlargement of the EU has provided the applicant states from Central and

Eastern Europe with a ready-made set of coherent laws for competing in market economies. In a matter of a few years, the applicant countries introduced a system of laws that had been tested, amended, and improved upon for decades.

Yet interventionism has important shortcomings too. Cost is perhaps the most significant. The production of regional law is a very time-consuming and complex process. Enormous quantities of resources are spent anticipating problems, consulting the interested parties, drafting laws, amending laws, and overseeing compliance. A complex judicial system is bound to arise, as the grounds for conflict are in some ways increased. Moreover, players in all sorts of industries and actors in all those spheres of social life affected by regional law must incur adjustment costs to new regional regulatory regimes. These adjustment costs are likely to be high initially, when the transition from national to regional rules is made, and low thereafter. Of course, costs must be considered in light of the associated benefits—in this case, as just discussed, lower transaction costs in import-export activities, a bigger market, more rational allocation of resources, and so on.

Interventionism also introduces a widening gap between legislators and common citizens. A Uruguayan citizen could at one time think of having some influence over the course of her country's legislative processes (through elections and other means). She was one of almost three million citizens of the country. With the arrival of Mercosur laws, the locus of legislative activity has moved very far away indeed. That citizen is now one in almost 210 million individuals: her impact has been diluted by a factor of almost 10. When we consider that regional lawmaking is a process largely controlled by members of the executive branches, references to "a democratic deficit" seem perfectly appropriate. The terminology has thus far been applied most often to the EU, where complex legislative processes in Brussels (guided by appointed regional bureaucrats and members of the executive branches of the member states, with only some influence from the European Parliament) have alienated EU citizens for decades (Zweifel 2002). Yet it is a problem that is bound to afflict any regional legislative process—even those that are designed with the question of democratic representation in mind.

Third, interventionism can introduce inefficiencies in industries and beyond. A benign interpretation of regional regulation assumes that regional law always helps business and other types of activities. Yet regional law may also prove quite harmful. This is likely to happen when one of several conditions are met: when overwhelming technical knowledge is needed for compliance, when powerful actors push for laws that undermine competition, when an industry is undergoing fast change, when pressure is high for generating laws rapidly, and so on. Officials operating under any of these conditions are likely to produce laws that make life more difficult, rather than easier, for societal actors.

Examining the merits and limitations of minimalism and interventionism is more than a scholarly exercise. As we discussed, there were certainly pressures for minimalism in NAFTA and interventionism in the EU and Mercosur. Yet the eventual choices were not inevitable; moreover, one need not think of the choice as one between two options, but instead as a matter of degrees. Indeed, in the EU itself, scholars have noted a move toward mutual recognition or external standardization bodies, especially in the case of technologically sophisticated products. Harmonization was "cumbersome and slow" and possibly not necessary (Mattli 2001: 328). The shift took place in the 1980s (Nikolaïdis and Egan 2001: 461).

The so called New Approach to harmonization, devised in 1985, restricted directives to define the "essential requirements" that products must meet in terms of health, safety, and environmental and consumer protection. It then delegated the task of articulating more detailed requirements to three private European standardization organizations: the European Committee for Standardization, the European Committee for Electrotechnical Standardization, and the European Telecommunications Standards Institute (Mattli 2001: 329). We see the move towards minimalism in the EU in policy areas also not strictly related to technical standards for products. Stevis and Mumme (2000) argue that the EU has moved away from harmonization and towards subsidiarity and mutual recognition in the realm of environmental policy, for instance.[3]

Selective policy harmonization remains an option as well in a number of otherwise minimalist RTAs. For example, AFTA member states have made wide use of a number of mutual recognition agreements in various industries.[4] At the same time, by August 2003, they had also developed harmonized standards for twenty priority products groups, including items such as motors, engines, rubber condoms, and medical rubber gloves. A large number of procedural and safety standards were also developed for the medical and drug industries.[5] All this suggests that there are reasons to consider at some length the merits and limitations of interventionism and minimalism.

[3] Though, as noted in chapter 3, the overall number of directives and regulations with harmonizing content has systematically increased in the EU throughout the 1980s and 1990s. See Fligstein and Stone Sweet (2001: 44), Fligstein and McNichol (1998: 77), and Duina (2003).

[4] See the ASEAN Framework Agreement on Mutual Recognition Arrangements of 1998 and its application to electronic products and cosmetics.

[5] For key documents, see the Internet site of the ASEAN's Secretariat: http://www.aseansec.org/4951.htm.

The presence of minimalist and interventionist approaches to integration brings us to a second point of reflection. How will the differences in cognitive approaches to integration affect trade *between* RTAs? Indeed, we must wonder what takes place when two interventionist blocs intensify their trade relations. We must also ask what takes place when trade intensifies between one minimalist and one interventionist RTA or between two minimalist RTAs. Ultimately, what this book identified as a regional problem will become a cross-regional or global problem. Officials may opt for a minimalist solution. On the other hand, they might embark on the articulation of a global system of agreements and even laws (Jameson and Miyoshi 1998). To the degree that such exchanges between markets already take place, we would expect to find evidence of initial strategies. Some interesting evidence is available on the EU and Mercosur. In response to increasing trade between the two regions, officials—in keeping with their own interventionist approaches—have already taken steps to address some regulatory differences though a process of harmonization.

The Interregional Framework Cooperation Agreement between the European Community and the Southern Common Market of 1999 is a good example. Article 6(1) states that "the Parties agree to cooperate in promoting the approximation of quality standards for agri-food products and industrial goods and certification." As a second example, Mercosur reports with Decision 23/97 that the "progressive harmonization of statistical methodologies" would facilitate trade between the two blocs (Annex II) by making possible the comparison of data on tariffs, technological matters, and industrial activities. As a result, the two RTAs have committed resources and working groups (such as EUROSTAT for the EU and the four national statistical institutes for Mercosur) to this task. The result will most likely be the harmonization of methods for representing social reality.

These and other initiatives reflect a strong interest on the part of the EU in particular in generating a cross-regional regulatory framework. The EU Commission's Latin America Directorate (Mercosur Desk), in an important overview of its strategic plans for increased EU-Mercosur trade for the period 2002–2006, summarized its position as follows:

> In the area of the single market policy the EU's strategy is the reinforcement of the economic integration process with a liberalisation of markets and the development of a *legislative framework* compatible with this objective, which ensures an adequate and effective protection of intellectual and industrial property rights, prevents money laundering, protects personal data and guarantees minimum standards for public procurement without being trade restrictive. Such a legislative framework would be economically bene-

ficial to the EU and Mercosur, facilitating trade, the investment and the establishment of companies on both sides. (European Commission 2002: 23, emphasis added)

As we read this text more closely, we also note the effort on the part of the EU to push Mercosur legislators to produce laws that are very similar to those of the EU, so as to make cross-regional agreements all the more feasible. Consider this passage:

In the area of competition the EU is *stimulating Mercosur to adopt legislation on competition which is basically inspired by the EU competition policy*. Mercosur will create the Competition Authority and in our negotiation for the Association Agreement a co-operation will be established between the two authorities. A [*sic*] technical assistance could be provided to Mercosur. (European Commission 2002: 24, emphasis added)

Funds have thus been allocated to help Mercosur's "insitutionalisation." In 2003, funds for the harmonization of Mercosur's technical standards were €4 million, those for statistics €2 million (European Commission 2002: 57).

In contrast to this aggressive approach, initial evidence on agreements between minimalist RTAs points to a preference for continued minimalism. Officials stress the importance of mutual recognition and regulatory transparency. Both approaches safeguard the integrity of existing regulatory approaches. Consider, for example the ongoing trade negotiations between AFTA and the Closer Economic Relations Trade Agreement (CER). The latter is an economic agreement between Australia and New Zealand. The founding Framework for the AFTA-CER Closer Economic Partnership was signed in September 2002. When it comes to regulatory issues, it lists the promotion of "transparency of regulations" as an objective (Article 4). In 2003, after the first year of operations, emphasis was put on the need for mutual recognition agreements for standards for fast moving consumer goods, such as food and electronics (Othman 2003). More transparent investment regimes were also urged. There will be no major cross-regional regulatory effort in Southeast Asia.[6]

A different approach among minimalist RTAs seems almost impossible. Those RTAs lack rich regional legislative texts. There is therefore relatively little that can be subject to harmonization. If interested in cross-regional regulatory frameworks, officials would have to devise those frameworks without building on regional precedents—a very difficult task. An alternative might be to develop cross-regional regulatory frameworks that

---

[6] At the same time, we should also note that the possibility of developing common approaches to regulation in certain areas has not been dismissed (Fallow 2002).

harmonize national regimes, whatever those might be. Yet it is almost impossible to imagine that countries that have hesitated in the first place to enter into deep regional agreements would be willing to join deep crossnational agreements.

Trade agreements between an interventionist and a minimalist RTA are to date difficult to find. Yet, we can safely hypothesize that the outcome would point towards some form of minimalism again. Disparities in regulatory regimes would, in fact, be between the whole interventionist RTA and each individual member state of the minimalist RTA (and with the minimalist RTA as a whole only on those policy areas where otherwise minimalist officials have engaged in heavy regulation). Such an asymmetry is unlikely to lead to harmonization: again, those member states that were unwilling to coalesce around an interventionist RTA of their own are sure to hesitate to undergo some form of harmonization with a distant RTA.

If this reasoning holds, then we can hypothesize a world segmented into areas where interventionist RTAs have developed rich cross-national regulatory regimes and areas where minimalist RTAs engage in mildly regulated trade with other minimalist RTAs and interventionist RTAs. The emerging picture is one where we do not observe a global legislative system but rather the presence of two systems of regulation.

The conclusion is tentative, however. It is premised on the notion that RTA officials will continue to differ in their evaluation of the merits and limits of interventionism and minimalism. Should NAFTA break apart partly because of a lack of regulatory principles (not an impossible scenario) and a more interventionist approach be pursued, the course of events could dramatically change across the globe. Similarly, should the EU collapse on the weight of its own legislative maze or—more realistically—should EU officials abandon heavy regulation in words and deeds (and possibly hand the task over to international organizations, as they have already done in part), tendencies worldwide would shift. In such a scenario, one can imagine the institutionalization of international organizations as the sources of regulation. This could apply not only to technical matters but also to other topics such as labor. One can easily imagine a strengthened role for the International Labor Organization in setting worldwide standards on a much larger number of topics than it currently addresses.

A third point of reflection concerns the question of change in any given RTA. To some, the arguments and evidence presented in the preceding chapters might appear to point to a picture of a predetermined path of evolution for each RTA. The language of constraints and limited choice seems to leave little room for unexpected outcomes in relation to both the construction of RTAs and their evolution through time. Put differently, the book may appear to paint a fundamentally static picture—a picture of little change in each RTA—rather than a story of dynamism and novelty.

This reading of the book is, however, inaccurate. As we noted in the first two chapters, continuity does not affect every member state in the same manner. Indeed, when we consider the high number of laws that are produced in RTAs, it inevitably means some departure for most, if not all, member states at some point or another. More importantly, though, there is a difference between continuity with the past and absence of change. In continuity there is, in fact, change—but a specific type of change. In continuity we observe that the present builds upon, and contains elements of, the past; yet we do not mistake the present for the past. From the perspective of continuity, the present brings novelty much as in music new notes generally follow preceding ones. Hence, throughout the book, much of our attention was spent on understanding how actors, given certain constraints, pursued their aspirations and interests. The assumption was that several outcomes within a certain range were possible.[7]

We can recall, for instance, the crafting of NAFTA's NAALC. We learned that this was an explicit attempt on the part of President Bill Clinton to assuage the concerns of trade unions fearful that NAFTA would undermine their established rights. That concern, however, could have been met in multiple ways. The NAALC was ultimately a strategic initiative of a sitting president eager (indeed, desperate) to retain the support of his political base. The expansion of dairy companies in the Mercosur region, in turn, could have happened in a number of ways. Changing domestic policies and a free-market environment in the 1980s certainly prepared dairy companies in Argentina and Brazil for international competition. Mercosur legislation created the regulatory underpinnings for a single dairy market. Yet the strategy of executives to transform their companies from national to international players in a short time was but one of several reasonable responses. They could have chosen a more gradual approach. As María Juana Rivera of the Ministerio de Economía y Producción in Argentina explained to the author, "the big dairy players saw Mercosur as a great opportunity to grow. . . . They were there from the start, pushing for market liberalization and the elimination of regulatory asymmetries, so that they could grow . . . but, certainly, they could have been more cautious too."[8]

---

[7] As pointed out in chapter 2, when framed in these terms, the argument of this book is aligned with path dependence theory—a school of thought in political science, sociology, and economics that emphasizes the importance of the past is delineating and limiting, but not defining, the future (Mahoney 2000).

[8] Interview with the author, Buenos Aires, Argentina, August 2003. See chap. 3, n. 25 for Rivera's full job title.

In the EU too, we can state without hesitation that the absence of EU law on the rights of labor to strike and form unions is ultimately one of several results that could have come from a clash between conflicting preferences. British business made it clear that the country could be crippled by the introduction of those rights. Their view was fully shared by Margaret Thatcher and, possibly with some convincing, by Tony Blair. Yet as they fought other Europeans, matters could have followed a different course than the crafting of declarations with questionable legal clout. A number of outcomes, then, were possible and would have been consistent with the political-institutional perspective of this book. A similar observation can be made with regard to the specific laws that EU officials developed on behalf of women. As we saw, the EU member states had rich but also diverse national legal traditions on this subject. We can safely assert that the resulting EU system did not replicate any one national tradition in full; rather, it represented one of many possible combinations of those systems.

These observations bring us to two more important points related to change. This book ultimately offers the reader a "snapshot" of three RTAs at a given point in time. If change is indeed possible, we cannot rule out the possibility that today's observable differences across RTAs may no longer be there at some point in the future. The EU and NAFTA might one day move towards more standardization in the realm of dairy products (or Mercosur towards a more minimalist approach). Women's groups will probably gain a more powerful voice in South America, while their counterparts in North America might find the desire and collective will to influence the course of integration there. The EU might in turn recognize the rights to strike and form associations, while migrant workers might be given unemployment rights in NAFTA and Mercosur. On the other hand, where today we find similarities, tomorrow we might find differences. RTAs are open-ended projects, whose evolution cannot be easily predicted. The objective of this book was not to paint a final, static picture of RTAs, but to delineate a logic for their rather different evolutions.

We should also remember that we observed significant dynamism and novelty in the specific types of laws that RTA officials crafted. The area of dairy products in the three RTAs is but one example. Those laws do deviate to some degree from existing practices: they do not replicate everything from those practices, but rather add, amend, and delete in small degrees. The same applies for organizational change. The regional expansion of women's groups in the EU had no precedent in the region, though of course we saw that it was in the making for decades as women gained more and more power in each member state. RTAs in themselves, then, very much embody change and novelty.

GLOBALIZATION, MARKET BUILDING, AND NEOLIBERALISM

In chapter 1, we discussed three important topics of much current debate: the limits of globalization, how markets are constructed, and the spread of neoliberalism across the world. This book speaks to those debates. Often, the evidence supports one side of those debates over another; at the same time, however, it also demands that we reframe those debates to take into account the presence of RTAs.

Consider globalization first. The debate was sparked in the early 1990s by a number of scholars who believed that the arrival of a global society (or elements of a global society, such as a global economy or a global polity) was imminent and inevitable. Those claims were soon met by those who firmly believed in the nation state and, over the years, by more moderate claims of partial globalization—according to which only certain elements of nation states were acquiring a global dimension. This book sides with the critics of globalization but, in so doing, does not necessarily share their optimism about the continuing relevance of nation states.

We can summarize the book's insights into the globalization debate as follows:

- We are *not* moving towards a single global economic system; because market activity requires supporting legal structures and generates organizational expansions, the prerequisites for a global system of law or global organizations are also absent.
- At the same time, we do *not* live in a world where nation states remain the sole building blocks of society: nation states have lost some of their economic, legal, and organizational integrity.
- We are instead witnessing the rise of *distinctive regional markets*: economic, and therefore legal and organizational, spaces comprising *several* nation states. These regional markets draw from the shared institutional and political traditions of their member states: this guarantees not only their uniqueness but also, at times, departures from existing conditions in any given member state.
- The globalization debate should be reframed. With the advent of RTAs, the world is experiencing the pull of three competing forces: the global, the regional, and the national. Any thorough analysis of current events requires that we investigate closely each of these forces and how they relate to each other.

From a tri-polar perspective of the world, global forces and nation states are not engaged in a zero-sum struggle. A weakening of the nation state need not mean a strengthening of global structures and trends: it could instead reflect the arrival of invasive regional trade arrangements. Nation states may continue to assert themselves as relevant actors in the world without direct consequences for globalization: they could be shaping in profound ways the course of regional integration. Importantly, from this perspective we should resist thinking of RTAs as stepping-stones towards a global world or as links between the national and the global. RTAs are stable and enduring entities: coupling market activity with legislative and organizational structures, they bring together countries with fairly similar histories, as well as complementary economic needs and outlooks.

The emphasis on regions is, of course, in line with the works of scholars such as Huntington (1997) and Ohmae (1993). They, too, have emphasized the increasing importance of regions. At the same time, these scholars hold quite different understandings of what might constitute a region.[9] In some cases, culture and religion define regional spaces; in other cases, adjacent segments of nation states involved in heavy trading constitute a region; in yet other cases, regions are mostly geographical entities, such as South America or sub-Saharan Africa. This book understands regions to be areas comprising a number of member states with deeply integrated economies, supporting legal structures, and actors with regional capabilities and outlooks. This amounts to an economic-political-societal understanding of regions.

This book has important implications for our understanding of how markets emerge and function. In response to the claim made by traditional economists about the natural and unaided rise of markets and economic activity, sociologists and others have recently argued that markets are, in fact, socially constructed in rich political, historical, and cultural environments. There is little work, however, on whether *transnational* market building is also a social process (Fligstein and Stone Sweet 2001; Fligstein and McNichol 1998). But for some exceptions, such as Dobbin (1997) for instance, most of the work on market building tends also to be noncomparative (Zelizer 1992; Campbell and Lindberg 1990; Hanley et al. 2002). This is especially so for works on transnational markets, whose focus has been the EU. These single-case analyses offer evidence that markets are socially constructed but do not tell us much about *how* and *why* market building can differ across geographies. This book addresses both of these issues.

The book shows that regional market building is—much like national market building, if not more—a *social* project. This is so for a number of reasons. First, RTAs constitute planned and explicit efforts to create a

[9] As discussed in chapter 1, Huntington's emphasis is on culture and religion while Ohmae's is mostly on economic activity across adjacent segments of nation states without significant supporting legal or organizational structures.

market space. In that regard, they are imagined and willed by a collective set of actors, often with a model of an ideal RTA in mind. Second, officials actively engage in the crafting of RTAs: regional markets do not "just happen"; on the contrary, thousands of concrete steps (such as the making of laws) are taken to create those markets. Third, institutional, political, and many other forces guide and influence the process of crafting markets. Fourth, markets stimulate and depend upon the participation of various societal players (economic, political, administrative) to function. Importantly, not everyone is "invited to play": only those who are prepared for life in a broader marketplace, and for whom a regional space for action is being created, have the opportunity.

The book then shows how and why market building is a remarkably different endeavor in different geographies. Fligstein and McNichol conclude their important study of the EU by underlining that "rule structures and market integration became linked" in the European experience, leading to an exponential production of laws over the decades (Fligstein and McNichol 1998: 1219). They proceed by hypothesizing—without empirical support—that much the same is either happening in other RTAs or will have to happen: "as trade grows, pressure will build on [other RTAs] to expand rule-making capacities and procedures" (1998: 1237). Our comparative analysis of the EU, NAFTA, and Mercosur suggests otherwise. The relationship between market building and rules can vary significantly across markets both in quantitative terms (how many laws) but also in qualitative terms (the target and content of laws). It can also involve remarkably different realms of society and societal organizations. This suggests that *there exists no single blueprint* for market building: markets require supporting structures and the participation of actors, but those needs can clearly be met in a variety of ways. This observation is made with data from regional markets but likely applies to national market building as well.

What, we are then bound to ask, determines the specific characteristic of each market-building effort? This book points to the importance of institutional and political factors—and ultimately *continuity* with local conditions—in shaping regional market efforts. Continuity suggests that markets must *"fit in"* in a given society, that they are molded to ensure a *correspondence* with other structures and dimensions of social life. As they are introduced in a given social system, they take on forms that are acceptable to that system.[10] Other variables, such as efficiency consider-

---

[10] The reader familiar with my previous book, *Harmonizing Europe*, will recall that I have emphasized the importance of "fit" before. In that book, however, the argument was somewhat different. There, I showed that when a regional law challenges the institutional conditions in a given member state, that law is unlikely to be properly implemented in that

ations, exposure to external and perhaps competing models of integration, and the placement of a given RTA in the international economic system, seem less important. Again, these observations about continuity were obviously made in light of data from three RTAs; they too, however, should apply to both regional and national market building, though only a systematic program of comparative analysis of market building at both the regional and national levels is needed to confirm our observations.

The book has implications for a third debate: the spread of neoliberalism throughout the world at the end of the twentieth century. That debate focuses on the implementation of this new free market ideology in different geographies. Countering claims by economists and others that the adoption of that ideology would lead to ever greater uniformity in terms of policies and outcomes (Boltho 1996), political scientists and sociologists have emphasized that abstract ideas were articulated and implemented quite differently in different countries. Often institutional and political variables were responsible for that variation. The evidence presented in the preceding chapters confirms, but also challenges, these insights into the nature and impact of neoliberalism. The book's contributions to this debate can be summarized as follows.

Neoliberalism, at least as it has informed the regional movement towards free trade, is a fairly generic ideology—much as is the case with many other economic as well as political and social ideologies. It is a deceivingly simple system of ideas in need of much conceptual articulation. It promotes free trade but does not define unambiguously key terms such as "free," "trade," "non-tariff barriers," "services," "growth," "economy," "regulation," and so on. Neoliberalism offers a *general vision* of trade across countries rather than a detailed set of ideas and concepts. To complicate matters, neoliberalism also *lacks instructions for its practical implementation* in the real world. The ideology says little about the types of regulation, deadlines, landmarks, and other processes and mechanisms that can ensure its realization in practice.

Both the conceptual articulation and the implementation planning for neoliberal projects occur at the local level. Market officials work in rich institutional and political contexts to translate general concepts into concrete reality. Because those officials and contexts differ across geogra-

---

member state. This did not lead me to conclude that regional law is, by and large, in line with the institutional conditions of the member states—a major point of this book. The arguments of the two books can nonetheless be combined rather nicely. This book argues that RTAs generally match the institutional conditions in the member states but also acknowledges that, inevitably, at times RTAs can challenge conditions in the member. *Harmonizing Europe* argues that when such challenges occur, the demands of RTAs are, in practice, rejected.

phies, neoliberalism *manifests itself differently in different locations.*[11] Thus, only in some cases, for instance, does the pursuit of free trade lead to the harmonization of environmental regulations. Similarly, only in other cases does it lead to the imposition of high sanitary requirements for food packaging processes. We note as well the importance of local institutions and politics in shaping outcomes—in line with the beliefs of those who doubt that neoliberalism has spread evenly across countries.

Once again, however, this book does not fully side with one side of the argument. Most scholars proposing that neoliberalism has not been uniformly implemented across geographies present evidence from *nation states*. This book actually undermines that position. The pursuit of free trade has led to some degree of convergence across the member states of any given RTA—whether in terms of legislative parameters or the structures and programs of organizations in certain spheres of social life, if not other areas. In this regard, neoliberalism *has acted as a force of uniformity*, bringing the member states into cooperative arrangements that diminish their distinctiveness. The debate over the spread of neoliberalism at the closing of the twentieth century should not be limited to questions of convergence or divergence across nation states and should instead recognize the presence and implications of RTAs.

COMPARATIVE REGIONAL MARKET BUILDING:
A NEW RESEARCH AGENDA

This book identifies and makes an initial contribution to an emerging field of study: the comparative analysis of regional market building. Much exciting research lies ahead. Some can build directly from this book's approach and empirical output. A different strand can depart significantly from this book's perspective, in ways that both challenge and complement that perspective. Both approaches are discussed here.

Building on This Book

Regional market building is a complex process. This book addresses only very particular dimensions of market building: the use of law for cognitive standardization and the adjustments of certain organizations to integration. A great number of additional dimensions require investigation.

[11] Here, a note on world society theory seems appropriate. World society theorists (Meyer et al. 1997; Frank et al. 2000) posit that global "models" for the behavior and organization of collectivities (states, companies, associations) and individuals are shaping life across the world, leading to a convergence effect. This book argues otherwise: global models exist but they do not, by themselves, produce convergence.

I coded the entire body of NAFTA texts and then three important sections of the laws of the EU and Mercosur. Within those sections, the high number of definitional and normative notions for the EU and Mercosur greatly exceeded the number of notions found in all the NAFTA texts. It seemed safe to conclude that officials from the EU and Mercosur have indeed taken a more aggressive definitional and normative approach to integration. When we considered variation in the specific targets and content of regional law, however, the analysis was by necessity more limited. Much of the empirical discussion centered on three topical areas: working women, dairy products, and labor rights. We observed strong evidence of variation in those areas. Yet those are only three possible areas of investigation. We remain unclear about how representative such variation is of the entire legal system of each of the three RTAs. Future research projects could thus undertake comparative analyses of different types of laws in the three RTAs to test for further variance. They could consider, for instance, the environment, real estate, education, transportation, welfare, and many other areas.

The book has also considered a very selected set of organizations. Indeed, attention turned to only one set of interest groups (women's groups), competitors in one type of industry (dairy), and a certain type of state administrative unit (departments of labor and employment). The observed variation was certainly impressive and, moreover, matched fairly well with the variation found in the legal dimension. Yet we did not consider how representative—statistically speaking—such variation is. Can we conclude from the evidence that there is systematic variation in organizational adjustments across RTAs? Future studies could broaden the data set and test for the extent of variation in and across RTAs. This would apply to interest groups, businesses, and state units.

We must also recognize that other types of organizations exist as well. Consider, for instance, political parties, professional associations (such as those for physicians or university professors), civic associations (such as poker players, automotive clubs, literary clubs, and so on), think tanks and independent policy institutes, university systems, and others. Future studies could examine the responses of these organizations to regional integration. Is it possible that expansion has happened with certain types of organizations (perhaps those most directly affected by regional law) and not others?

Future research could also challenge the measurements used for organizational expansion. In the case of business, for instance, our attention turned to the productive infrastructure of firms. Companies may retain a national profile on that dimension but still expand regionally in other respects: with exports, with foreign sales forces, with informal and formal cooperation agreements with foreign companies, and so on.

Attention should also go to additional RTAs. This book said little about the legal and organizational landscapes of any other RTA, such as AFTA. The EU and Mercosur are likely to be the two most legalistic RTAs in existence. Through certainly prominent, they may also be a minority. Because we argued that law was a significant driver of regional expansion for organizations, it follows that organizational expansion may have been less significant in other RTAs. We wonder as well whether the political-institutional framework presented in this book can apply to ten or twenty RTAs. A study of the legal architecture of RTAs and the common- versus civil-law traditions of the member states would be both relatively easy to execute and quite instructive. It is indeed possible that a political-institutional approach carries validity in some RTAs but not others—a disturbing thought for those social scientists eager to discover universal laws that hold true across time and space.

Most importantly, perhaps, future studies could investigate the question of variation beyond law and organizations. The literature on the EU is extremely rich and, as such, discusses trends in the EU that might apply to other RTAs. Yet the same literature is almost always noncomparative. A similar statement can be made about the smaller literatures on NAFTA, Mercosur, and other RTAs: on the whole, they lack a comparative dimension. This is understandable in light of the relatively young age of most of these efforts. The number of topics for possible analysis is overwhelming. Consider, for instance, the question of culture. Does regional integration generate a regional culture (or elements of that)? Recent studies on the EU certainly state so (Kurzer 2001; Duina and Breznau 2002). If so, what exactly becomes regional and why? Is it different across RTAs? This is a fundamental question, of course. Such a study could very well begin with an analysis of the impact of the definitional and normative notions found in regional law on the lives of everyday people.

Scholars should consider as well questions of language and framing. Proponents of RTAs have surely encountered opposition and, in an effort to overcome obstacles, have developed a discourse for what regional integration is and what its benefits might be. An analysis of discourse surrounding regional integration would be fascinating. Questions of symbolism, legitimacy, economic terminology, and much more would need to be addressed. Parallel studies could carry out comparative studies of protest discourse across RTAs. Who objects to regional integration across RTAs? What reasoning do they offer? What explains their opposition? Much as already been written on opposition movements in specific RTAs (especially NAFTA). A rich literature in the area of social movements can already provide interested scholars with the conceptual framework for analysis.

Researchers should also examine the varied impact of RTAs on the integrity of nation states. This is of course a major topic of discussion among scholars of the EU. The traditional split between intergovernmentalists and neofunctionalists that shaped much of the writing on the EU in the 1970s, 1980s, and even 1990s was ultimately about the continuing relevance of the nation state (Duina 2000). Integration is sure to challenge the structural part of nation states in countless ways: legislatively, administratively, judicially, and so on. It is also likely to alter their substantive core: national identity, ideas of citizenship, ethnic composition, language, geographical boundaries, and so on. Yet, the specific nature of those challenges is sure to vary across RTAs. We can speak of the "Europeanization" of nation states in Europe and of the "Mercosurization" of nation states in South America. We wonder what such a process entails in each case and why differences are sure to exist.

Beyond Institutions and Politics

In this book, I put forth a political-institutional explanation for the evolution of law and organizations in RTAs. As outlined in figure 2.1, I argued that preexisting legal and power contexts influence in fundamental ways the nature of regional law in each RTA. I then argued that those same contexts plus regional law (itself an institution) shape how organizations respond to regional integration. Much attention was therefore paid to institutions and politics. A number of other explanatory approaches, however, could shed light on the observed course of events. These approaches could both complement and challenge the political-institutional approach of this book.[12] Further research should articulate and test those approaches in some detail.

One line of research should consider the objectives of the three RTAs in question. We noted that Mercosur has the largest overall number of definitional and normative notions in the realms of economics, the environment, and public health. We noted that the EU comes in a close second, and NAFTA has the fewest. Perhaps the differences between Mercosur and the EU on the one hand, and NAFTA on the other are most easily explained by the fact the first two RTAs aim at a common market rather than a simple free-trade area. More ambitious goals call for more ambitious supporting structures: closer integration calls for more potential targets of standardization. Mercosur and the EU aim at the liberalization of all services, capital, and labor. NAFTA is mostly about goods and, to a lesser extent, capital and services. It does not consider labor. The relatively small difference between the EU and Mercosur could itself be attributed

---

[12] I borrow from Lockhart (1999) the idea that alternative approaches can often complement, rather than invalidate, each other. This viewpoint is, in my view, the most likely to yield a reliable picture of reality.

to factors other than objectives—such as technical approaches to standardization, a clearer commitment to standardization on the part of Mercosur officials, and even imprecision in the coding methodology used in this book. Taking the objectives of integration into consideration may thus shed light on perhaps the most obvious differences among RTAs.

A few words of caution are, however, in order. I have shown elsewhere that Mercosur officials have so far barely addressed labor as well as capital and services (Duina 2003). Most of Mercosur's laws target goods. In the case of goods, a direct comparison with NAFTA can easily be made: Mercosur has significantly more laws than NAFTA. In addition, if objectives can account for some of the differences in the volume of law between the EU and Mercosur on the one side and NAFTA on the other, they probably cannot account for variation in the specific target and content of regional law. Recall, for instance, that NAFTA recognizes the right to strike and form unions, but the EU does not. The focus on grand objectives probably also explains little of the organizational developments we discussed. We observed variation across RTAs in the types of organizations that develop regionally, and not in the volume of those organizations.

A second line of research should consider the gap in development levels among the member states. The EU has industrialized and developed countries as member states. Mercosur has semideveloped countries as member states. NAFTA is quite different: there we have two of the most sophisticated economies in the world interacting with a developing country. Moreover, in NAFTA we have a major superpower that cannot be expected to surrender the integrity of its legal system. Given all this, we should expect that EU and Mercosur officials would find it relatively easy (and therefore attractive) to harmonize differences in legal systems: that is a way to seek closer and more intimate integration. In the NAFTA region, by contrast, from the very beginning officials voiced their preference for cautious and limited integration.

This explanation can probably help us understand differences in the volume of legislation produced. The legal systems of the United States and Canada support very different economies than that of Mexico. Legislation on intellectual property, services, e-commerce, consumer rights, the environment, public health, product safety, and workers' health (to name a few areas) is quite different in the United States and Canada from that in Mexico. Harmonization is thus likely to appear both daunting and unnecessary. Why, the public would ask, is a shared rich and detailed legal system needed for Mexico, the United States, and Canada? Integration—albeit of a limited sort—can happen without harmonization. In the case of Mercosur and the EU, aspirations were loftier. As Manuel Olarreaga of the Secretaría del Mercosur explained to the author, there "are important but also surmountable differences among the member states: solving them is an important step in the integration of our economies."[13] A similar attitude has clearly driven the process of European integration.

At the same time, we can see that a focus on economic similarities or gaps among the member states has important limitations that any future study would have to address. It can say little about variation in the specific targets and content of law. Why, for instance, have EU officials hesitated to standardize the world of dairy products or recognize the rights of workers to strike and form unions? Why were those rights recognized in NAFTA and Mercosur? Similarly, this explanation offers little insight into the question of variance in organizational developments. Had this book offered evidence on variation in the number of organizations expanding regionally (with few doing so in NAFTA and more in the EU and Mercosur—as indeed one would expect if the link between regional law and organizations proposed in this book is valid), then perhaps this perspective could shed some light. Given the evidence presented here, however, this explanatory perspective seems to have limited application.

An additional theoretical approach seems promising. A turn to institutions and politics has seemed quite powerful throughout the study. Yet at times, institutions and politics almost appeared as "givens" and, therefore, as somewhat causally irrelevant. A broader variable seemed to be responsible for the observed patterns: culture. Social scientific theories of culture emphasize the importance of shared beliefs, values, and norms for the unfolding of social phenomena. Actors are relevant, of course, but only as conduits through which those collectively held beliefs, values, and norms express themselves. Religious, political, economic, and other types of institutions also reflect the cultural contexts in which they operate: they, too, are conduits for the expression of culture (Goldstein and Keohane 1993). In the 1980s and 1990s, social scientists often criticized cultural explanations as unconvincing: they found it difficult to identify the causal mechanisms linking culture to outcomes (Hall 1986). Moreover, they noted that culture could not account for variation in outcomes within a given society at any given point in time. What could explain, for instance, the disparate voting behavior of individuals who shared virtually identical cultural backgrounds? Yet cultural explanations retain a certain appeal, especially when one is considering differences in outcomes across societies, and recent comparative scholarship has once again turned to culture (Hall and Soskice 2001b: 13). Culture almost always varies across societies: such variation is likely to have an impact on the behavior of individuals and institutions and, thus, on societal outcomes.

A cultural perspective could probably explain some of the most im-

---

[13] Interview with the author, Montevideo, Uruguay, July 2003. See chap. 3, n. 24 for Olarreaga's job title.

portant differences across the EU, Mercosur, and NAFTA that were described in this book. Consider the presence of common-law and civil-law traditions in the different regions. Common law reflects a certain Anglo-Saxon pragmatism: a tendency to shy away from abstraction and to avoid a priori moral or other types of principles, a predilection for accepting reality as is, and a propensity to allow societal institutions to emerge from social life rather than to allow visions of a wished-for world to mold those institutions. The Anglo-Saxon pragmatist would never dream of codifying the world, let alone of devising countless laws to regulate, a priori, the lives of citizens. Civil-law traditions, on the other hand, are certainly a reflection of some form of continental idealism. Such idealism embodies a desire for completeness and perfection, both in understanding reality and in the future evolution of human beings and societies. The continental idealist cringes at the prospect of letting social life take its course without the guidance of preestablished limits and rules. Such an approach is both basic and devoid of any hope: it represents a surrender to reality as opposed to an optimistic (if not romantic) effort to depart from the common and strive for something better.

When we consider the design choices of RTA officials, then, pointing to the presence of common- versus civil-law traditions in the member states may be appropriate but not truly enlightening. The choices of RTA officials might be most clearly explained by a set of deeply engrained approaches to social life in general—of which common- or civil-law traditions are but one expression. NAFTA's minimalism might reflect a widely shared pragmatism in the societies of the United States and Canada. The more legalistic approaches of EU and Mercosur officials might represent instead a collective tendency of people in those areas to impose onto reality artificial forms of control. That which explains the common- versus civil-law split among the member states of RTAs also explains the general character of regional law.

Similarly, preexisting legal approaches to particular spheres of social life—which were argued in this book to have influenced the specific targets and content of regional law—can themselves be seen as reflections of powerful cultural contexts. The rich protectionist legacies in the area of dairy products in Italy, France, and Spain unquestionably were the result of a societal celebration of farming life and of food. In all three countries, there exists a close bond between agriculture and life. Farming is a way of life. Recall the words of France's Minister of Agriculture, Hervé Gaymard: "For us, agricultural products are more than marketable goods; they are the fruit of a love of an occupation and of the land, which has been developed over many generations" (Economist 2002b: 18). Similarly, the absence of progressive laws on women in Mercosur is itself clearly a reflection of certain viewpoints about women and their role in society. In this case, a culture of machismo exists in those countries, and this certainly has limited what could be contemplated and achieved at the transnational level.

Yet we should remember that cultural theories suffer from their own limitations. They seem especially powerful when outcomes seem highly consistent with other events or configurations in society. In those cases, the observer is naturally inclined to move beyond the specificity of the situation at hand and to investigate the consistency itself in search of the common causal variable. In so doing, the most immediate causal variables—typically individuals or groups of individuals—are lost. They are seen as conduits for the expression of more powerful forces. The same can be said, of course, for institutional variables. The observer hesitates to attribute to human agency the necessary freedom of action that would make it responsible for the events at hand. Cultural explanations lose their power, however, when one notices that the same outcomes could have easily happened (or have already happened) in totally different societal contexts or when one notices that the given outcomes could not possibly have happened a few years prior. In those cases, other causal mechanisms must have been at work—ones that are far less linked to large-scale and relatively stable cultural systems.

There are additional alternative explanatory frameworks worth considering. Three can be briefly mentioned. One concerns legislative legitimacy. Two interviewees in South America suggested that Mercosur's rich legislative output is itself a function of the lack of implementation of national law. The turn to regional law constitutes a hopeful trend towards the creation of a new set of laws that have more legitimacy. Another explanation focuses on levels of exposure to world society. Mercosur in many ways imitates the EU; it also borrows heavily from regulations already promulgated by international organizations. María Juana Rivera, of Argentina's Ministerio de Economía y Producción and an active participant in Mercosur lawmaking, admitted openly that her assistant uses the Internet extensively to see what others have done.[14] There are instances where the EU too has borrowed from Mercosur.[15] NAFTA is possibly less reliant on the outside world. Yet another approach could be macroeconomic and efficiency-centered. Somewhat in line with the new trade theories discussed in chapter 3, one could argue that RTAs represent, with their differences, ideal configurations for economic activity: they

---

[14] Interview with the author, Buenos Aires, Argentina, August 2003. See chap. 3, n. 25 for Rivera's full job title.

[15] For a verbatim example of Mercosur's borrowing from the EU, see EU Directive 88/378 of 1988 and Mercosur Resolution 54/92 of 1992 and their stipulations about toys and their safety requirements.

integrate those industries that withstand the rigor of international competition but not others, they remove nontariff barriers to trade by harmonizing laws when this is truly beneficial to a given industry, and so on. Future research could articulate and test these and other explanatory frameworks.

Concluding Remarks

The pursuit of free trade across nation states has given rise to a large number of RTAs: economic spaces where a combination of goods, services, capital, and labor circulate freely across national borders. Such a pursuit, however, has been far more than a simple matter of economic exchange. It has required the articulation of complex legal systems and has stimulated, in turn, the expansion of important societal organizations, such as interest groups, businesses, and state administrations. Local conditions on the ground have shaped both legal and organizational developments. The result is a world of highly distinctive, historically rooted, and thus enduring RTAs.

This book represents one of the earliest efforts to examine the pursuit of free trade in comparative terms. But for the European exception, where writing on market building is at this point extensive, we still know very little about RTAs. We lack the necessary frameworks and tools for analysis. A great number of questions about the nature of RTAs, their impact on everyday life, and their implications for pressing topics of much current debate remain without answers. This book is a first step toward a sophisticated understanding of free trade and its pursuit in various geographies: it offers an argument for the social foundations and distinctiveness of RTAs. It is, at the same time, an invitation for more research and work.

APPENDIX

CHAPTER 3 EXPLAINS only in part how I identified which EU and Mercosur laws affect economic life, the environment, and public health. It also does not explain how—when the number of laws with definitions or normative content in a given realm was too high for coding (economics for both the EU and Mercosur, public health for Mercosur)—I selected a sample of laws to estimate the overall number of definitional and normative passages for all laws in that realm.

Chapter 3 also does not provide information about the basic character (international versus supranational, whether obligatory and superior to national law) of NAFTA, EU, and Mercosur law. This appendix addresses both the selection and basic character of regional law.

The coding is for EU and Mercosur laws related to economic life, public health, and the environment. How did I determine whether a given law belonged to any one of these three realms?

Laws related to economic life were those concerned with the production and exchange of goods, labor, capital, and services. For the environment, they were those related to the preservation of natural habitats, animal life, eco-systems, and natural resources. For public health, they were laws related to the well-being of human populations. The EU's own classification schemes of its laws into subject areas helped me identify which laws to examine.[1] Official directories of Mercosur law do not group de-

---

[1] The EU's official database (Euro-Lex) organizes its laws into topical sections. EU laws were considered to affect economic life if they were found in these sections: free movement of goods, agriculture, fisheries, workers, services, transportation, competition, taxation, economic policy, capital movement, industrial policy, regional development, regional funding, consumer rights, and undertakings. They were considered related to the environment if they were found in the section titled "environment." They were considered related to public health if they were found in the section titled "health protection." In addition, given the possibility that one may overlook important laws because they may be categorized differently even if they affect our spheres of interest, keyword searches of the EU's database were executed (keywords used were "environment" and "public health").

cisions and resolutions by topic. I thus reviewed all laws first to determine their proper subject areas. The total number of EU and Mercosur laws thus categorized as belonging to one of the three realms exceeded three thousand.

The number of definitional and normative passages in EU and Mercosur law became very large early on in the coding. I thus opted for the following methodology to arrive at an estimate of total definitional and normative passages in the two legal systems. At times, the number of directives or regulations (for the EU) and decisions and resolutions (for Mercosur) with cognitive content affecting any one of the three realms under consideration (economics, environment, public health) exceeded one hundred. When less than a hundred, I coded all laws. When over a hundred, I selected a representative and stratified (through time) random sample of those laws.[2] I coded the laws in the sample and calculated the average number of definitional and normative passages in each law. I applied that average to the larger set of laws and then totaled all the results.

The General Character of NAFTA, EU, and Mercosur Law

NAFTA is purely an intergovernmental affair: there are no supranational bodies seeking to advance the interests of NAFTA as an entity independent of the member states.[3] Accordingly, all of NAFTA's legal outputs have thus far been produced by the member states themselves coming to consensual agreement. These agreements are also intended to regulate, above all, the relationship among the member states, as opposed to impose direct rights and obligations on private parties. The consensual nature and regulatory focus of these agreements make them *international law*, as opposed to supranational law.

The NAFTA text asserts the *obligatory* nature of its content in Article

---

[2] The size of the sample was based on a margin of error of ±10%, a confidence level of 95%, and a *p* value of .05. The stratification through time is most important for the EU, where the tendency of officials to standardize is supposed to have diminished somewhat over time. The stratification was done by decade for the EU and by year for Mercosur. Note as well that for the EU, given that officials have promulgated more and more laws through time, the number of sample laws taken for later decades was adjusted. Thus, if the total sample size of laws for economics (the only area were a sample was needed) was around 90, approximately 75% of that sample came from the 1980s and 1990s, since about 75% of all directives and regulations were produced in those years. Note that there was separate sampling and analysis (for a given policy realms) of directives and regulations (for the EU) and decisions and resolutions (for Mercosur).

[3] Implementation of NAFTA law is the responsibility of the Free Trade Commission, which has cabinet-level representatives from the three member states. The Commission is assisted by the NAFTA Secretariat; this too, however, has national "sections."

105: "The Parties shall ensure that all necessary measures are taken in order to give effect to the provisions of this Agreement, including their observance, except as otherwise provided in this Agreement, by state and provincial governments." At the same time, NAFTA law is not *superior* to national law, insofar as this would mean that, by virtue of a special status, it automatically supercedes existing national laws. In all three member states, NAFTA law enjoys the status of national law and is largely implemented as such (Fried 1994).[4] Conflicts between existing law and NAFTA law, however unlikely,[5] are addressed as any other conflict between national laws.

In the case of the EU, I coded directives and regulations: the TEC, in its various reincarnations, specifies that these shall be the instruments to be used for the creation of a common market. Directives have been broader and more sweeping in scope. Regulations have been typically more subject-specific and practical in their aim (Nugent 1994). Both are generally drafted by the European Commission (a supranational organ composed of bureaucrats working on various subject areas) and approved by the Council of Ministers (a body composed of national ministers) and, with increasing importance, by the European Parliament (as the Commission, a supranational body composed of elected national representatives).[6] Thus, EU law is *supranational law*, in so far as it is produced at least in part by legislative bodies whose mission entails the promotion of the EU as a whole, independently of the interests of the single member states.

EU directives and regulations are both *obligatory* in the member states and *superior* to national law. As to the obligatory nature of EU law, the TEC states the following with regard to directives. Article 249 states: "A directive shall be binding, as to the result to be achieved, upon each Member State to which it is addressed, but shall leave to the national authorities the choice and form of methods [of implementation]." In the case of regulations, the treaty makes a similar assertion, though it allows less latitude in the area of implementation methods, since regulations are such that they take immediate effect upon their enactment at the EU level: "A

---

[4] Thus, in the United States, for instance, the NAFTA text was adopted as an ordinary law requiring majority votes by both the House of Representatives and the Senate followed by approval of the President. However, because it dealt with a foreign power, it was given the status of a congressional-executive agreement.

[5] As law primarily concerned with the relationship between countries, NAFTA law is not likely to conflict with national law, which primarily regulates the relationships between state and private actors, and between private actors.

[6] Directives require transposition into national legal texts, while regulations take immediate legal effect on a specified date across the EU. Note that the EU has also utilized decisions to achieve its goals. More administrative than legislative acts (e.g., the decision to initiate a pilot program) decisions are not considered in this book.

regulation shall have general application. It shall be binding in its entirety and directly applicable in all Member States" (Article 249).

Nowhere in the TEC or other EU treaties and amendments, however, is the superiority of EU directives and regulations clearly asserted. Such an omission is understandable when one recalls that EU law was initially thought to be primarily international law regulating the relationship between states rather than a system of legal principles intent on regulating the behavior of public and private legal entities and persons within national territories (Weiler 1991). Under that early vision, the possibility of conflicting overlaps between national and supranational laws might have seemed reasonably small, and thus states were generally expected to simply ensure the realignment of national laws whenever necessary (Stone Sweet and Caporaso 1998).

The issue of superiority was asserted by a series of rulings of the European Court of Justice.[7] Empowered, and in fact created, by the TEC to ensure that EU law is observed (Article 220), the European Court of Justice early on faced the problem of national laws precluding the acceptance of EU directives and regulations in the member states (Folsom et al. 1996: 23–26). The first crucial ruling came in 1964 with *Costa vs. Enel* when the Court argued for the superiority of EU law vis-à-vis national laws that are created after the promulgation of EU law (Borchardt 2000):

> By contrast with ordinary international treaties, the EEC Treaty [later TEC Treaty] has created its own legal system which, on the entry into force of the treaty, became an integral part of the legal systems of the member states and which their courts are bound to apply. . . . [T]he executive force of Community law cannot vary from one state to another in deference to subsequent laws. (Case 6/64, *Costa vs. ENEL* [1964])

There remained the issue of national laws that predate the promulgation of EU law. In 1978, in Case 106/77, *Simmenthal* (1978), the Court added that from the moment of entry into force every EU law "renders automatically inapplicable any conflicting provision of . . . national law."

The case of directives, however, presented additional difficulties. Because they require transposition into national law, the repeated occurrence of directives being only partially transposed or not at all transposed (Duina 1999) raised the important question of whether national law may reign supreme in areas where directives have been enacted at the EU level but are not transposed nationally. The European Court of Justice addressed that problem directly by making EU directives, regardless of their

---

[7] The court is the final interpreter of EU law, and its decisions are superior to those of national courts.

status in the legal system of member states, relevant in the member states (Case 41/74, *Van Duyn* [1974a]). By implication, this made all conflicting national laws invalid. In Case 106/89, *Marleasing* (1990b), the court resolved that same problem by empowering national judges to consider incomplete national versions of EU directives *as if* they stated all the principles of EU directives. This de facto rewriting of national legislation in turn allowed for the invalidation of any national law conflicting with the full versions of EU law (Stone Sweet and Caporaso 1998).

In the case of Mercosur, I coded decisions and resolutions. The Protocol of Ouro Preto identifies these as the main legal tools to be used for the creation of the common market. Decisions are produced by the Consejo del Mercado Común (an intergovernmental organ composed of the ministers of foreign affairs, finance, and the heads of state). Similar to EU directives, these have tended to be rather abstract and intent on establishing broad principles (Article 40, Protocol of Ouro Preto). Resolutions are the product of the Grupo Mercado Común (also an intergovernmental organization composed of four permanent members, the ministries of foreign affairs and the economy, and national central bankers).[8] Similar to EU regulations, these have tended to be more practical and specific in nature. Decisions and resolutions stem from intergovernmental bodies and are not, therefore, supranational in nature (Haines-Ferrari 1993). They are technically closest to *international law*, though they very often present requests that do more than regulate the relationship between member states. For instance, after 1998 Mercosur laws regulating production standards for countless sectors were to be applied to both products destined for exportation (as international law might require) but also sale within a given member state.

Mercosur asserts with clarity the *obligatory* nature of its decisions and resolutions in the Protocol of Ouro Preto, which finalized Mercosur's existence after an initial period of transition. The assertion is found in four key passages. Article 9 concerns decisions, and states: "The Consejo del Mercado Común will promulgate Decisions, whose adoption will be obligatory for the Member States." Article 15 affirms the same for resolutions: "The Grupo Mercado Común will promulgate Resolutions, whose adoption will be obligatory for the Member States." Article 42 reiterates the obligatory nature of both decisions and resolutions: "The laws emanated from Mercosur's organs, which are discussed in Article 2 of this Protocol, have an obligatory character." Finally, in the Protocol of Ouro Preto, we read: "The Member States agree to undertake all measures nec-

[8] Both decisions and resolutions become effective in Mercosur thirty days after the last member state announces the adoption of the principles in question (Article 40, Protocol of Ouro Preto).

essary to ensure, in their respective countries, the realization of Mercosur laws" (Article 38).

Mercosur's founding documents do not address the question of the *superiority* of Mercosur law anywhere. The intergovernmental character of Mercosur law (like that of NAFTA law) and its related incorporation into national legal systems as, ultimately, national law do not grant it an a priori privileged status over existing laws. At the same time, most Mercosur laws interfere in practice directly with the behavior of private actors. They also require incorporation into national legal systems. This necessarily involves the repeal or overriding of those national laws whose principles preclude the realization of decisions and resolutions. Article 40 states as much, albeit indirectly: "Once the laws are approved, the Member States will adopt *the necessary measures* for their *incorporation* into the *national legal system*" (Article 40, emphasis added). Thus, while Mercosur law does not enjoy formal superiority over existing national law, it enjoys a de facto form of superiority.[9]

We should add that case law unfortunately cannot provide us with additional guidance as to the superiority of Mercosur law. The principal reason for this is the absence of such law in the first place. Mercosur lacks a formal supranational court dedicated to the interpretation of Mercosur law. Until 1998, it left dispute resolution in the hands of an informal procedure that relied on ad hoc arbitration tribunals or a group of experts depending on whether the issue involved member states only or also private parties (as specified in the Protocol of Brasilia of 1991). In 1998, the Acuerdo sobre Arbitraje Comercial Internacional del Mercosur (International Commercial Arbitration Agreement of Mercosur) was signed (though not functional until 2003, following ratification by all the member states). This introduced arbitration before a panel of three referees. It is, however, unlikely that such a mechanism will generate proclamations on the general superiority of Mercosur law, though of course this will only be known as cases are considered and resolved.

[9] There are indications that Mercosur may in the near future move towards a more supranational model of lawmaking. The EU has already sent a specialized team to Mercosur's headquarters to provide advice on the design and function of the EU Parliament (interview between the author and Michel Coat, Co-Director of the EU Support Project to the [now purely intergovernmental] Joint Parliamentary Commission, Montevideo, Uruguay, August 2003). Under the leadership of President Luiz Inácio "Lula" da Silva, the Brazilians have expressed a strong interest in the creation of a Mercosur Parliament similar to the EU's equivalent and in collaborating further with the EU (Agence France Presse 2003b). Mercosur officials' explicit rejection of a European supranational model of lawmaking (Haines-Ferrari 1993) is thus being revisited.

REFERENCES

Abbott, Frederick M. 2000. "NAFTA and the Legalization of World Politics: A Case Study." *International Organization* 54 (3): 519–47.

Abolafia, Mitchel Y. 1996. *Making Markets: Opportunism and Restraint on Wall Street*. Cambridge, MA: Harvard University Press.

Abu-Lughod, Janet L. 1989. *Before European Hegemony: The World System, A.D. 1250–1350*. New York: Oxford University Press.

Administrative Commission of the European Communities on Social Security for Migrant Workers. 1996. *Your Social Security Rights When Moving within the European Union: A Practical Guide*. Luxembourg: Office for Official Publications of the European Communities.

Agence France Presse. 2001a. "Brasil Quiere Armonizar las Medidas Fitosanitarías en el Mercosur." *Agence France Presse*, February 12.

———. 2001b. "Gira de Lafer Enfatiza Prioridad del Mercosur para Brasil." *Agence France Presse*, February 13.

———. 2001c. "En Plena Crisis, la Industria Uruguya Redobla su Apuesta al Mercosur." *Agence France Presse*, November 12.

———. 2003a. "SADC Chief Renews Calls for a Free Trade Area, Customs Union." *Agence France Presse*, January 21.

———. 2003b. "Propuesta de Parlamento Común en la Mira de Poderes Legislativos del Mercosur." *Agence France Presse*, September 24.

———. 2003c. "Centrales Sindicales del Mercosur Reclaman Cambio de Rumbo en el Bloque." *Agence France Press*, December 15.

Agri Service International Newsletter. 1993. "Milk: Problems over Standardization." *Agri Service International Newsletter*, February 11.

AllAfrica. 2001. "SADC Free Area in 8 Years Remains a Dream." *AllAfrica*, October 19.

Amnesty International. 2000. "AI on Human Rights and Labor Rights." In *The Globalization Reader*, ed. Frank J. Lechner and John Boli, 187–91. Malden, MA: Blackwell Publishers.

Arrighi, Giovanni. 2000. "Globalization, State Sovereignty and the 'Endless' Accumulation of Capital." In *The Ends of Globalization*, ed. Don Kalb et al., 125–48. Lanham, MD: Rowman and Littlefield.

Atkinson, Glen. 1998. "Regional Integration in the Emerging Global Economy: The Case of NAFTA." *Social Science Journal* 35 (2): 159–69.

———. 1999. "Developing Global Institutions: Lessons to Be Learned from Regional Integration Experiences." *Journal of Economic Issues* 33 (2): 335–41.

Baer, M. Delal. 1991. "North American Free Trade." *Foreign Affairs*, 132–49.

Bagwell, Kyle, and Robert W. Staiger. 1998. "Will Preferential Agreements Undermine the Multilateral Trading System?" *Economic Journal* 108 (449): 1162–82.

Bailey, Kenneth W. 2002. "Comparison of the U.S. and Canadian Dairy Industry." Staff Paper No. 349, April. Department of Agricultural Economics and Rural Sociology, The Pennsylvania State University.

Baldwin, Richard E. 1997. "The Causes of Regionalism." *World Economy* 20 (7): 865–88.

Banks, Cara. 2000. "The Solidarity Network: A Report on the State of the Social Justice Movement." *Briarpatch Magazine* 29 (3): 7–8.

Beccalli, Bianca. 1984. "Italy." In *Women and Trade Unions in Eleven Industrialized Countries*, ed. Alice H. Cook, Val. R. Lorwin, and Arlene Kaplan Daniels, 184–214. Philadelphia: Temple University Press, 1984.

———. 1985. "Le Politiche del Lavoro Femminile in Italia: Donne, Sindacati e Stato tra il 1974 e il 1984." *Stato e Mercato* 15: 423–59.

Becker, Gary. 1986. *Accounting for Tastes*. Cambridge: Cambridge University Press.

Bentley, Jerry H. 1993. *Old World Encounters: Cross-Cultural Contacts and Exchanges in Pre-Modern Times*. New York: Oxford University Press.

Berger, Peter L., and Samuel P. Huntigton, eds. 2002. *Many Globalizations: Cultural Diversity in the Contemporary World*. New York: Oxford University Press.

Bergsten, Fred C. 1996. "Globalizing Free Trade." *Foreign Affairs* 75 (3): 105–20

Betts, Paul. 1984. "French Farmers in EEC Protest." *Financial Times*, May 30.

Bhagwati, Jagdish. 1993a. "Regionalism and Multilateralism." In *New Dimensions in Regional Integration*, ed. Jaime de Melo and Arvind Panagariya, 22–51. Cambridge: Cambridge University Press.

———. 1993b. "Beyond NAFTA: Clinton's Trading Choices." *Foreign Policy* 91 (Summer): 155–62.

Bhagwati, Jagdish, and Anne O. Krueger. 1995. *The Dangerous Drift to Preferential Trade Agreements*. Washington, DC: American Enterprise Institute.

Bhagwati, Jagdish, David Greenaway, and Arvind Panagariya. 1998. "Trading Preferentially: Theory and Policy." *Economic Journal* 108 (449): 1128–48.

Blum, Jonathan S. 2000. "The FTAA and the Fast Track to Forgetting the Environment: A Comparison of the NAFTA and the MERCOSUR Environmental Models as Examples for the Hemisphere." *Texas International Law Journal* 35 (3): 435–57.

Blythman, Joanna. 1992. "A Step in the Right Directive." *Independent* (London), November 21.

Boltho, Andrea. 1996. "Has France Converged on Germany? Policies and Institutions since 1958." In *National Diversity and Global Capitalism*, ed. Suzanne Berger and Ronald Dore, 89–104. Ithaca, NY: Cornell University Press.

Borchardt, Klaus-Dieter. 2000. *The ABC of Community Law*. Luxembourg: Office for Official Publications of the European Communities.

Börzel, Tanja. 2001. "Europeanization and Territorial Institutional Change: Toward Cooperative Regionalism?" In *Transforming Europe: Europeanization and Domestic Change*, ed. Maria Green Cowles, James Caporaso, and Thomas Risse, 137–58. Ithaca, NY: Cornell University Press.

Bradsher, Keith. 1993. "Side Agreements to Trade Accord Vary in Ambition." *New York Times*, September 19.

Brasher, Philip. 1993. "Who Speaks for the Farmer?" *Associated Press*, October 23.

Bronstein, Arturo S. 1995. "Societal Change and Industrial Relations in Latin America: Trends and Prospects." *International Labour Review* 134 (2): 163–86.

Brunke, Henrich. 2002. "Commodity Profile with an Emphasis on International Trade: Dairy Products." Agricultural Marketing Resource Center (Agricultural Issues Center), University of California at Davis.

Buchanan, Paul G., and Kate Nicholls. 2001. "Neoliberal Labor Relations in Two Small Open Democracies: Contemporary New Zealand and Uruguay." Center for Iberian and Latin American Studies Working Paper No. 20, University of California, San Diego.

Burfisher, Mary E., Sherman Robinson, and Karen Thierfelder. 1998. "Farm Policy Reforms and Harmonization in the NAFTA." In *Regional Trade Agreements and U.S. Agriculture* (Economic Research Service, AER No. 771), ed. Mary E. Burfisher and Elizabeth A. Jones, 66–74. Washington, DC: U.S. Department of Agriculture.

Burtless, Gary, et al. 2000. "Globaphobia: Confronting Fears about Open Trade." In *The Globalization Reader*, ed. Frank J. Lechner and John Boli, 181–86. Malden, MA: Blackwell Publishers.

Byrne, Justin. 2000. "NAFTA Dispute Resolution: Implementing True Rule-Based Diplomacy through Direct Access." *Texas International Law Journal* 35 (3): 415–34.

Cable, Vincent. 1994. "Overview." In *Trade Blocs? The Future of Regional Integration*, ed. Vincent Cable and David Henderson, 1–16. London: Royal Institute of International Affairs.

Cain, Peter. 1999. "British Free Trade: 1850–1914: Economics and Policy." *Recent Findings of Research in Economics & Social History* 29 (Autumn): 1–4.

Calloni, Stella. 1996. "Centrales Sindicales del Mercosur Rechazan las Políticas Neoliberales." *La Jornada*, October 10.

Cameron, David. 1998. "Creating Supranational Authority in Monetary and Exchange Rate Policy: The Sources and Effects of EMU." In *European Integration and Supranational Governance*, ed. Wayne Sandholtz and Alec Stone Sweet, 188–216. Oxford: Oxford University Press.

Campbell, John L. 2004. *Institutional Change and Globalization*. Princeton, NJ: Princeton University Press.

Campbell, John L., and Leon N. Lindberg. 1990. "Property Rights and the Organization of Economic Activity by the State." *American Sociological Review* 55 (5): 633–47.

Campbell, John L., and Ove K. Pedersen, eds. 2001a. *The Rise of Neoliberalism and Institutional Analysis*. Princeton, NJ: Princeton University Press.

———, eds. 2001b. "The Second Movement in Institutional Analysis." In *The Rise of Neoliberalism and Institutional Analysis*, ed. John L. Campbell and Ove K. Pedersen, 249–81. Princeton, NJ: Princeton University Press.

———, eds. 2001c. "The Rise of Neoliberalism and Institutional Analysis." In *The Rise of Neoliberalism and Institutional Analysis*, ed. John L. Campbell and Ove K. Pedersen, 1–23. Princeton, NJ: Princeton University Press.

Campbell, Ricardo G. 1991. "New Argentina Unemployment Program." *Social Security Bulletin* 54 (12).

————. 1993. "Argentina's New Unemployment Program Generates Little Interest." *Social Security Bulletin* 56 (2).

Canada NewsWire. 1996. "A Deal is a Deal." *Canada News Wire*, February 26.

————. 1999. "First-ever Canada/U.S.A. Businesswomen's Trade Summit Opens, Business and Government Spearhead Landmark Event for Women Entrepeneurs." *Canada News Wire*, May 18.

Canadian Dimension. 1992. "Women Fight Free Trade." *Canadian Dimension* 26 (5): 20.

Carlyle, Elizabeth. 2002. "NAC Attack." *Canadian Dimension* 36 (1): 14–16.

Carranza, Mario. E. 2003. "Can Mercosur Survive? Domestic and International Constraints on Mercosur." *Latin American Politics & Society* 45 (2): 67–103.

Castañeda, Jorge G. 1994. *Utopia Unarmed: The Latin American Left after the Cold War*. New York: Vintage Books.

Castle, Stephen. 2000. "New EU Charter Enshrines the 'Right to Strike.'" *Independent* (London), September 21.

Cavanagh, John, and Sarah Anderson. 2002. "Happily Ever NAFTA? A Bad Idea that Failed." *Foreign Policy*, September/October (132): 58–60.

Chew, Diana, and Richard A. Posthuma. 2002. "International Employment Dispute Resolution under NAFTA's Side Agreement on Labor." *Labor Law Journal* 1 (53): 38–45.

Chiarelli, Carlos Alberto G. 1976. "Social Security for Rural Workers in Brazil." *International Labour Review*: 113 (2): 159–69.

Cichowski, Rachel A. 1998. "Integrating the Environment: the European Court and the Construction of Supranational Policy." *Journal of European Public Policy* 5 (3): 387–405.

————. 2003. "Women's Transnational Activism: Political and Legal Mobilization in Europe." Paper presented at the Conference on National Feminism in a Transnational Arena: The European Union and the Politics of Gender, University of Wisconsin, Madison, April 4–6.

Cieza, Daniel. 1998. "Argentine Labor: A Movement in Crisis." *NACLA Reports on the Americas* 31 (6).

Coeffard, Alain. 1982. "Regulations Governing Social Security for Persons Moving within the European Community." *International Labour Review* 121 (3): 243–58.

Cohen, Marjorie G. 1996. "Macho Economics—Canadian Women Confront Free Trade." *Off Our Backs* 26 (3): 12–14.

Cohen, Marjorie Griffin, et al. 2002. "Globalization: Some Implications and Strategies for Women." *Canadian Women Studies* 21/22 (4/1): 6–14.

Collins, Randall. 1980. "Weber's Last Theory of Capitalism: A Systematization." *American Sociological Review* 45:925–42.

Coleman, James. 1990. *Foundations of Social Theory*. Cambridge, MA: Harvard University Press.

Commission of the European Communities. 1979. *Report of the Commission to the Council on the Application as of 12 February 1978 of the Principle of Equal Pay for Men and Women*. Brussels.

Commission for Labor Cooperation. 2001. *Annual Report*. Washington, DC: Secretariat of the Commission for Labor Cooperation.

————. 2003. *Protection of Migrant Agricultural Workers in Canada, Mexico and the United States*. Washington, DC: Secretariat of the Commission for Labor Cooperation.

Compa, Lance. 2001. "NAFTA's Labor Side Agreement and International Labor Solidarity." *Antipode* 33:451–67.

Condon, Bradley. 1997. "NAFTA at Three-and-One-Half Years: Where Do We Stand and Where Should We Be Headed?" *Canada–United States Law Journal* 23:347–67.

Connolly, Michelle. 1999. "Mercosur: Implications for Growth in Member Countries." *Current Issues in Economics & Finance* 5 (7): 1–5.

Cook, María Lorena. 2002. "Labor Reform and Dual Transitions in Brazil and the Southern Cone." *Latin American Politics & Society* 44 (1): 1–34.

Costa, Olivier. 2003. "The European Court of Justice and Democratic Control in the European Union." *Journal of European Public Policy* 10 (5): 740–61.

Cowles, Maria Green. 1998. "The Changing Architecture of Big Business." In *Collective Action in the European Union: Interests and the New Politics of Associability*, ed. Justin Greenwood and Mark Aspinwall, 108–25. London: Routledge.

————. 2001. "The Transatlantic Business Dialogue and Domestic Business-Government Relations." In *Transforming Europe: Europeanization and Domestic Change*, ed. Maria Green Cowles, James Caporaso, and Thomas Risse, 159–179. Ithaca, NY: Cornell University Press.

Crijns, Léo, and André Laurent. 1978. "Action by the Commission of the European Communities in the Field of Social Security." *International Labour Review* 117 (5): 569–81.

Cullen, Pauline P. 1999. "Coalitions Working for Social Justice: Transnational Non-Governmental Organizations and International Governance." *Contemporary Justice Review* 2 (2): 159–77.

Curtin, Philip D. 1984. *Cross-Cultural Trade in World History*. Cambridge: Cambridge University Press.

Cypher, James M. 2001. "NAFTA's Lessons: From Economic Mythology to Current Realities." *Labor Studies Journal* 26 (1): 5–21.

De Melo, Jaime, and Arvind Panagariya. 1993. Introduction to *New Dimensions in Regional Integration*, ed. Jaime de Melo and Arvind Panagariya, 3–21. Cambridge: Cambridge University Press.

De Montigny, André E., and Dieter Schmahl. 1970. "Planning Benefits in Europe: The Problem of Consistency." *Columbia Journal of World Business* 5 (3): 40–48.

De Oliveira, Francisco, Eduardo Barreto, and Kaizō Iwakami Beltraō. 2001. "Brazil: The Brazilian Social Security System." *International Social Security Review* 54 (1): 101–12.

De Roest, Kees, and Alberto Menghi. 2000. "Reconsidering 'Traditional' Food: The Case of Parmigiano Reggiano Cheese." *Sociologia Ruralis* 40:439–51.

Deeprose, Jenny. 1997. "Through the French Window." *Dairy Industries International* 62 (12): 18–19.

Deere, Carolyn L., and Daniel C. Esty, eds. 2002. *Greening the Americas: NAFTA's Lessons for Hemispheric Trade*. Cambridge, MA: MIT Press.

Delgado, Dora. 1994. "Official Standards Become the Norm." *Business Mexico*, September.

Deutsche Presse-Agentur. 1999. "African Trade Ministers Agree on Trade Protocol." *Deutsche Presse-Agentur*, July 14.

Diamond, Larry. 2000. "The Globalization of Democracy." In *The Globalization Reader*, ed. Frank J. Lechner and John Boli, 246–54. Malden, MA: Blackwell Publishers.

Diaz, Carolina Lasén. 2001. The EC Habitats Directive Approaches Its Tenth Anniversary: An Overview." *Review of European Community & International Environmental Law* 10 (3): 287–95.

Diebel, Linda. 1993. "Key U.S. Democrat Won't Back NAFTA." *Toronto Star*, September 22.

DiMaggio, Paul. 1994. "Culture and Economy." In *The Handbook of Economic Sociology*, ed. Neil J. Smelser and Richard Swedberg, 27–57. Princeton, NJ: Princeton University Press.

Dobbin, Frank. 1997. *Forging Industrial Policy: The United States, Britain, and France in the Railway Age*. Cambridge: Cambridge University Press.

Domínguez, Edmé R. 2002. "Continental Transnational Activism and Women Workers' Networks within NAFTA." *International Feminist Journal of Politics* 4 (2): 216–39.

Donnelly, Rob. 1998. "NAFTA Falls Short for Many Workers." *Novedades Editores*, March 2.

Douglas, Mary, and Aaron Wildavski. 1983. *Risk and Culture: An Essay on the Selection of Technological and Environmental Dangers*. Berkeley: University of California Press.

Dowdy, Timothy W. 1990. "The Emergence of the Social Dimension of the European Community." *Brigham Young University Law Review* (4): 1667–86.

Doyon, Maurice A., and Andrew M. Novakovic. 1996. "Trade Liberalization and the U.S. and Canadian Dairy Industries." Paper prepared for the Program on Dairy Markets and Policy, Department of Agricultural Economics, Cornell University.

Dubal, Veena, et al. 2001–2. "Why Are Some Trade Agreements 'Greener' Than Others?" *Earth Island Journal* 16 (4): 44, 47.

Duina, Francesco. 1997. "Explaining Legal Implementation in the European Union." *International Journal of the Sociology of Law* 25 (July): 155–79.

———. 1999. *Harmonizing Europe: Nation States within the Common Market*. Albany: State University of New York Press.

———. 2000. "Gauging the Strength of the Nation-State in the European Union," *Polity* 33 (3): 455–62.

———. 2001. "Important but Not Pervasive: The Shared Limits of Secondary Law in the Common Markets of Europe and South America." *Current Politics and Economics of Europe* 10 (4):351–379.

———. 2003. "National Legislatures in Common Markets: Autonomy in the European Union and Mercosur." In *The Nation-State in Question*, ed. T. V. Paul, G. John Ikenberry, and John A. Hall, 183–212. Princeton, NJ: Princeton University Press.

———. 2004. "Regional Market Building as a Social Process: An Analysis of Cognitive Strategies in NAFTA, the European Union, and Mercosur." *Economy and Society* 33 (3): 359–89.

Duina, Francesco, and Frank Blithe. 1999. "Nation States and Common Markets: The Institutional Conditions for Acceptance." *Review of International Political Economy* 6 (4): 494–530.

Duina, Francesco, and Nathan Breznau. 2002. "Constructing Common Cultures: The Ontological and Normative Dimensions of Law in the European Union and Mercosur." *European Law Journal* 8 (4): 574–95.

Duina, Francesco, and Paulette Kurzer. 2004. "Smoke in Your Eyes: The Struggle for Tobacco Control in the European Union." *Journal of European Public Policy* 11 (1): 57–77.

Earth Island Journal. 1993. "Stop NAFTA." *Earth Island Journal* 8 (3): 8.

Echikson, W. 1998. "When Cheese Is Not Just Cheese: Getting Picky about Origin." *Christian Science Monitor*, January 22.

Ecologist. 2002. "NAFTA—Placing Investors' Rights Before the Environment." *Ecologist* 32 (7): 16.

Economist. 1975a. "Social Affairs: Getting Warmer." *Economist*, December 27.

———. 1975b. "Life on the Dole." *Economist*, March 1.

———. 1975c. "German Workers: Why Bother?" *Economist*, September 13.

———. 1975d. "Italy's Hand-Out State." *Economist*, December 27.

———. 1976. "Women: Less Equal than Others." *Economist*, April 17.

———. 1989. "The EEC's Social Dimension: Louder than Words." *Economist*, July 8.

———. 1990. "The Economics of Free Trade." *Economist*, September 22.

———. 1991. "Cheesed Off." *Economist*, December 7.

———. 1993a. "A Target for Protection." *Economist*, March 27.

———. 1993b. "Businessmen for NAFTA." *Economist*, October 16.

———. 1996. "All Free Traders Now?" *Economist*, December 7.

———. 2002a. "Every Man for Himself." *Economist*, November 2.

———. 2002b. "A Survey of France: The French Exception." *Economist*, November 16.

———. 2003a. "The Douha Round." *Economist*, September 20.

———. 2003b. "Where to File It." *Economist*, June 6.

———. 2003c. "Tidying Up or Tyranny?" *Economist*, May 31.

Egan, Michelle. 1998. "Regulatory Strategies, Delegation and European Market Integration." *Journal of European Public Policy* 5 (3): 485–507.

Ehrick, Christine. 1998. "Madrinas and Missionaries: Uruguay and the Pan-American Women's Movement." *Gender & History* 10 (3): 406–24.

El Pais. 2003. "Conaprole: Exportaciones de Productos Lácteos Aumentan 12% en 2002." *El Pais*, July 3.

Ekelund, Robert B., Jr., and Robert D. Tollison. 1997. *Politicized Economies: Monarchy, Monopoly, and Mercantilism.* College Station: Texas A&M University Press.

Epstein, Jack. 1994. "Brazilian Women Leaders in Fight for Equal Rights." *National Catholic Reporter* 30 (29): 6.

Espino, Maria Alma. 2000. "Women and Mercosur: The Gendered Dimension of Economic Integration." In *United Nations Development Fund for Women: Women's Empowerment and Economic Justice,* 16–26. New York: UNDFW.

External Affairs and International Trade Canada. 1993. *NAFTA: What's It All About?* Ottawa: Government of Canada.

Europe Agri. 2003. "Commission Registers Designations of Origin for Spanish Regional." *Europe Agri,* December 5.

European Commission. 1996. "Equal Opportunities for Women and Men in the European Union." Luxembourg: Office for Official Publications of the European Communities.

———. 1998. "Equal Opportunities for Women and Men in the European Union: Annual Report 1997." Luxembourg: Office for Official Publications of the European Communities.

———. 2002. *Mercosur-European Community Regional Strategy Paper: 2002–2006.* Brussels: EC External Relations Directorate General—Directorate Latin America.

European Report. 1995. "Women's Lobby 'Devastated' by Social Council Decision." *European Report,* December 13.

———. 1996. "Commission Public Relations Campaign for Traditional Food Products." *European Report,* June 26.

———. 1997. "European Farmers Oppose Sale of 'Fake Roquefort.'" *European Report,* March 5.

———. 1998. "European Parliament." *European Report,* April 10.

———. 2002. "Farm Lobby Defends Italian Producers on Trade Names." *European Report,* May 25.

———. 2003. "New Protected Designation of Origin for Italian Cheese." *European Report,* December 24.

———. 2004. "Social Policy: New Support for Gender-Equality Organizations." *European Report,* February 14.

European Women Lawyers Association. 2002. *The European Women Lawyers Association.* Brussels.

European Women's Lobby. 2000. *Annual Report.* Brussels.

Fagnani, Jeanne. 2002. "Why Do French Women Have More Children than German Women? Family Policies and Attitudes Towards Child Care Outside the Home." *Work & Family* 5 (1): 103–19.

Fallow, Brian. 2002. "Cautious Southeast Asian Ministers Agree to Frame Trade Rules." *New Zealand Herald,* September 17.

Federal News Service. 1996. "Prepared Testimony of Ambassador Ira Shapiro, Office of the United State Trade Representative before the House Committee on Agriculture, Subcomittee on Dairy, Livestock and Poultry." *Federal News Service,* September 25.

Feld, Werner J. 1979. "Implementation of the European Community's Common Agricultural Policy: Expectations, Fears, Failures." *International Organization* 33 (3): 335–63.

Ferreira, María Carmen. 2001. *The Social Dimension of Integration: The Mercosur Experience.* Lima: International Labour Office—Regional Office for the Americas.

Financial Post. 1996a. "US Strikes Hard at Dairy." *Financial Post* (Toronto), March 26.

————. 1996b. "Supply Management Gets a Reprieve: NAFTA Panel Decision on Canada's High Poultry, Egg and Dairy Tariffs Will Have Mixed Results." *Financial Post* (Toronto), July 29.

————. 1996c. "Canada NAFTA Victor in Dairy and Poultry Fight." *Financial Post* (Toronto, Vancouver Edition), December 3.

Financial Times. 1990. "'British Destiny Is a Full Member of the European Community': Margaret Thatcher's Speech in Aspen." *Financial Times*, August 6.

Fligstein, Neil. 1996. "Markets as Politics: A Political-Cultural Approach to Market Institutions." *American Sociological Review* 61 (4): 656–73.

————. 2001. *The Architecture of Markets: An Economic Sociology of Twenty-first Century Capitalist Societies*. Princeton, NJ: Princeton University Press.

Fligstein, Neil, and Alec Stone Sweet. 2001. "Institutionalizing the Treaty of Rome." In *The Institutionalization of Europe*, ed. Alec Stone Sweet, Wayne Sandholtz, and Neil Fligstein, 29–55. Oxford: Oxford University Press.

————. 2002. "Constructing Polities and Markets: An Institutionalist Account of European Integration." *American Journal of Sociology* 7: 1206–43.

Fligstein, Neil, and Jason McNichol. 1998. "The Institutional Terrain of the European Union." In *European Integration and Supranational Governance*, ed. Wayne Sandholtz and Alec Stone Sweet, 59–91. Oxford: Oxford University Press.

Folsom, Ralph, et al. 1996. *European Union Law after Maastricht: A Practical Guide for Lawyers outside the Common Market*. Boston: Kluwer Law International.

Food and Agriculture Organization of the United Nations. 1997. *The Political Economy of the Common Market in Milk and Dairy Products in the European Union*. Rome: FAO.

Forero, Juan. 2003. "Brazil Pushes for South American Trade Pact." *New York Times*, September 17.

Fourcade-Gourinchas, Marion, and Sarah L. Babb. 2002. "The Rebirth of the Liberal Creed: Paths to Neoliberalism in Four Countries." *American Journal of Sociology* 108 (3): 533–79.

Fowlie, Laura. 1993. "Unions Told to Join Forces on NAFTA." *Financial Post* (Toronto), May 7.

Frank, Andre Gunder. 1998. *ReOrient: Global Economy in the Asian Age*. Berkeley: University of California Press.

Frank, David J., Ann Hironaka, and Evan Schofer. 2000. "The Nation State and the Natural Environment, 1900–1995." *American Sociological Review* 65 (1): 96–116.

Frankel, Jeffrey A. 1997. *Regional Trading Blocs in the World Economic System*. Washington, DC: Institute for International Economics.

Fried, Jonathan T. 1994. "Two Paradigms for the Rule of International Trade Law." *Canada–United States Law Journal* 20:39–56.

Fukuyama, Francis. 1992. *The End of History and the Last Man*. New York: Free Press.

Gabriel, Christina, and Laura Macdonald. 1994. "NAFTA, Women and Organising in Canada and Mexico: Forging a 'Feminist Internationality.'" *Millennium: Journal of International Studies* 23 (3): 535–62.

Gallie, Duncan, and Serge Paugam, eds. 2000. *Welfare Regimes and the Experience of Unemployment in Europe*. Oxford: Oxford University Press.

Galperin, Hernan. 1999. "Cultural Industries Policy in Regional Trade Agreements: The Cases of NAFTA, the European Union and Mercosur." *Media, Culture & Society* 21 (5): 627–48.

García, A. Alonso. 2002. "The General Provisions of the Charter of Fundamental Rights of the European Union." *European Law Journal* 8 (4): 492–514.

Gardels, Nathan. 1993. "The Post-Atlantic Capitalist Order." *New Perspectives Quarterly* 10 (2): 2–3.

Gardner, Brian. 1996. *European Agriculture: Policies, Production, and Trade*. New York: Routledge.

Gazeta Mercantil. 2003. "We Must Create Strong Commercial Bloc, Says Lula." *Gazeta Mercantil Invest News*, September 17.

Gazeta Mercantil Online. 1997a. "Minister of Agriculture Signs 27 Decrees on Dairy Sector." *Gazeta Mercantil Online* (Brazil), September 11.

———. 1997b. "Argentine Midwest Grows with Mercosur." *Gazeta Mercantil Online* (Brazil), May 27.

Gazette. 1996. "Agricultural Agencies Warn of Job Losses if US Wins." *Gazette* (Montreal), January 30.

Gibb, Richard. 1994. "Regionalism in the World Economy." In *Continental Trading Blocs: The Growth of Regionalism in the World Economy*, ed. Richard Gibb and Wieslaw Michalak, 1–35. West Sussex: John Wiley & Sons, Ltd.

Gitterman, Daniel P. 2003. "European Integration and Labour Market Cooperation: A Comparative Regional Perspective." *Journal of European Social Policy* 13 (2): 99–120.

Glenn, H. Patrick. 2001. "Conflicting Laws in a Common Market? The NAFTA Experiment." *Chicago-Kent Law Review* 76 (3): 1789–819.

———. 2003. "Harmony of Laws in the Americas." In *Legal Harmonization in the Americas: Business Transactions, Bijuralism and the OAS*, ed. Office of the Assistant Secretary for Legal Affairs, 29–48. Washington, DC: Organization of American States.

Glenn, John K. 2001. *Framing Democracy: Civil Society and Civic Movements in Eastern Europe*. Stanford, CA: Stanford University Press.

Goldsmith, Charles. 1990. "European Leaders Divided over World Trade Talks." *United Press International*, October 28.

Goldstein, Judith, and Robert O. Keohane. 1993. "Ideas and Foreign Policy: An Analytical Framework." In *Ideas & Foreign Policy: Beliefs, Institutions, and Political Change*, ed. Judith Goldstein and Robert O. Keohane, 3–30. Ithaca, NY: Cornell University Press.

Golob, Stephanie R. 2003. "Beyond the Policy Frontier: Canada, Mexico, and the Ideological Origins of NAFTA." *World Politics* 55 (3): 361–98.

Gordon, Bernard K. 2003. "A High-Risk Trade Policy." *Foreign Affairs* 82 (4): 105–18.

Grant, Wyn, Duncan Matthews, and Peter Newell. 2000. *The Effectiveness of European Union Environmental Policy*. New York: St. Martin's Press.

Gray, Tricia. 2003. "Electoral Gender Quotas: Lessons from Argentina and Chile." *Bulletin of Latin American Research* 22 (1): 52–78.

Greenwood, Justin. 1997. *Representing Interests in the European Union*. New York: St. Martin's Press.

———. 2003. *Interest Representation in the European Union*. Houndmills, UK: Palgrave Macmillan.

Greenwood, Justin, and Mark Aspinwall, eds. 1998. *Collective Action in the European Union: Interests and the New Politics of Associability*. London: Routledge.

Grieco, Joseph M. 1997. "Systemic Sources of Variation in Regional Institutionalization in Western Europe, East Asia, and the Americas." In *The Political Economy of Regionalism*, ed. Edward D. Mansfield and Helen V. Milner, 164–87. New York: Columbia University Press.

Griswold, Daniel T. 2002. "NAFTA AT 10: An Economic and Foreign Policy Success." *Free Trade Bulletin* 1 (December): 1–2.

Guerrina, Roberta. 2002. "Mothering in Europe: Feminist Critique of European Policies on Motherhood and Employment." *European Journal of Women's Studies* 9 (1): 49–68.

Guillén, Mauro F. 2001. *The Limits of Convergence: Globalization and Organizational Change in Argentina, South Korea, and Spain*. Princeton, NJ: Princeton University Press.

Gwynne, Robert. 1994. "Regional Integration in Latin America: The Revival of a Concept?" In *Continental Trading Blocs: The Growth of Regionalism in the World Economy*, ed. Richard Gibb and Wieslaw Michalak, 189–207. West Sussex: John Wiley & Sons, Ltd.

Hadekel, Peter. 1994. "Too Many Barriers to Free Trade." *Ottawa Citizen*, November 10.

Haines-Ferrari, Marta. 1993. "Mercosur: A New Model of Latin American Economic Integration?" *Case Western Reserve Journal of International Law* 25 (3): 413–47.

Hall, Carl T. 1993. "New Trade Talks Open Today: U.S. Wants to Boost Mexican Standards in North American Pact." *San Francisco Chronicle*, March 17.

Hall, John A. 2000. "Globalization and Nationalism." *Thesis Eleven* 63 (1):63–79.

———. 2003. "Nation-States in History." In *The Nation-State in Question*, ed. T. V. Paul, G. John Ikenberry, and John A. Hall, 1–26. Princeton, NJ: Princeton University Press.

Hall, Peter A. 1986. *Governing the Economy: The Politics of State Intervention in Britain and France*. New York: Oxford University Press.

Hall, Peter A., and David Soskice, eds. 2001a. *Varieties of Capitalism: The Institutional Foundations of Comparative Advantage*. New York: Oxford University Press.

———. 2001b. "An Introduction to Varieties of Capitalism." In *Varieties of Capitalism: The Institutional Foundations of Comparative Advantage*, ed. Peter A. Hall and David Soskice, 1–68. New York: Oxford University Press.

Hallstein, Walter. 1963. "Industry and Agriculture in the European Economic Community." *Nebraska Journal of Economics & Business* 2 (1): 3–14.

Hamilton Spectator. 1997. "Saputo an Even-larger Big Cheese." *Hamilton Spectator* (Ontario, Canada), November 11.

Hanley, Eric, et al. 2002. "The State, International Agencies, and Property Transformation in Postcommunist Hungary." *American Journal of Sociology* 108 (1): 129–67.

Hansen, Patricia Isela. 2003. "Judicialization and Globalization in the North American Free Trade Agreement." *Texas International Law Journal* 38 (3): 489–503.

Hanson, Kim. 1999. "Women Urged to Play Bigger Role in Exports: Cultural Bias at Play—Trade Summit Supports Woman Entrepeneurs." *National Post*, May 19.

Harvard Law Review. 2000. "Recent Cases: Constitutional Law." *Harvard Law Review* 113 (5): 1234–39.

Heide, Ingeborg. 1999. "Supranational Action Against Sex Discrimination: Equal Pay and Equal Treatment in the European Union." *International Labour Review* 138 (4): 381–410.

Heinrich, Jeffery, and Denise Eby Konan. 2001. "Prospects for FDI in AFTA." *ASEAN Economic Bulletin* 18 (2): 141–60.

Helfand, Steven M. 1999. "The Political Economy of Agricultural Policy in Brazil: Decision Making and Influence from 1964 to 1992." *Latin American Research Review* 34 (3): 41.

———. 2000. "Interest Groups and Economic Policy: Explaining the Pattern of Protection in the Brazilian Agricultural Sector." *Contemporary Economic Policy* 18 (4): 462–76.

Henderson, David. 1992. "International Economic Integration: Progress, Prospects and Implications." *International Affairs* 68 (4): 633–53.

Hicks, Alexander, and Lane Kenworthy. 1998. "Cooperation and Political Economic Performance in Affluent Democratic Capitalism." *American Journal of Sociology* 103 (6): 1631–72.

Higgott, Richard. 1998. "The International Political Economy of Regionalism: The Asia Pacific and Europe Compared." In *Regionalism & Global Economic Integration*, ed. William A. Coleman and Geoffrey R. D. Underhill, 42–67. London: Routledge.

Hirst, Paul. 2000. "The Global Economy: Myth or Reality?" In *The Ends of Globalization*, ed. Don Kalb et al., 107–23. Lanham, MD: Rowman and Littlefield.

Hochstetler, Kathryn. 2003. "Fading Green? Environmental Politics in the Mercosur Free Trade Agreement." *Latin American Politics & Society* 45 (4): 1–31.

Hoekman, Bernard, and Pierre Sauvé. 1994. "Regional and Multilateral Liberalization of Service Markets: Complements or Substitutes? *Journal of Common Market Studies* 32 (3): 283–317.

Hormats, Robert D. 1994. "Making Regionalism Safe." *Foreign Affairs* 10 (March/April): 97–108.

Hoskyns, Catherine. 1986. "Women, European Law and Transnational Politics." *International Journal of the Sociology of Law* 14:299–315.

Htun, Mala. 2002. "Puzzles of Women's Rights in Brazil." *Social Research* 69 (3): 733–51.

Human Rights Watch. 2001. "Trading Away Rights: The Unfulfilled Promise of NAFTA's Labor Side Agreement." *Human Rights Watch Report* 13 (2).

Huntington, Samuel P. 1997. *The Clash of Civilizations and the Remaking of World Order*. New York: Touchstone.

Imig, Doug, and Sidney Tarrow, eds. 2001. *Contentious Europeans: Protest and Politics in an Emerging Polity*. Lanham, MD: Rowman & Littlefield.

Inglehart, Ronald, Neil Nevitte, and Miguel Basañez. 1996. *The North American Trajectory: Cultural, Economic, and Political Ties among the United States, Canada, and Mexico*. New York: Aldine de Gruyter.

INTAL (Institute for the Integration of Latin America and the Caribbean, Inter-American Development Bank). 1998. *Mercosur Report No. 4, January–June*. Buenos Aires, Argentina.

———. 2001. *Mercosur Report No. 7: 2000–2001*. Buenos Aires, Argentina.

International Monetary Fund. 1994. *International Trade Policies: The Uruguay Round and Beyond: Volume II (Background Papers)*. Washington, DC: IMF.

———. 1995. *Direction of Trade Statistics Yearbook 1995*. Washington, DC: IMF.

———. 2000. *Direction of Trade Statistics Yearbook 2000*. Washington, DC: IMF.

———. 2002. *Direction of Trade Statistics Yearbook 2002*. Washington, DC: IMF.

Jameson, Fredric, and Masao Miyoshi. 1998. *The Cultures of Globalization*. Durham, NC: Duke University Press.

Jayasuriya, Kainsha. 2003a. "Embedded Mercantilism and Open Regionalism: The Crisis of a Regional Political Project." *Third World Quarterly* 24 (2): 339–55.

———. 2003b. "Introduction: Governing the Asia Pacific—Beyond the New Regionalism." *Third World Quarterly* 24 (2): 199–215.

Jelin, Elizabeth, Teresa Valdes, and Line Bareiro. 1998. *Gender and Nationhood in Mercosur: Notes for Approaching the Subject*. Paris: United Nations Educational, Scientific and Cultural Organization.

Jenson, Jane. 1988. "The Limits of 'and the' Discourse." In *The Feminization of the Labor Force: Paradoxes and Promises*, ed. Jane Jenson, Elizabeth Hagen, and Ceallaigh Reddy, 155–72. Cambridge: Polity Press.

Johansson, Karl Magnus. 1999. "Tracing the Employment Title in the Amsterdam Treaty: Uncovering Transnational Coalitions." *Journal of European Public Policy* 6 (1): 85–101.

Jordan, Andrew. 1999. "The Implementation of EU Environmental Policy: A Policy Problem without a Political Solution?" *Environment & Planning C* (Government & Policy) 17 (1): 69–90.

Kahler, Miles. 1995. *Regional Futures and Transatlantic Economic Relations*. New York: Council of Foreign Relations Press.

Kerremans, Bart. 2000. "The Links between Domestic Political Forces, Inter-Bloc Dynamics and the Multilateral Trading System." In *The Political Importance of Regional Trading Blocs*, ed. Bart Kerremans and Bob Switky, 119–67. Aldershot: Ashgate Publishing Ltd.

Kerremans, Bart, and Bob Switky. 2000. Introduction to *The Political Importance of Regional Trading Blocs*, ed. Bart Kerremans and Bob Switky, 1–9. Aldershot: Ashgate Publishing Ltd.

Knill, Christoph. 2001. *The Europeanization of National Administrations: Pat-*

terns of Institutional Changes and Persistence. Cambridge: Cambridge University Press.

Kono, Daniel Yuichi. 2002. "Are Free Trade Areas Good for Multilateralism? Evidence from the European Free Trade Association." *International Studies Quarterly* 46 (4): 507–27.

Korzeniewicz, Miguel. 2000. "Commodity Chains and Marketing Strategies: Nike and the Global Athletic Footwear Industry." In *The Globalization Reader*, ed. Frank J. Lechner and John Boli, 155–66. Malden, MA: Blackwell Publishers.

Krueger, Anne O. 1999. "Are Preferential Trading Arrangements Trade Liberalizing or Protectionist?" *Journal of Economic Perspectives* 13 (4): 105–24.

Krugman, Paul. 1990. *Rethinking International Trade*. Cambridge, MA: MIT Press.

———. 1993. "The Uncomfortable Truth about NAFTA." *Foreign Affairs* 72 (5): 13–19.

Kurzer, Paulette. 2001. *Markets and Moral Regulation: Cultural Change in the European Union*. Cambridge: Cambridge University Press.

La Jornada. 1996a. "Reprimene en Brasil a Sindicalistas de Cuatro Paises que Protestaron en la Cumbre del Mercosur." *La Jornada*, December 18.

———. 1996b. "Paraliza Argentina la Huelga General." *La Jornada*, September 27.

Lalonde, Michelle. 1992. "NAC Membership Votes to Take Firm Stance Against Three-way Free-trade Pact." *Gazette* (Ottawa Citizen), June 7.

Lamas, Marta. 1998. "The Mexican Feminist Movement and Public Policy-Making." In *Women's Movements and Public Policy in Europe, Latin America, and the Caribbean*, ed. Geertje Lycklama à Nijeolht, Virginia Vargas, and Saskia Wieringa, 113–42. New York: Garland Publishing, Inc.

Larudee, Mehrene. 1998. "Integration and Income Distribution under the North American Free Trade Agreement: The Experience of Mexico." In *Globalization and Progressive Economic Policy*, ed. Dean Baker, Gerald Epstein, and Robert Pollin, 273–92. Cambridge: Cambridge University Press.

Lawrence, Robert Z. 1996. *Regionalism, Multilateralism, and Deeper Integration*. Washington, DC: Brookings Institution.

Lechner, Frank J., and John Boli, eds. 2000. *The Globalization Reader*. Malden, MA: Blackwell Publishers.

Lecuona, Rafael A. 1999. "Economic Integration: NAFTA and Mercosur—A Comparative Analysis." *International Journal on World Peace* 16 (4): 27–52.

Liebert, Ulrike. 1999. "Gender Politics in the European Union: The Return of the Public." *European Societies* 1 (2): 197–239.

Liebowitz, Debra J. 2002. "Gendering (Trans)National Advocacy." *International Feminist Journal of Politics* 4 (2): 173–96.

Lockhart, Charles. 1999. "Cultural Contributions to Explaining Institutional Form, Political Change, and Rational Decisions." *Comparative Political Studies* 32 (7): 862–93.

Lognonne, Anna. 1998. "Farmers Fight European Agricultural Reform Plan—Brussels Venue Ringed by Barbed Wire Fence." *Journal* (Newcastle, UK), April 1.

Loney, Martin. 1998. *The Pursuit of Division: Race, Gender, and Preferential Hiring in Canada*. Quebec: McGill-Queen's University Press.

Lorée, Marguerite. 1980. "Equal Pay and Equal Opportunity Law in France." In *Equal Employment Policy for Women: Strategies for Implementation in the United States, Canada and Western Europe*, ed. Ronnie Steinberg, 79–107. Philadelphia: Temple University Press.

MacDonald, Ian Thomas. 2003. "NAFTA and the Emergence of Continental Labor Cooperation," *American Review of Canadian Studies* 33 (2): 173–96.

Macdonald, Laura. 2002. "Globalization and Social Movements." *International Feminist Journal of Politics* 4 (2): 151–72.

Mahoney, James. 2000. "Path Dependence in Historical Sociology." *Theory & Society* 29 (4): 507–48.

Majone, Giandomenico, ed. 1996. *Regulating Europe*. London: Routledge Press.

Malaysia General News. 2002. "AFTA Not Affecting Domestic Trade." *Malaysia General News*, January 17.

Mansfield, Edward D., and Helen Milner. 1997a. "The Political Economy of Regionalism: An Overview." In *The Political Economy of Regionalism*, ed. Edward D. Mansfield and Helen V. Milner, 1–19. New York: Columbia University Press.

———, eds. 1997b. *The Political Economy of Regionalism*. New York: Columbia University Press.

Marsh, John. 1977. "Europe's Agriculture: Reform of the Cap." *International Affairs* 53 (4): 604–14.

Martin, Paul. 1998. "Sovereignty and Food Safety in a NAFTA Context." *United States Law Journal* 24:369–76.

Mattli, Walter. 1999. *The Logic of Regional Integration: Europe and Beyond*. Cambridge: Cambridge University Press.

———. 2001. "The Politics and Economics of International Institutional Standards Setting: An Introduction." *Journal of European Public Policy* 8 (3): 328–44.

Mazey, Sonia. 1995. "The Development of EU Equality Policies: Bureaucratic Expansion on Behalf of Women?" *Public Administration* 73 (4):591–609.

———. 1998. "The European Union and Women's Rights: From the Europeanization of National Agendas to the Nationalization of a European Agenda." *Journal of European Public Policy* 5 (1):131–52.

———. 2000. "Integrating Gender-Intellectual and 'Real World' Mainstreaming." *Journal of European Public Policy* 7 (3): 333–45.

Mazey, Sonia, and Jeremy Richardson. 2001. "Interest Groups and EU Policy Making: Organizational Logic and Venue Shopping." In *European Union: Power and Policy-Making*, ed. Jeremy Richardson, 217–31. London: Routledge.

McAnany, Emile G., and Kenton T. Wilkinson, eds. 1996. *Mass Media and Free Trade: NAFTA and the Cultural Industries*. Austin: University of Texas Press.

McConnell, James, and Alan MacPherson. 1994. "The North American Free Trade Area: An Overview of Issues and Perspectives." In *Continental Trading Blocs: The Growth of Regionalism in the World Economy*, ed. Richard Gibb and Wieslaw Michalak, 163–87. West Sussex: John Wiley & Sons, Ltd.

McCormick, John. 2001. *Environmental Policy in the European Union*. Houndmills, UK: Palgrave.

McEvoy, Janet. 1994. "Women's Lobby Campaigns for Equitable Share of Seats:

Women Throughout Europe Are Demanding Better Representation in the European Parliament." *Irish Times*, May 18.

McGuire, J. Powers. 1987. "A Comparison of the Right of Public Employees to Strike in the United States and Canada." *Labour Law Journal*, May: 304–10.

Meade, Goeff. 1989. "Pressure Mounting on Thatcher over Social Charter Plan." *Press Association*, September 24.

———. 2000. "EU Charter's 'Right to Strike' Won't Affect UK." *Press Association*, September 20.

Mecham, Michael. 2003. "Mercosur: A Failing Development Project?" *International Affairs* 79 (2): 369–87.

Melnik, W. Joseph. 1994. "A Comparative Analysis of Proposals for the Legal Protection of Computerized Databases: NAFTA vs. the European Communities." *Case Western Reserve Journal of International Law* 26 (1): 57–114.

Mendelson, Sarah E., and John K. Glenn, eds. 2002. *The Power and Limits of NGOs: A Critical Look at Building Democracy in Eastern Europe and Eurasia*. New York: Columbia University Press.

Mény, Yves, Pierre Muller, and Jean-Louis Quermonne, eds. 1996. *Adjusting to Europe: The Impact of the European Union on National Institutions and Policies*. London: Routledge.

Meyer, John W., et al. 1997. "World Society and the Nation-State." *American Journal of Sociology* 103 (1): 144–81

Merryman, John Henry. 1985. *The Civil Law Tradition: An Introduction to the Legal Systems of Western Europe and Latin America*. Stanford, CA: Stanford University Press.

Michalak, Wieslaw. 1994. "The Political Economy of Trading Blocs." In *Continental Trading Blocs: The Growth of Regionalism in the World Economy*, ed. Richard Gibb and Wieslaw Michalak, 37–72. West Sussex: John Wiley & Sons, Ltd.

Milner, Helen. 1997. "Industries, Governments, and Regional Trade Blocs." In *The Political Economy of Regionalism*, ed. Edward D. Mansfield and Helen V. Milner, 77–106. New York: Columbia University Press.

———. 1998. "Regional Economic Co-operation, Global Markets and Domestic Politics: A Comparison of NAFTA and the Maastricht Treaty." In *Regionalism & Global Economic Integration*, ed. William A. Coleman and Geoffrey R. D. Underhill, 19–41. London: Routledge.

Milward, Alan. 1992. *The European Rescue of the Nation-State*. London: Routledge.

Moeller, Robert G. 1989. "Protecting Mother's Work: From Production to Reproduction in Postwar West Germany." *Journal of Social History* 22 (3): 413–37.

Moles, R. R. 1982. "Social Security for Migrant Workers in Latin America." *International Labour Review* 2 (121): 155–68.

Montpetit, Éric. 2000. "Europeanization and Domestic Politics: Europe and the Development of a French Environmental Policy for the Agricultural Sector." *Journal of European Public Policy* 7 (4): 576–92.

Moravcsik, Andrew. 1998. *The Choice for Europe: Social Purpose and State Power from Messina to Maastricht*. Ithaca, NY: Cornell University Press.

Morton, Peter. 1993. "Talks Set for Next Month on 'Parallel' NAFTA Deals." *Financial Post* (Toronto), February 18.

Navarro, Marysa. 2001. "Argentina: The Long Road to Women's Rights." In *Women's Rights: A Global View*, ed. Lynne Walter, 1–14. Westport, CT: Greenwood Press.

Nepomuceno, Eric. 1995. "Entra en Vigor el Mercosur, con la Mira Puesta en el Beneficio de las Elites." *Proceso*, September 1.

Nicolaïdis, Kalypso, and Michelle Egan. 2001. "Transnational Market Governance and Regional Policy Externality: Why Recognize Foreign Standards?" *Journal of European Public Policy* 8 (3): 454–73.

Niemann, Michael. 2000. *A Spatial Approach to Regionalism in the Global Economy*. New York: St. Martin's Press.

Nofal, María Beatriz, and John Wilkinson. 1999a. "La Producción y el Comercio de Productos Lácteos en el Mercosur." In *Impacto Sectorial de la Integración en el Mercosur*, ed. Juan José Taccone and Luis Jorge Garay, 235–394. Buenos Aires: Banco Interamericano de Desarollo, Departamento de Integración y Programas Regionales (Instituto para la Integración y Programas Regionales).

———. 1999b. "Production and Trade in Dairy Products in Mercosur." *Integration & Trade Journal* 78 (January–August): 147–69.

Notimex. 1997. "Avanzan Negiocaciones para Armonizar Leyes Mineras en el Mercosur." *Notimex*, September 26.

Nugent, Neill. 1994. *The Government and Politics of the European Union*. Durham, NC: Duke University Press.

Nusa Dua, Andrew Burrell. 2003. "Asian Leaders Opt for Common Market." *Australian Financial Review*, October 8.

Nye, Jospeph Vincent. 1991. "The Myth of Free-Trade Britain and Fortress France: Tariffs and Trade in the Nineteenth Century." *Journal of Economic History* 51 (1): 23–46.

Ohmae, Kenichi. 1993. "The Rise of the Region-State." *Foreign Affairs* 72 (2): 78–87.

O'Meara, Patrick, et al., eds. 2000. *Globalization and the Challenges of the New Century*. Bloomington: Indiana University Press.

O'Reilly, Dolores, and Alec Stone Sweet. 1998. "The Liberalization and European Regulation of Air Transport." In *European Integration and Supranational Governance*, ed. Wayne Sandholtz and Alec Stone Sweet, 164–87. Oxford: Oxford University Press.

Othman, Mohd Kamel. 2003. "Need to Establish MRA to Reduce Transaction Costs, Says Raifah." *Bernama: The Malaysian National News Agency*, September 4.

Outlaw, Joe, et al. 1994. *NAFTA and the U.S. Dairy Industry*, Leaflet P14, Dairy Markets and Policy, Department of Agricultural Economics, Cornell University.

Panagariya, Arvind. 2000. Preferential Trade Liberalization: The Traditional Theory and New Developments." *Journal of Economic Literature* 38 (2): 287–331

Patroni, Viviana. 1998. "The Politics of Labour Legislation Reform in Mexico." *Capital & Class* 65:107–32.

Paul, T.V., G. John Ikenberry, and John A. Hall, eds. 2003. *The National State in Question*. Princeton, NJ: Princeton University Press.

Pelletier, Debi. 1993. "NAFTA 'Challenge' to Equality: Women Urged to Take to the Streets to Fight Free Trade." *Record* (Kitchener-Waterloo, Ontario), February 22.

Phelps, Constance. 2001. "Social Work and Labor: A Look at the North American Agreement on Labor Cooperation." *Journal of Sociology and Social Welfare* 28 (1): 23–41.

Pierson, Paul. 2000. "Increasing Returns, Path Dependence, and the Study of Politics." *American Political Science Review* 94 (2): 251–67.

Pitanguy, Jaqueline. 1998. "The Women's Movement and Public Policy in Brazil." In *Women's Movements and Public Policy in Europe, Latin America and the Caribbean*, ed. Geertje Lycklama à Nijeholt, Virginia Vargas, and Saskia Wieringa, 97–112. New York: Garland Publishing.

Poitras, Guy, and Raymond Robinson. 1994. "The Politics of NAFTA in Mexico." *Journal of Interamerican Studies & World Affairs* 36:1–35.

Polanyi, Karl. 1944. *The Great Transformation*. Boston: Beacon Press.

Pollack, Mark. A., and Emilie Hafner-Burton. 2001. "Mainstreaming Gender in the European Union." *Journal of European Public Policy* 7 (3):432–56.

Pomeranz, Kenneth, and Steven Topik. 1999. *The World That Trade Created: Society, Culture, and the World Economy, 1400 to the Present*. Armonk, NY: M.E. Sharpe.

Powell, Walter W. 1991. "Expanding the Scope of Institutional Analysis." In *The New Institutionalism in Organizational Analysis*, ed. Walter W. Powell and Paul J. DiMaggio, 183–203. Chicago: University of Chicago Press.

Presidents & Prime Ministers. 1997. "Dairy Sector." *Presidents & Prime Ministers* 6 (3): 22–27.

Press Association. 1989. "Social Charter a Threat to Economic Prosperity." *Press Association*, October 28.

Prestowitz, Clyde V. 1992. "Setting New Priorities." *National Forum* 72 (4): 7–9.

Profit. 1993. "NAFTA Support Growing Despite Competitive Concerns." *Profit*, Summer.

Quintero-Ramírez, Cirila. 2002. "The North American Free Trade Agreement and Women." *International Feminist Journal of Politics* 4 (2): 240–59.

Ramirez, Miguel D. 2003. "Mexico Under NAFTA: A Critical Assessment." *Quarterly Review of Economics and Finance* 43 (5): 863–92.

Rapid. 1996. (Commission of the European Communities). "Commission Approves the Registration of Agricultural and Food Products." *Rapid*, June 12.

———. 2003. (Commission of the European Communities). "Women and the Future Treaty: High Level Conference Tomorrow in Brussels," *Rapid*, March 3.

Rebella, Jorge. 1999. "Conaprole: Milking the Marketplace." *Economist Intelligence Unit*, February 22.

Reuveny, Rafael, and William R. Thompson. 2000. "Trade, Regionalization, and Tariffs: The Correlates of Openness in the American Long Run." In *The Political Importance of Regional Trading Blocs*, ed. Bart Kerremans and Bob Switky, 55–83. Aldershot: Ashgate Publishing Ltd.

Reyes, Alejandro. 2000. "Tariff Troubles." *Asiaweek*, September 1: 51.

Ricardo, David. 1984 [1817]. *Principles of Political Economy and Taxation*. London: Dent.

Richards, Donald G. 1999. "Dependent Development and Regional Integration: A Critical Examination of the Southern Cone Common Market." *Latin American Perspectives* 24 (6): 133–55.

Roberts, Bob. 2003. "Strike Out the Rights: Britain to Bloc EU bid for All-out Action." *Mirror*, May 28.

Roederer-Rynning, Christilla. 2002. "Farm Conflict in France and the Europeanisation of Agricultural Policy." *West European Politics* 25 (3): 105–24.

Roell, Sophie. 1993. "Tradition Takes a Back Seat in Mozarella Market—A Victory for Cows Over Buffaloes." *Financial Times*, August 19.

Rohter, Larry. 2001. "Slow to Yield: Brazil Passes Equal Rights for Its Women." *New York Times*, August 18.

Rojo, Oscar. 1992. "Where to Learn About NAFTA Standards." *Toronto Star*, October 19.

Ronzoni, Raul. 1995. "Women-Uruguay: High Participation in the Workforce but Low Wages." *Inter Press Service*, December 13.

Ross, George. 1995. *Jacques Delors and European Integration*. New York: Oxford University Press.

Rossilli, Mariagrazia. 1999. "The European Union's Policy on the Equality of Women." *Feminist Studies* 25 (1): 168–82.

———, ed. 2000. *Gender Policies in the European Union*. New York: Peter Lang.

Salinas, Carlos de Gortari. 1995. "The More Trade *Blocs* The Better." *New Perspectives Quarterly* 12 (1): 38–39.

Sanchez, Roberto A. 2002. "Governance, Trade, and the Environment in the Context of NAFTA." *American Behavioral Scientist* 45 (9): 1369–83.

Sanguinetti, Ingacio. 2004. "Sector Lácteo Busca Negociar Trabas para Ingresar a Brasil." *La Voz del Interior* (Argentina), February 24.

Sandholtz, Wayne. 1998. "The Emergence of a Supranational Telecommunications Regime." In *European Integration and Supranational Governance*, ed. Wayne Sandholtz and Alec Stone Sweet, 134–163. Oxford: Oxford University Press.

Sardegna, Paula Costanza. 2001. *La Trabajadora Migrante en el Mercosur*. Buenos Aires: LexisNexis, Abelado-Perrot.

Schiek, Dagmar. 1998. "Sex Equality Law After Kalanke and Marschall." *European Law Journal* 4 (2): 148–66.

Schlaeger, Hilke. 1978. "The West German Women's Movement." *New German Critique* 13:59–68.

Schmidt, Vivien A. 2002. *The Futures of European Capitalism*. New York: Oxford University Press.

Scollay, Robert. 2001. "The Changing Outlook for Asia-Pacific Regionalism." *World Economy* 24 (9): 1135–60.

Seabright, Paul. 2004. *The Company of Strangers: A Natural History of Economic Life*. Princeton, NJ: Princeton University Press.

Serra, Jaime, and Enrique J. Espinosa. 2002. "Happily Ever NAFTA? The Proof Is in the Paycheck. *Foreign Policy*, September/October (132): 58–60.

Shaw, Jo. 2000. "Importing Gender: The Challenge of Feminism and the Analysis of the EU Legal Order." *Journal of European Public Policy* 7 (3): 406–31.

Skjaerseth, Jon Birger, and Jorgen Wettestad. 2002. "Understanding the Effectiveness of EU Environmental Policy: How Can Regime Analysis Contribute?" *Environmental Politics* 11 (3): 99–120.

Smith, Lee. 1993. "Needy NAFTA." *Fortune* 128 (9): 14–15.

Smith, Mitchell P. 2001. "In Pursuit of Selective Liberalization: Single Market Competition and its Limits." *Journal of European Public Policy* 8 (4): 519–40.

Snower, Dennis J. 1995. "Unemployment Benefits: An Assessment of Proposals for Reform." *International Labour Review* 13 (4–5): 625–47.

Snyder, Francis G. 1985. *Law of the Common Agricultural Policy*. London: Sweet & Maxwell.

———. 1996. "The Use of Legal Acts in EC Agricultural Policy." In *Sources and Categories of European Union Law: A Comparative and Reform Perspective*, ed. Gerd Winter, 348–84. Baden-Baden: Nomos.

Soldon, Norbert C. 1978. *Women in British Trade Unions, 1874–1976*. Totowa, NJ: Rowman and Littlefield.

Solinger, Dorothy J., et al., eds. 1999. *States and Sovereignty in the Global Economy*. London: Routledge.

Sornberger, Joe. 1992. "Coalition Ready for Fight Over Free Trade Deal." *Ottawa Citizen*, November 13.

Southern Cone Report. 2003. "Rejuvenated Mercosur Commits to Agenda of Broadening and Deepening." July 1.

Spanish Newswire Services. 1998. "Sindicatos Piden se Preserven los Derechos de los Trabajadores." *Spanish Newswire Services*, December 9.

———. 1999a. "Lácteos Argentinos Deberá Demostrar Cumplimiento Sanitario," *Spanish Newswire Services*, September 15.

———. 1999b. "Productores de Leche se Declaran Víctimas Guerra 'No Declarada.'" *Spanish Newswire Services*, September 15.

———. 1999c. "Mujeres Piden Base Institucional Sólida Que Las Tenga en Cuenta." *Spanish Newswire Services*, May 24.

———. 1999d. "Mujeres en Pie de Guerra para Reclamar Espacios de Mando." *Spanish Newswire Services*, August 13.

———. 1999e. "Empresa Sancor, Líder Lácteo, Se Asociará con Cooperativa Brasil." *Spanish Newswire Services*, October 14.

———. 2000a. "Argentina: Exportadores Proponen Formalmente Nuevo Tratado Para El Bloque." *Spanish Newswire Services*, March 7.

———. 2000b. "Mercosur no Desistirá de Lucha Contra Proteccionismo Agrícola UE." *Spanish Newswire Services*, February 23.

———. 2001a. "Exportación Quesos Denominación Origen Crecerá, Según Consorcio." *Spanish Newswire Services*, April 30.

———. 2001b. "Argentina y Brasil Solucionaron Conflicto por Leche en Polvo." *Spanish Newswire Services*, February 15.

———. 2001c. "Mexico Se Convierte en el Segundo Comprador de Lácteos Argentinos." *Spanish Newswire Services*, February 15.

———. 2002. "Mujeres Analizan en Brasil su Participación en el Mercosur." *Spanish Newswire Services*, November 18.

———. 2003a "Empresarios Brasileños Premian a Lavagna y a Marco Aurelio García." *Spanish Newswire Services*, December 19.

———. 2003b. "Ministro Destaca Creciente Calidad Quesos, con 18 Denominaciones." September 25.

Sperling, Liz, and Charlotte Bretherton. 1996. "Women's Policy Networks and the European Union." *Women's Studies International Forum* 19:303–14.

Spicers Centre for Europe. 1998. "Application Re Protected Geographical Indications: Cheese." *Spicers Centre for Europe*, November 12.

Spillman, Lyn. 1999. "Enriching Exchange: Cultural Dimensions of Markets." *American Journal of Economics and Sociology* 58 (4): 1047–73.

Steger, Manfred B. 2003. *Globalization: A Very Short Introduction*. Oxford: Oxford University Press.

Steinberg, Richard H. 1997. "Trade-Environment Negotiations in the EU, NAFTA, and WTO: Regional Trajectories of Rule Development." *American Journal of International Law* 91 (2): 231–67.

Stephen, Lynn. 1997. *Women and Social Movements in Latin America: Power from Below*. Austin: University of Texas Press.

Stetson, Dorothy McBride. 1987. *Women's Rights in France*. New York: Greenwood Press.

———. 1997. *Women's Rights in the U.S.A.: Policy Debates and Gender Roles*. New York: Garland Publishing.

Stevis, Dimitris, and Stephen Mumme. 2000. "Rules and Politics in International Integration: Environmental Regulation in NAFTA and the EU." *Environmental Politics* 9 (4): 20–42.

Stone Sweet, Alec, and James A. Caporaso. 1998. "From Free Trade to Supranational Polity: The European Court and Integration." In *European Integration and Supranational Governance*, ed. Wayne Sandholtz and Alec Stone Sweet, 92–133. Oxford: Oxford University Press.

Strid, Sofia. 2003. "European Institutionalisation of Gendered Interests and Women's Organisations." Paper presented at the European Consortium for Political Research Conference, Marburg, Germany.

Stryker, Robin. 2003. "Mind the Gap: Law, Institutional Analysis and Socioeconomics." *Socio-Economic Review* 1 (3): 335–67.

Stubbs, Richard. 2000. Signing on to Liberalization: AFTA and the Politics of Regional Economic Cooperation." *Pacific Review* 13 (2): 297–318.

Summers, Larry. 1991. "Regionalism and the World Trading System." In *Policy Implications of Trade and Currency Zones*, ed. Larry Summers, 11–21. Kansas City: Federal Reserve Bank of Kansas City.

Switky, Bob. 2000. "The Importance of Trading Blocs: Theoretical Foundations." In *The Political Importance of Regional Trading Blocs*, ed. Bart Kerremans and Bob Switky, 13–53. Aldershot: Ashgate Publishing Ltd.

Tate, Jay. 2001. "National Varieties of Capitalism." In *Varieties of Capitalism: The Institutional Foundations of Comparative Advantage*, ed. Peter A. Hall and David Soskice, 442–473. New York: Oxford University Press.

Taylor, Rupert J. 1997. "Labour History: The Struggle for Workers' Rights." *Canada and the World Backgrounder* 63 (3): 1–50.

Teague, Paul. 2003. "Labour-Standard Setting and Regional Trading Blocs." *Employee Relations* 25 (5): 428–52.

Terry, Edith. 1996. "Regional Trade Blocs Are In; Global Group Draws Yawns." *Christian Science Monitor* 88 (109): 7.

Thapanachai, Somporn. 1999. "Looking Ahead—2000 ASEAN Trade: AFTA an Apprenticeship for Liberalizing under the WTO." *Bangkok Post*, December 22.

Thatcher, Margaret. 1998. "A Family of Nations." In *The European Union: Readings on the Theory and Practice of European Integration*, ed. Brent F. Nelsen and Alexander C.-G. Stubb, 49–54. Boulder, CO: Lynne Rienner Publishers.

Thelen, Kathleen. 1999. "Historical Institutionalism in Comparative Politics." *Annual Review of Political Science* (2): 369–404.

Thurow, Lester. 1992. "New Rules for Playing the Game." *National Forum* 72 (4): 10–12.

Times. 2000. "France to Lead EU Drive for Basic Rights Charter." *Times* (London), May 5.

Torfing, Jacob. 2001. "Path-Dependent Danish Welfare Reforms: The Contributions of the New Institutionalism to Understanding Evolutionary Change." *Scandinavian Political Studies* 24 (4): 277–309.

Toronto Star. 1992. "Business Likes Liberals' Plan on Trade Pact." *Toronto Star*, November 27.

———. 1993. "Don't Change NAFTA, Business Groups Tell U.S." *Toronto Star*, October 30.

———. 1998. "Free Trade's Many Broken Promises." *Toronto Star*, January 15.

Tussie, Diana. 1998. "In the Whirlwind of Globalization and Multilateralism: The Case of Emerging Regionalism in Latin America." In *Regionalism & Global Economic Integration*, ed. William A. Coleman and Geoffrey R. D. Underhill, 81–96. London: Routledge.

Ulshoefer, Petra. 1998. *Mercosur and the Challenges for the Integration and Participation of Women in the World of Work*. Geneva: International Labour Organization.

United Press International. 1990. "Thousands of Farmers Demonstrate Against Dropping Prices." *United Press International*, April 25.

United States Department of Agriculture. 1997. *Agricultural Outlook: January–February*. Washington, DC: USDA Economic Research Service.

Urata, Shujiro. 2002. "Globalization and the Growth in Free Trade Agreements." *Asia-Pacific Review* 9 (1): 20–32.

van Doorne-Huiskes, Anneke, Jacques van Hoof, and Ellie Roelofs, eds. 1995. *Women and the European Labour Markets*. London: P. Chapman Publishers.

Vernon, Raymond. 1996. "Passing Through Regionalism: The Transition to Global Markets." *World Economy* 19 (6): 621–33.

Verucci, Florisa. 1991. "Women and the New Brazilian Constitution." *Feminist Studies* 17 (3): 557–68.

Villars, C. 1981. "Social Security for Migrant Workers in the Framework of the Council of Europe." *International Labour Review* 120 (3): 291–302.

Viner, Jacob. 1950. *The Customs Union Issue*. New York: Carnegie Endowment for International Peace.

Walker, Martin. 1993. "Free Trade Battle Puts Class Back on the US Agenda; Clinton Still Short of Majority for Key Vote on Deal with Mexico and Canada." *Guardian*, November 9.

Walter, Lynne. 2001. "Denmark." In *Women's Rights: A Global View*, ed. Lynne Walter, 57–70. Westport, CT: Greenwood Press.

Warde, Alan. 2000. "Eating Globally: Cultural Flows and the Spread of Ethnic Restaurants." In *The Ends of Globalization*, ed. Don Kalb et al., 299–316. Lanham, MD: Rowman and Littlefield.

Warner, Herriet. 1984. "EC Social Policy in Practice: Community Action on Behalf of Women and Its Impact in the Member States." *Journal of Common Market Studies* 23 (2): 141–67.

Weber, Max. 1978 [1922]. *Economy and Society*. Berkeley: University of California Press.

———. 1992 [1923]. *General Economic History*. New Brunswick, NJ: Transaction Publishers.

Wedel, Joachim. 1970. "Social Security and Economic Integration." *International Labour Review* 102 (5): 455–74.

Weiler, Joseph H. H. 1991. "The Transformation of Europe." *Yale Law Journal* 100:2403–83.

Weiss, Linda, ed. 2003. *States in the Global Economy: Bringing Domestic Institutions Back In*. Cambridge: Cambridge University Press.

White, Marceline, Carlos Salas, and Sarah Gammage. 2003. *Trade Impact Review: Mexico Case Study—NAFTA and the FTAA: A Gender Analysis of Employment and Poverty Impacts in Agriculture*. Washington, DC: Women's Edge Coalition.

Wiktorow, Alexandra. 2001. *An Impact of Enlargement of the European Union on Social Security Schemes in Central and Eastern European Countries—Polish Case (Administrative Approach)*. Paper prepared for the November 22–23, 2001 meeting of the International Social Security Association (Social Security and the Changing World of Work), Dresden.

Williamson, Oliver E. 1985. *The Economic Institutions of Capitalism*. New York: Free Press.

Wise, Mark. 1994. "The European Community." In *Continental Trading Blocs: The Growth of Regionalism in the World Economy*, ed. Richard Gibb and Wieslaw Michalak, 75–109. West Sussex: John Wiley & Sons, Ltd.

Women's International Network. 1993. "Uruguay." *Women's International Network News* 19 (2): 25.

———. 1995. "Brazil." *Women's International Network News* 21 (2): 17.

———. 1996. "Canada." *Women's International Network News* 22 (2): 20.

———. 2003. "Mexico: Legislation Passed to Protect Women's Rights." *Women's International Network News* 29 (3): 63.

Woo-Cumings, Meredith. 2003. "Diverse Paths towards the 'Right Institutions': Law, the State, and Economic Reform in East Asia." In *States in the Global Economy: Bringing Domestic Institutions Back In*, ed. Linda Weiss, 200–224. Cambridge, Cambridge University Press.

World Commission on Environment and Development. 2000. "From One Earth to One World." In *The Globalization Reader*, ed. Frank J. Lechner and John Boli, 374–79. Malden, MA: Blackwell Publishers.

———. 2003. "Free Trade Areas in Southern Africa." *Xinhua General News Service*, August 20.

Xinhua General News Service. 1989. "Britain's Labor Party Favors EC Social Charter." *Xinhua General News Service*, October 4.

Xinhua General Overseas News Service. 1991. "Uruguay Sells Tariffs-Free [*sic*] Milk to Brazil, Argentina." *Xinhua General Overseas News Service*, August 10.

Yarbrough, Beth V., and Robert M. Yarbrough. 1997. "Dispute Settlement in International Trade: Regionalism and Procedural Coordination." In *The Political Economy of Regionalism*, ed. Edward D. Mansfield and Helen V. Milner, 134–63. New York: Columbia University Press.

Yeung, May T., Nicholas Perdikis, and William A. Kerr, eds. 1999. *Regional Trading Blocs in the Global Economy: The EU and ASEAN*. Cheltenham, UK: Edward Elgar.

Zakaria, Fareed. 2000. "The Rise of Illiberal Democracy." In *Globalization and the Challenges of a New Century*, ed. Partick O'Meara, Howard D. Mehlinger, and Matthew Krain, 181–95. Bloomington: Indiana University Press.

Zeff, Eleanor E., and Ellen B. Pirro, eds. 2001. *The European Union and the Member States: Cooperation, Coordination, and Compromise*. Boulder, CO: Lynne Rienner Publishers.

Zelizer, Vivana A. 1992. "Human Values and the Market: The Case of Life Insurance and Death in 19th Century America." In *The Sociology of Economic Life*, ed. Mark Granovetter and Richard Swedberg, 285–304. Boulder, CO: Westview Press.

Zweifel, Thomas D. 2002. ". . . Who Is without Sin Cast the First Stone: The EU's Democratic Deficit in Comparison." *Journal of European Public Policy* 9 (5): 812–40.

INDEX

S